Leisure Settings

LEISURE SETTINGS

Bourgeois Culture,

Medicine,

and the Spa

in Modern France

DOUGLAS PETER MACKAMAN

The University of Chicago Press
Chicago and London

DOUGLAS P. MACKAMAN is assistant professor of modern European history and director of French studies at the University of Southern Mississippi. He holds degrees from the University of Wisconsin, Madison, and the University of California, Berkeley, where he earned his Ph.D. in 1994. Mackaman resides in Hattiesburg, Mississippi.

The University of Chicago Press, Chicago, 60637
The University of Chicago Press, Ltd., London
© 1998 by The University of Chicago
All rights reserved. Published 1998
Printed in the United States of America
07 06 05 04 03 02 01 00 99 98   1 2 3 4 5

ISBN: 0-226-50074-8 (cloth)
ISBN: 0-226-50075-6 (paper)

Library of Congress Cataloging-in-Publication Data

Mackaman, Douglas Peter.
    Leisure settings : bourgeois culture, medicine, and the spa in modern France / Douglas Peter Mackaman.
        p.   cm.
    Includes bibliographical references and index.
    ISBN 0-226-50074-8 (alk. paper). — ISBN 0-226-50075-6 (pbk. : alk. paper)
    1. Health resorts—Social aspects—France—History—19th century.
    2. Balneology—Social aspects—France—History—19th century.
    3. Middle class—France—Social life and customs—19th century.
    4. France—Social life and customs—19th century. I. Title.
RA863.M25 1998
613′.122′094409034—dc21   98-15570
                                                                           CIP

♾ The paper in this publication meets the minimum requirements of the American National Standard for Information Sciences—Permanence of Paper for Printed Library Materials, ANSI Z39.48-1992.

Contents

Illustrations

Acknowledgments

Few pleasures associated with scholarship go beyond the joy I feel in acknowledging my gratitude to the colleagues, institutions, friends, and family who have offered this book and its author such boundless support.

My editors at the University of Chicago Press, Douglas Mitchell and Matthew Howard, together with Jenni Fry and helpful assistants, were my friends and critical fans throughout the four years it took to write this book. Their confidence in my project and steady encouragement can never be repaid but will never be forgotten.

In France, I received much assistance from the knowledgeable staffs of the Archives Nationales and Bibliothèque Nationale in Paris, the Archives Départementales of Savoie, Haute-Savoie, Allier, and the Archives des Thermes Nationaux of Aix-les-Bains. In particular, I thank Michel Bouille and Serban Cantacuzino, both of whom offered invaluable advice on materials and operational tactics within the Archives Nationales. For endless discussion on the history of French thermalism, not to mention their help in gaining me access to archives that otherwise were closed, I thank Yvan Cuesta and Geneviève Frieh of Aix-les-Bains and Francine Glière of Chambéry. Finally, for much help on foreign soil, sumptuous dinners, and innumerable tips on life and nightlife in Paris, I thank my dear friend Jean-Pierre Chamayou.

Funding for the research and writing of this book was provided by the Office of the Vice President for Research and Planning, the College of Letters and Sciences, and the College of International and Continuing Education at the University of Southern Mississippi, which built on generous grants I received while this work was in the dissertation stage at the University of California at Berkeley. In particular, I thank the Department of History at Berkeley for the Heller Fellowship it awarded me so that I could begin my work in France. I am also grateful to the Mellon Foundation for its sustained support of my research and writing.

Susanna Barrows must be acknowledged as the intellectual mother of a whole generation of cultural historians to come out of Berkeley. As an advisor, critic, mentor, and friend, she has been a steadfast and gracious shepherd of my research and writing for many years now. Sharing her personal time more generously than anyone would have asked her to, Susanna encouraged a nervous flock of dissertators to form a writing salon in her home. There, among friends and trusted critics, her students found humanity and sanity on a weekly basis—all the while, of course, we improved our abilities as writers and cooks. No one read my work more intently and encouragingly than did Susanna and the floating membership of her dissertation seminar. My chapters are all better for their having been read by David Barnes, Megan Koreman, Jeffrey Ravel, Sylvia Schafer, Vanessa Schwartz, Regina Sweeney, Matt Truesdell, and Tamara Whited.

Thomas Laqueur and Allan Pred also gave generously of their time and talents in support of my dissertation. Each read the chapters in draft form more than once, consistently offering invaluable advice on matters of argumentation, organization, source materials, methodology, and style. I thank both scholars for the encouragement they gave my work in its early stages. Each directed a research project of mine in my second year at Berkeley, and from their support I derived much of the courage necessary to choose a dissertation topic.

Other colleagues at Berkeley and beyond have read all or part of the book, and I have gained from their advice in many instances. For this help, I especially thank Leif Brown, Lisa Cody, Paul Friedland, George Mosse, Robert Magnan, and Rachel Fuchs. At the University of Southern Mississippi, I have enjoyed a wonderfully rich and stimulating academic home. Colleagues and friends who have helped me with my work and offered constant encouragement include Orazio Ciccarelli, Neil MacMillen, R. Geoff Jensen, Jon Sensbach, Kathryn Edwards, David Wheeler, Marjorie Spruill Wheeler, and Michael Mays. I note with special gratitude the support and inspiration I have received from two of my colleagues at USM, Tim Hudson and President Emeritus Aubrey K. Lucas, just as I warmly thank my students for their interest in this project.

At home, where I might have feared writing the most, I found nothing but companionship and loving encouragement from my family. Clare and Richard Mackaman, my parents, were proud of me when I needed that most. Just as important, they did not think I was crazy to devote a decade to the study of spas! David and Cordy Strand brought me to France for the first time, perhaps not knowing the many effects this would have on my future, and I thank them for their solidarity. The late Eva Mackaman and her daughter, Doris Corrie, taught me to love history, a gift that has helped me through writing this book. Daniel Mackaman, my family's first writer and a reliable champion of my best interests, has spurred me intellectually and otherwise in ways that only gracious and charitable older siblings can. My children, Henry and Owen Mackaman, have done all that babies and little boys can do to make a parent feel like writing—they napped every day and let me talk in paragraphs while I walked them. I dedicate this book to Meredith Strand Mackaman, who remembers well before this research was ever begun and whose friendship and support made me know many things, among them that I would find a book at the end of ten years' work.

for Meredith

Introduction

The French will not find it curious that a book about their social identity has been written with bathtubs and drinking fountains in the foreground. With a fevered anticipation for each summer's vacation, this people seems to believe that whatever France is, it is at least partly that because of rest cures and vacationing. Anything but trivial or adjunctive to social life, leisure and its modern manifestations all but embody France's claims of mastery in the category of joie de vivre. Spas and the curing one still does at them are of obvious importance to the contemporary scene. For even if there are fewer of them today than there were in the nineteenth century, French spas—some of which are still state owned and administered—are almost universally regarded as medically potent places.[1] Thus for an eager American to refer to Le Mont-Dore, Challes-les-Eaux, or some other national bath in a quick and chatty way is to set a conversational table for a banquet-length story about everyone's favorite uncle with a rheumatic hip.

In their beloved vacations and in their still medically respected bathing places, the French see not just a contemporary importance but a significant history. What holidays are today, they clearly were not just a century ago, for although cherished relatives, broken-backed factory workers, and footsore functionaries are the denizens of most baths now, it was for the socially ambitious ranks of the bourgeoisie that the nineteenth century's thermal milieu was made. Surrounding the great and luxurious vacation sites of then, once opulent hotels and "palaces" with their decayed promenades but still panoramic vistas onto natural beauty stand today as abandoned, crumbling markers of what the "bourgeois century" built but could not sustain. Although the now quiet paths to and from these places might reveal that war and depression changed the nature of holiday life for the French, what the abandonment of these hulking edifices signals more dramatically is that there was very recently a society whose expectations, commitments, pleasures, and confidences differed

I

dramatically from the sensibilities of today. Into that world of mineral water cures, casinos, and pleasant excursions, a world which is now only a boarded-up grandeur, nearly a million people each year by 1900 went to spend their vacations. Why people went to spas, what they did while there, and how watering places both made and were made by the vacationing middle classes—these questions dangle in the air of so many dull towns where it once was so gay to go.

This book is about spas and the culture of being at them from the latter years of the Old Regime to the end of the nineteenth century. What I seek to explore is how spas helped France's emerging bourgeoisie create and refine an acceptable practice of leisure and pleasure on vacation. It is my largest argument that spas, because of how they would come to stand as architectural and administrative governors of proper leisure, constituted a discursive field where the emerging bourgeoisie would first move en masse to the peculiar rhythms of its rest. Until the last decade or so, research related to identity formation tended to focus on work and other "productive" aspects of experience. More recently, however, cultural critics and historians have turned from the study of labor to explore the complex sociological, economic, and cultural grids of everyday life. After the work of Michel de Certeau in particular, the subtle and quiet politics of opposition—produced by anyone's passage through the lived experience of an average day—have given an important scholarly imperative to the seemingly banal features of existence.[2] Similarly, the rise of "cultural history" since the 1980s has contributed to a now widespread belief that the history of seemingly simple or even silly things is serious indeed. Outstanding work on pet keeping, the politics of furniture, fashion, the history of odor, and so on has been invaluable in silencing the snickers one might have heard in the 1970s upon announcing to an audience of American scholars that the hour of the spa's history was almost at hand.[3]

My decision to study health resorts was driven in large part by an interest in the intersections of medicine and class identity in the nineteenth century. Reading the work of Michel Foucault and of French historians who were deeply influenced by his histories, especially Alain Corbin and Michelle Perrot, had prepared me to find in the spas both the proliferation of medical discourse in the 1800s and its hidden-hand mode of authorship.[4] Similarly, reading in this genre had schooled me to search for ways in which the body figured, historically, as an entity for scrutinization and as an organ—both physiological and metaphorical—where dominance, authority, and normalization would inevitably become governors. Even with this theoretical grounding, however, I was puzzled to find in my early work on spas just how much medicine the French bourgeoisie took with it on vacation.

Enduring (or seeking) endless medical directives, adopting (whole- or half-heartedly) complicated regimes, and weathering (or enjoying) cures that seemed to be thinly disguised forms of punishment—this was how I found most French spa-goers spending their leisure, at least in the first five or six decades of the nineteenth century. Guidebooks from this period reveal that everyday life at the spas, notwithstanding the balls and social functions that were its pleasured punctuations, was overarchingly a medical matter. Sick people were so present at Vichy in the 1830s that one promotional writer found it necessary to warn his readers that their spa vacations might feel from time to time like a hospitalization of sorts. For example, the author revealed that although most guests at Vichy's hotel tables enjoyed eating and talking, diners would invariably be joined by "a small number of individuals whose health does not permit them to engage in either of these functions." Weak and understandably sullen, these invalid guests, the author wished to warn his readers, could "indeed diminish the gaiety of the table."[5]

But medicine at Vichy or elsewhere in the decades prior to midcentury was more about a routine and a regimen than it was the variously high or low percentage of desperately sick guests one would encounter during an average day. Life on vacation in this era was ordered according to the dictates of medical curing, as even socially oriented guides to the spas did not fail to note. Very early morning hours were the rule at most baths; commonly, "by 6 or 7, virtually all visitors [were] awake and getting on with the day."[6] Getting on with the day, even for many vacationers who had no health complaints, meant obeying the orders of a doctor. At Vichy, Aix-les-Bains, and most other spas, daily curing began with the drinking of mineral water. This serious business, guidebooks revealed, caused patients to "dispatch quickly and without pretensions with the morning toilette," just as it demanded a curtailment of sociability. "When one meets acquaintances, one greets them but speaks very little," one writer noted in characterizing water drinking at a spa, because "everyone's attention is directed toward the two mineral water sources."[7] Following an hour or so of water drinking, most curists went on to prescribed baths, rest periods, and epochs of exercise. Even social functions and evening meals assumed medical importance in this era, as doctors made it a rule of law at most spas that everyone who bathed in mineral waters had to seek a physician's counsel and establish at least some kind of a curative regimen.

For Foucault, the dispersal of medicine's social authority in the eighteenth and nineteenth centuries was chartable without explicitly invoking the category of class. To consider medicalization and the spa, however, is necessarily to investigate how doctors and doctoring were symbiotically related to the formation of bourgeois identity. Although medicine was omnipresent at the spas, its popularity as an experience of leisure was not constant. The historiography on modern medicine, in France and elsewhere, had led me to expect that medicine's peak as a factor in spa culture and bourgeois leisure would have occurred somewhere in the Belle Époque. By then, the professionalization of medicine was an accomplished fact, just as medicine's spread as a social authority had achieved vast dimensions. Yet in the decades prior to the Great War, what one sees at the spas is not only a less obvious medical presence than was the case earlier in the century, but, moreover, a diminished percentage of people taking the waters. Framing an explanation to account for why medicine at the spas seemingly saw a significant "fall" in the very period when the medicalization of society and culture was reaching such a pervasive extent became a problem I grappled with in my investigations of leisure and bourgeois identity formation.

In exploring the shifting fortunes of hydrotherapeutic medicine, I felt initially that doctors had simply sought to achieve too much control over the spas and their patients. Cures had taken an unduly sharp turn toward pain, I thought. And bourgeois tourists who had typically also agreed to be curists did so no longer when bathing seemed to approximate torture. That explanation for the ebbing of hydrotherapy's hold over the vacation was but partly successful, however, because cures had always been demanding. Similarly, the fact that hydrotherapy persisted as a leisure pursuit for a not insignificant segment of the spa population—a great many of whom doctored even though they were quite fully in the pink—meant that cures must not have more or less suddenly been seen as onerous or unbearable. If cures had simply become too intrusive and doctors too lordly and demanding, then it would have been odd for bathing to persist as a practice of leisure, which, by all accounts, it did.

An alternative argument presented itself on the question of pleasure. Might it have been that pain and discomfort did not increase inside the spas, but, instead, that pleasure and fun found greater privilege in the social spaces and cultural practices beyond the baths? With the improvement and expansion programs almost all the spas pursued during the Second Empire, the place of pleasure on vacation clearly came to be underscored around midcentury. New casinos, larger hotels, lavish promenades, public parks, and expanded shopping districts were but the main civic commitments to a pleasant life in public that most French watering places made after the midcentury mark. This explanation of medicine's partial removal from the repertoire of bourgeois leisure practice, however, was unsatisfactory on purely chronological grounds. The perceptible drift of vacationers away from hydrotherapy began around 1850, but the pleasures of spa culture were in full swing long before that date. Fun had never not been featured at the nineteenth-century watering places. If civic improvements highlighted pleasure in the latter half of the century, those changes increased fun but did not invent it.

My conclusion is that medicine never disappeared from spa culture in the nineteenth century, just as I contend that pleasure was always there. The great decades for spa medicalization were the three that came after the fall of the first Bonaparte. That the period 1815 to 1850 was also the indisputable era when France's bourgeoisie saw its social, political, economic, and cultural ascension is no mere coincidence. Indeed, I argue that in the bourgeoisie's making of an identity, it calibrated at the spas a way to do leisure that no other environment would have so easily accepted. Webbed together with overarching concepts like rationality, anticlericalism, respectability, and science, which together stood for something like an emerging bourgeois worldview, medicalization was an effective and appealing mode of order at the spas precisely because spa-goers knew it in other guises, understood it, and welcomed it.

The extent to which medicine was bound to the bourgeoisie and the French state in the administration of public health structures, the legal system, and in other contexts of nineteenth-century social life has been well documented by social historians and cultural critics.[8] But the complete and comfortable lodging of medicalization within a locale like the bourgeois spa is no plain matter, that is until one sees leisure as a problem instead of as an ahistorical given. In all of its variations and unscripted possibilities, leisure was associated both with great promise and with potential pitfalls. Popular leisure, with its festive excesses and carnal components, presented one largely unappealing model for bourgeois commentators to observe. Aristocratic cultural sensibilities were somewhat more satisfactory, with visiting, promenading, dancing, reading, and the annual pleasures of the social season constituting respectable ways of spending free time, but courtly uses of leisure had frivolous and sexual aspects that hardly conformed well with the rising bourgeoisie's notions of productivity and respectability. Similarly, although leisure of the everyday was a solvable problem very early on, as Carol Harrison's work on scientific societies and betterment clubs from the Restoration and July Monarchy reveals, the matter was less easily addressed when the quantity of leisure was increased to three weeks' duration.[9]

Spa medicine became the bourgeoisie's way to reconcile a productive ethos to the fact that consuming an extended holiday was a socially advantageous course of action. Medicine in this scheme did what it always endeavored to do as science's hand on the formation of a modern society. It debunked mystery. It surveyed so much chaos and offered an authoritative will toward order and wellness. To the partly cocky, partly timid, somewhat risen, and somewhat nascent social group that was the French bourgeoisie, spa medicine offered precise prescriptions according to which leisure was to be practiced. Thus medicine let the bourgeoisie have its rest, all the while making that rest impermeable to waste, indecency, excess, sloth, and the other social attributes the still forming bourgeoisie took to be antithetical to the dual guises of productivity and respectability. As I endeavor to explore within this book, the more "set" that bourgeois identity became, the less need spa vacationers seemed to have for the strict dictates of mineral water curing. Moreover, as the middle class came increasingly to join the bourgeoisie at France's spas in the later decades of the century, these new tourists and curists would seek holiday versions of the pleasures and public life that they enjoyed in Paris and elsewhere.[10] Daily routines at most spas reflected the rise of pleasure as early morning cures gave way to excursion travel, concerts, and the frenetic activity of social intercourse.[11]

Alain Corbin's masterful history of the beaches of England and France as leisure settings, entitled *Le territoire du vide: L'Occident et le désir du rivage, 1750–1840,* has stimulated much of my thinking for this project, just as it has pushed me to ask questions of agency and historical causality that Corbin at least partly avoids.[12] The project of his book, which is both extraordinarily broad and minutely detailed, is to chart the ways in which cultural sensibilities regarding the seaside changed in the century after 1750. Corbin reveals how seaside settings, a maligned place in the minds of most eighteenth-century contemporaries, emerged in the nineteenth century as objects of great desire. Imagining a locale like Margate or Dieppe no longer meant that one conceived of danger, indecency, or the attending uncertainties of life among the peoples of a poorly defined border region. Rather, one now understood the seaside as a territory whose vast vistas and geographical precariousness inspired romantic reflection and the muses of art.

As Corbin states it, the new image of the European beach as a decent and worthy place to think about and even visit was in large part due to its first having been recast as a culturally safe environment. Doctors and medical authority, Corbin convincingly argues, were among the chief architects of beach "safety." The medical codification and administration of sea bathing, for example, was effected in both England and France around the middle of the eighteenth century. Beyond rationalizing salt water hydrotherapy, making bathing a medical act signaled to observers near and far that a measure of scientific authority had been installed at the shore. Now, because of sea-bathing cures, people not only had reasons to go to a beach but also a variety of very specific things to do there.

Corbin's work is a history of what the French call *mentalités*. Thus he explores, in addition to the rise of medical authority at the seaside, the shifting place of the beach in the cultural calculus of those who imagined it. As medicine made beaches seem safe and worthy of consideration, Corbin argues that respectability too came to inform people's visions of the seashore. Medical bathing, after all, hardly made nymphs of its practitioners. On the contrary, as Corbin explains, sea bathing was an administered experience in which pain and discomfort were sometimes quite pronounced. At the same time, bathing of this sort was made as morally decent as possible. Even where there were no local ordinances ensuring that male bathers wore clothing of some kind, a peculiar sort of "bathing machine" was used to uphold a measure of modesty. Carried to an appropriate depth in an enclosed cart with enormous wheels, bathers were released from these machines through trap doors—their bobbing heads being all that curious onlookers could see.

As a more or less strictly cultural study, Corbin's work lacks the valuable institutional history that local studies of French leisure locales provide. Indeed, the book's deep bow to Michel Foucault leaves the issue of human agency in the construction of the beach more or less unexplored. This is obviously not to suggest that Corbin fails to show his readers a host of discourses implicated in the rise of beaches. But beyond beach doctors, who obviously had a vested interest in the improved fortunes of their locales—yet about whose motives in this regard Corbin has little to say—the author is not much interested in the economic and developmental history of beaches as leisure sites. Entrepreneurs and speculators hardly figure at all in the analysis, and neither, of course, do their variously successful and unsuccessful efforts to exploit and otherwise trade upon the vogue of beach-going.

For the English case, Corbin might have hastily ignored this aspect of the seaside's story because others have already given it a credible telling.[13] The same cannot be said, however, for France. Nor can it be said that such a history would not reveal a great deal about the collective cultural sensibilities of those historical actors who interpreted and internalized the new meanings of the beach. On the contrary, the endless promotional writings that beach developers produced in support of their hotels and casinos must surely constitute a valuable optic on the means by which beaches were invented, popularized, and made profitable.

In planning my book, I decided to look closely at a limited number of French spas and draw out whatever implications and generalizations I could for the thermal milieu and bourgeois vacationing generally. While I found this less-than-scientific methodology to have certain perils, I did my utmost to check my "data" and "findings" against different types of spas in different regions. Thus I devote a great deal of my analysis in chapter 2 to a comparative discussion of spa development in three municipalities, each in a different *département* and each boasting a very different kind of thermal establishment. But rather than doing all of my research and writing around such a comparison, which would have greatly limited the intellectual range of my analysis for the simple reason that spas shared too much of a common history to make their inevitable differences the centerpiece of a book, I opted to make tactical use of comparisons while creating an essentially composite portrait of my subject.

Before sketching the narrative and analytical contours of the book's five chapters, I would like to offer a working definition of the term "vacation leisure," which figures prominently in my discussion. Vacation leisure denotes a category of leisure that differs in my estimation from other forms of free time. Mainly, I make this distinction on temporal grounds. Leisure of the everyday, quite simply, has always been organized and passed in relatively brief bursts. One is away from one's place of work and the direct demands of that place, so one does what one will. Historically, the range of options available to those in the possession of everyday leisure has varied a great deal.[14] Principally, it has been class, gender, and race that have imposed the greater limitations on the practice of everyday leisure. Yet this leisure, whether spent in a café, garden, museum, or bedroom, has still maintained a direct relationship to everyday life that a vacation lacks, for vacation leisure has ultimately been a matter of some duration, best measured in increments of whole days if not always entire weeks.

My use of the term vacation leisure implies important spatial and geographical elements too.[15] Simply passing days or weeks in one's home, regardless of the ways in which one fills this leisure, has not historically constituted a form of leisure practice that conforms to my conception of a vacation. On the contrary, vacation leisure as I see it is based on at least a modest measure of displacement or motion.[16] The eighteenth-century Englishman's Grand Tour might well be taken as an example of vacationing in the early modern era.[17] An integral component of an elite male's cultural education, such tours routinely lasted for a year or more and saw their practitioners visit much of Latin Europe.

But the spatial dimension of vacation leisure should not be understood as being solely dependent upon travel. Rather, spa-going in the eighteenth century was a form of vacation leisure too, even though one's destination was more important than one's journey. The reason for this, as I see it, is that even back and forth travel of a limited distance—from, say, Marseille to Aix-en-Provence—was sufficient in the eighteenth century and much of the nineteenth to earn for the traveler the distinction of being a foreigner.[18] Having come to a place from somewhere "foreign," with plans to stay for awhile without working, therefore, would satisfy two of the three components in my conception of vacation leisure.

Finally, I ascribe a certain purposefulness to the practice of vacationing.[19] Religious pilgrimage, in both the early and late modern periods, is the strongest example of the utility I see in vacation leisure.[20] Pilgrims traveled to places like Rome, Venice, and Lourdes with a clear notion of why they had left home.[21] Seeking something spiritual, hoping to heal some physical ailment, wanting to offer gratitude to a patron saint—these and scores of other motives informed all aspects of pilgrim travel. Yet serious sojourns such as these still ought to be understood as practices of vacation leisure, for hotels, caravans, trains, guidebooks, and the experience of being a foreign traveler all conspired to remove pilgrims from the patterns and rhythms of work and everyday life.[22]

Sociability and other lighter motives have historically conferred purpose onto practices of leisure, too.[23] Plombières and other eighteenth-century spas, as I discuss in chapter 1, were great capitals of aristocratic leisure. To the French elites who scurried to these places each summer, a mixture of well-known motives girded the spa vacation. But regardless of whether one went seeking new friendships, camaraderie with old acquaintances, better health, sexual conquest, a carnivalesque season of excess, or merely something pleasant to do during the summer season, spa-goers all recognized that they would see enough interesting topography and meet enough curious foreigners to secure for themselves a purposeful and meaningful distance from their everyday lives.

What I seek to reveal in my main argument is the peculiarly contrapuntal essence of holiday-making in nineteenth-century France. From the resonating call for productive leisure that was exclaimed by developers and vacationers alike in the first years of the Restoration, therefore, I trace the shifting fortunes of the medicalized vacation into the latter years of the century. But spas were never mere health camps, not even when doctors sought zealously to make them that, thus I try to make audible the cries for fun, gaiety, and pleasure that always reverberated through the spa milieu.

In chapters 1 and 2, I offer a history of spa development and spa-going in France over the long term. Here, I investigate the structural continuities of the early modern spa and how these were radically altered in the first half of the nineteenth century. After considering medicine and culture at the Old Regime spas, my analysis traces the three principal strategies of spa development that emerged in France during the period of the Restoration and came to constitute the parameters of the modern thermal industry.

In the third chapter, I explore how spa developers attempted to "read" and in some cases anticipate the cultural expectations of the spa's bourgeois consumers in the period 1820–50. Further, I consider the ways in which representations of the spa underwent deliberate change, too, as developers and promoters initiated elaborate campaigns to advertise their locales. Much of the discussion is oriented around changes in architecture and administrative procedure as I seek to show how rising notions of respectability and modesty came to be defined in class-specific and gendered terms.

In chapter 4, I analyze the creation and proliferation of vacationing among the French bourgeoisie in the period 1820–50. I argue that through an elaborate process of medicalization, spas created for the first time a productive and, therefore, bourgeois model of vacationing. Through an examination of the medicalized rhythms and rituals of the spa vacation, I show how medicine organized the pleasures of vacationing such that bourgeois spa-goers could justify and otherwise account for their leisure.

In chapter 5, I look critically at the social applications of pleasure and leisure in spa vacationing in the period 1860–1900. In considering how holidays were used as a means of transferring economic capital into social standing, and how the various public venues at the spas were utilized in strategies of family formation, I reveal how and why spas emerged as centers where bourgeois identity was reproduced in a vacationing and consuming middle class.

Leisure has never been a "set" or "established" thing. Rather, it seems to be (even in its many forms of disorder) a socially ordering intersection of place and practice whose terms of interaction change over history's smaller and larger sweeps of time. So it is that today, while walking around Vittel, one sees not the same world that was there when "thermal fever" built the spa and its environs from a bucolic preserve into one of the great vacation sites of the late 1890s. Bathing suits hang from wrought iron balconies, dripping onto the sidewalks and the unsuspecting heads of those who move about this small city after morning cures. From the town's lush gardens, filtered through a summer's thick bouquet of flowering plants, one can hear at midday the unmistakable drone of a Wurlitzer in action. Pairs of aged couples, shuffling just behind the organ's beat, show that spa life still has its peculiar penchant for scheduled leisure. Smiling at each other and for the cameras, these dancers strike poses of happiness and hopefulness. For many of them, turning around the dance pavilion in the afternoon is a form of doctoring or an interlude between different kinds of mineral water curing. For others, dancing on vacation is romance in the present and a shared counterpoint to an everyday life where there is no cheek-to-cheek time at lunch. The soft press of individual time at Vittel and France's other spas, marked gently on the tired faces of people who use walkers to get around but remember well that they used to run, mirrors the larger push from the past that all of these places have seen in a century's time. Because even when the French warm so quickly to talk of their bathing places and what spa will help which ailment, and even when they proudly show a knee bending further than it had before a trip to Vichy, the structures of modern life, modern medicine, and holiday-making today depend on spas for a lineage without needing them very much to explain or organize patterns of leisure. That spas once served these larger functions so formidably as to encompass for a time the totality of bourgeois vacationing is reason enough to assess how these places and their particular way of setting leisure both reflected and constructed the sensibilities of that other epoch's noontime dancers, eager promenaders, and grim-faced curists.

— 1 —

BATHS AND CURING IN
THE OLD REGIME

𝒯he Sardinian doctor Joseph Despine was no young man in 1789, yet he would continue his practice of medicine in the municipality of Aix-les-Bains to the end of the Restoration. Aged and tired in his latter years, the doctor practiced during the 1820s with his son and grandson, both of whom were physicians affiliated with the largest bathing establishment in the Savoy. As he gradually turned over his profitable practice to his heirs, the senior Despine seems to have slipped increasingly away from the active role he had played for nearly five decades in the administration of the spa at Aix-les-Bains. His age may well have disinclined him to continue meeting each week with the other men who ran the bathing establishment. But perhaps just as likely, Dr. Despine may have disengaged himself from administering the thermal establishment because spas and the ways of managing them and making them profitable were changed beyond that which the old man could reckon. This chapter is about the baths that Joseph Despine had known and even helped to construct, just as it is about what caused those spas to be replaced.

GEOGRAPHY, TRAVEL, AND CLIENTELE

Geography has long been a constant in the history of France's spas. The principal spas have always been where mineral sources most abound: in the four mountainous regions of France (see fig. 1). Their greatest concentration lies within the Pyrenees mountains, where waters such as those of Ax-les-Thermes, Luchon, and Bagnères-de-Bigorre have been frequented steadily since antiquity. The mountains of the Vosges are home to more than a score of long-exploited springs too. Plombières and Luxeuil in particular have been associated with their mineral water sources for many

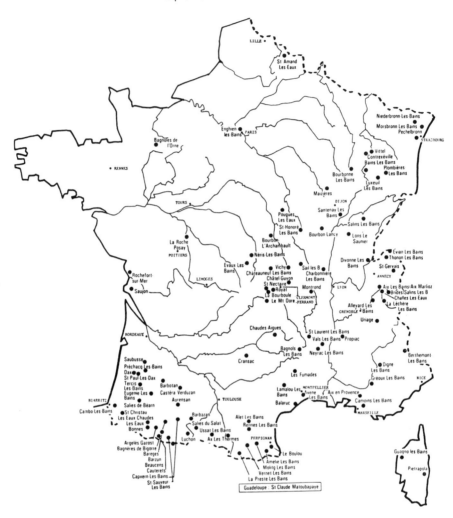

FIGURE I   Map of France showing major sources of mineral water exploitation. Reprinted from Institut Français d'Architecture, *Villes d'eaux en France*, 274.

centuries. Alpine France also boasts an abundance of mineral springs, some of which knew a great deal of notoriety as the sites of great Roman baths. And finally, there are the important springs of the Massif Central and the Bourbon plain—Vichy, Néris-les-Bains, Royat, Bourbon-l'Archambault, and le Mont-Dore—whose names have long been synonymous with their curative properties.

The typically remote geographical location of water sources was a determining factor in their early modern historical development—or lack thereof. Other than Enghien-les-Bains, situated in the northwestern environs of Paris, few important sources of mineral water were within easy traveling distance of the capital. Thus, for Parisians, spa-going meant travel to either the sources of the Vosges—Luxeuil and Plombières were favored destinations throughout the period—or one of the spas in France's interior. Geographical proximity to the spas was better for many but not all of France's provincial cities. Marseille and Montpellier, for example, were both within easy traveling distance of Aix-en-Provence. Similarly, Strasbourg had Niederbronn as its neighboring watering place; Toulouse had Luchon, Bagnères-de-Bigorre, and Ax-les-Thermes; Bordeaux had Dax; Dijon had Bourbon-Lancy; and both Lyon and Grenoble had Aix-les-Bains. But Rennes, Tours, and other important cities were not convenient to any of the country's principal springs.

While carriages made regularly scheduled trips to even the more remote areas of France, travel to the spas was never easy or convenient until the coming of the steamboat ferries and railroads of the nineteenth century. The traditional calendar of the spa season reflected the difficulties of mountain travel clearly enough. Through the months of winter, when heavy rains and snow combined to render mountainous roads almost impassable, spa towns were utterly deserted save for their local populations. The same was true for the months of early spring and late fall, when rains and flooding routinely subjected mountain travelers to bothersome delays. Spa-goers waited to travel until the best possible weather, thus the "season" seldom began before the end of May or continued past the middle of September.

Even under ideal conditions, traveling to a spa often involved a journey that was measured in days rather than hours. Parisians, for instance, had the main of France to cross in order to reach the many spas of the Pyrenees region. And although the noted waters of Forges were less than sixty miles from the capital city, even affluent travelers might spend eight days on the road between Paris and Vichy.[1] Less drastically, inhabitants of a northern city such as Lille had to travel for two days or more to reach the spas of the Alps or, for that matter, those of the Vosges. Knowing the amount of time required by voyages as well as the many challenges presented by them, spa-goers of the early modern period seldom went to a spa for anything less than three weeks.

Travel also cost a significant amount of money, particularly when one's journey was long and arduous. Thus spa-going was simply beyond most people's means in the early modern period, just as the thought of cross-country travel was outside the pale of their imaginations. Neither cost nor difficulty changed a great deal from the sixteenth to the eighteenth century, which is doubtlessly why the spas of France and Europe generally did not draw significantly larger crowds in the early 1800s than in the late sixteenth century, when Michel de Montaigne visited and wrote sardonically about them.[2]

Yet the barriers posed by the spas' geography were surmountable in the early modern period by a select set of persons.[3] Principally, of course, it was the court and nobility which could afford travel and knew how to negotiate a voyage's challenges. A Vichy newspaper, for instance, heralded with a certain excitement the arrival on one day, in May of 1676, of no fewer than ten members of the French nobility.[4] At nearby Bourbon-l'Archambault, as the most noted historian of French spas in the seventeenth century, Laurence Brockliss, has observed, aristocrats "came to the spa from all over France: Paris, Caen, Tours, Reims, Montauban, Brittany, and so on."[5] Determining how many nobles went to the spas is more difficult, however, than recognizing that most of them might have gone had they wanted to.[6] Beyond holders of high titles or those persons of otherwise great notoriety, aristocrats at a spa were not typically counted or otherwise recorded by spa administrators. Seasonal tallies of all visitors were sometimes made, but these did not dissect the spa population into sociological subgroups.[7] Thus one is left with little choice but to offer a crude estimate as to the number of spa-going nobles in this period. As none of the dozen or so principal spas had more than 1,000 visitors in any given summer, and we know that each spa had a steady stream of visitors from both the first and the third estates, the number of elite spa-goers most likely ranged from 6,000 to 9,000 persons per year.[8]

After the aristocracy and a sometimes significant population of "humble bourgeois, merchants, lawyers, simple *curés* and an endless stream of afflicted monks and nuns," destitute invalids constituted the greatest cohort among the spa's summer population.[9] At Vichy in 1752, for example, nearly two hundred poor visitors arrived in June and July.[10] People who could prove their poverty and medical necessity to the authorities of their village or region were often granted a modest sum of money with which to pay for travel to a spa. Parish priests as well sometimes made allowances to the poor. Paternalism from other sources saw to it that wounded soldiers, aging veterans, clerical authorities, and members of religious orders could obtain enough charity to travel to a spa.[11] And at the spas too, an enduring paternalism—dating in many cases from the Middle Ages—allowed these travelers to make free and unlimited use of a town's mineral waters and medical services.[12] Indigents typically went to the largest spa within their region, thus Vichy, Luxeuil, Aix-les-Bains, and Bagnères-de-Bigorre especially were frequented by these spa-goers. It is clear from various records that not even vouched-for and charity-bearing invalids were always given the right to bathe, however, the typical reception of the poor was doubtlessly better than that.[13]

What motivated the spa's various populations to travel in the first place was not that colorful and amusing sociability was waiting at the destination. Brockliss has observed, visitors "did not come seeking to meet new acquaintances or hatch marriage alliances."[14] Arriving with family members, servants, and sometimes friends, visitors apparently were met with a dull social season while taking their cures. The situation was evidently so bleak that even servants found the spa towns impossibly boring.[15] But if what Brockliss has observed is true, that "no one wanted to stay at a French spa if they could help it," then those who did stay must have done so for medicinal rather than social reasons.[16] Indeed, it seems clear that the sick and invalid who went to a bath brought with them a shared but vaguely considered belief in the power of mineral water to restore health.[17] It mattered little what medical complaints a person had, for local physicians and travel writers were eager to claim that their mineral waters were able to combat virtually every malady. Thus, cases of gout, rheumatism, skin disease, liver distress, arthritis, asthma, paralysis, and infertility were liberally represented among a spa's summer population. From the severely invalid to those whose sole complaint was indigestion or headaches, all summer curists expected some measure of rejuvenation from their spa visit. At the very least, urban spa-goers knew that they would feel better for having left the heat, airlessness, and overpowering stench of the summertime city behind them, while aristocratic visitors from the countryside looked forward to finding a tonic for the boredom and isolation that often went with provincial living.[18]

But why they expected to feel better, medically speaking, was not especially clear to anyone in the period. Doctors affiliated with the principal spas did what they could to establish a therapeutic rationale for spa curing.[19] But such little-known tracts as Dr. Jean-Baptiste de Cabias's *Les vertus merveilleuses des bains d'Aix en Savoie,* first published in 1623, did little to give spa cures a scientific grounding. On the contrary, Cabias and his fellow spa publicists tended to make such extravagant claims about the efficacy of their spas as to move mineral water curing all the further into the mysterious realm of water lore. Other writers and publicists endeavored to find a more balanced tone in their various descriptions of mineral water bathing. The larger and more frequented spas of the seventeenth and eighteenth centuries, for instance, all had eager publicists whose eyes were trained toward development and profit. Bourbon-Lancy and Forges had doctors and writers who were all too anxious to praise the local waters for their capacity to cure fertility problems.[20] Doctors affiliated with Bourbon-l'Archambault and Vichy made equally strident appeals to sufferers of rheumatic disorders.[21]

Curing was something that early modern spa-goers seemed to take seriously throughout their three-week holidays, even though most patients, regardless of their different maladies, tended to receive almost identical prescriptions from their doctors. The typical cure in the era involved both mineral water baths and the drinking of water from its source.[22] Still very much adhering to the theory of humors, spa physicians bled and purged most of their visitors before mineral waters were even introduced.[23] Once cleaned of noxious humors, the body was ready to be made well. If drinking water from a fountain seemed like it would be a pleasant enough way to cure, the lie was often put to this assumption once "patients" sampled their tonic for the first time. One visitor to Vichy toward the end of the eighteenth century recounted her own experience: "I took the waters this morning my dear friend, and oh were they bad! One goes at six in the morning to the fountain and finds that everyone is already there. One drinks, then walks around the fountain, then takes a longer promenade, and then drinks more of the disagreeable water. This is what one does until midday."[24] The extent to which water drinking was a medically supervised affair is open to some speculation. Doctors offered their visitors at least rough guidelines on how much water to drink and when to drink it. Yet prescriptions and regimens clearly varied widely, with some doctors insisting that water had to be drunk only at sunrise, while others cautioned against drinking when still sleepy.[25] Certainly, as historians have noted, a free-spirited curist like Montaigne could gulp as many as a dozen glasses of mineral water in a morning.[26] And visitors accustomed to the less potent waters of Bourbon-l'Archambault, where an imbiber would routinely drink as many as twenty glasses of water per day, were ill prepared for the comparative moderation common when drinking other waters. At Forges, for instance, four glasses in a day constituted a full curative dose.[27] Frequently, drinkers of water at a spa simply medicated themselves with whatever quantity of fluid they could ingest. As one bloated commentator reported in the seventeenth century, this crude method of self-curing could go on cup after cup: "I drink about a dozen glasses in the morning, and this makes me desperate to purge myself."[28] All water drinkers had enough medical instruction to know that what went into them had to come out of them, thus sheltered walkways were built close to spa fountains, allowing drinkers some privacy in which to eliminate the water they had consumed.[29]

Showering, or taking the "douche," was another form of curing in the early modern era. Reporting her experience in a shower to a close friend, one noblewoman called showering "a good re-creation of purgatory I am sure." This cure, she wished for her friend to know, was far from either comfortable or pleasant, involving as it did "a flow of water, hotter and more forceful than you could ever imagine." In showering, she warned her friend, "everyone suffers . . . a humiliating state of affairs."[30] It seems that patients who followed these cures very often endured pain. During this therapy, which doctors only prescribed with great care, hot water was poured from a height of several feet directly onto lesions or rheumatic limbs.[31]

Bathing, another common form of treatment, was not a terribly medical experience at the spas of this period.[32] Doctors seem to have gone only rarely with their patients to bathe. Similarly, medical attendants were not posted at all spas, though a concierge or *baigneur* was often on hand to charge an admission fee to those who could pay. Although promotional literature from the seventeenth and eighteenth centuries suggested that bathing at a spa was a highly ordered and medical experience, the gap between this rhetoric and the actual practice of curing was probably significant. For if "no one (took) meals in the basin," as one of Montaigne's assistants recounted, most people stayed long enough to acquire an appetite. As this witness remembered it, "hardly anyone left the bath without having passed an hour or so."[33] Doctors' advice to patients called for not only much shorter baths than this, but also insisted upon a quiet and reserved comportment.[34]

The bathing facilities featured at the principal spas did very little to affirm a medical essence. If anything, the particular organization of a spa's waters that was common throughout France until the end of the eighteenth century suggested sociability rather than science or medicine.[35] A basin for group bathing, called a bath, was the centerpiece of every spa's curative spatiality.[36] These communal pools, which were invariably open to the sky and located in the center of town, did nothing to segregate their users according to gender or class. On the contrary, such pools as the one at Plombières, (fig. 2), were open, without respect to social background or gender, to whomever wished to take the waters. As a local historian of Plombières noted in 1748, basins were public and social places that made no allowances for modesty. For in these baths, the historian described, people "bathe[d] indiscriminately, men, women, children, priests, monks, nuns all in the same pool and almost naked."[37] In certain locales, such as Aix-les-Bains in the duchy of Savoy, spa basins hardly even separated their human users from the lame or otherwise sick horses and cattle which were herded to town to seek the benefits of a mineral water cure.[38] Many of them still floored with the mud that had been there since their medieval or even Roman origins, spa baths could welcome as many as 150 curists at a time.[39]

It was not only at French watering places, however, that communal bathing characterized the spa experience. At England's famous Bath, which

FIGURE 2   Sixteenth-century etching of the public basin at Plombières. Reprinted from Institut Français d'Architecture, *Villes d'eaux en France*, 367.

FIGURE 3   This sixteenth-century depiction of the open bath at Néris-les-Bains suggests the erotic and public nature of bathing. Reprinted from Institut Français d'Architecture, *Villes d'eaux en France,* 169.

was far and away the most courtly watering place in all of eighteenth-century Europe, bathing was conducted in a basin that was strikingly similar to those at Plombières, Néris (fig. 3), or Aix-les-Bains.[40] The main facility at Bath until the 1770s, called the King's Bath, dated from the sixteenth century. This facility was a rectangle, approximately sixty by forty feet.[41] In shallow water that was warmed to a temperature of 116 degrees, bathers waded about and chatted with each other. Their experience—just like that of bathers at French watering places—was social, public, and collective. While women and men each had separate and private dressing rooms, they were together for the duration of their stay in the bath. Dressed for bathing in linen clothes and hats, men and women alike outfitted themselves with floating trays, the contents of which included a handkerchief, a snuff box, and a drink.[42] Thus equipped, Bath's bathers were prepared to engage in precisely the sort of social and sexual intrigue with which the place had become so rightfully associated.[43] And, like their French equivalents, these illustrious bathers conducted themselves while curing, without medical guidance or supervision of any sort.

Michel Foucault's theories on "bio power" and the advent of medicine as a politicized discourse with insidious social authority suggest why it is probably inaccurate to characterize spas and the cures one followed at them in the early modern period as "medicalized" in the critical sense of that term. If doctors held a certain sway over the routines that their visitors followed while at Vichy or Forges, that authority clearly was not girded by the epistemological shifts to a medicalized articulation of social relations that the eighteenth century would announce. Architecture, administration, the body as a vehicle for discourses on physical wellness and for social identity—these reconfigurations of knowledge and how knowledge was to be known were hardly even nascent in the baths and bathing practices of the seventeenth-century spa. That sick people bathed in the 1600s and tried to follow what their doctors prescribed is coincidental.[44] Patient compliance in this period was a thing that individual doctors might or might not cause to occur. Where strong-willed and ambitious doctors sought to advance their standing in the society of the Old Regime, as they built up their practices and gained personal profit, there can be no doubt that visitors to a bath became patients with mineral water medicine to take.[45] The logic of curing and of recognizing as authoritative a medicalized metering of a day or a three-week cure, however, was not an internalized sensibility in the early modern period. If individual doctors at one spa could bully their patients to perform a routinized and healthful day, the absence of such individuals at another spa left curing open to much interpretation.[46] Thus, while the variety of different cures available at spas, coupled with the large number of physicians one could find at the more popular bathing places, made medicine very much a part of the spa milieu, it is also important to understand that medicine in this context lacked the overarching if also unwitting authority it would come to have in the 1800s.

LOCAL ECONOMIES AND SPA DEVELOPMENT

Upon reaching the spa towns of France, what did travelers find beyond bathing pools, fountains, and each other? The residents of these towns were in most respects similar to residents of other small cities. Of the 1,300 persons counted in the 1743 census at Aix-les-Bains, for example, fully 277 persons were poor enough to be exempted from taxation and eight were officially registered as beggars.[47] At the other end of the social spectrum, 30 people were registered as notables, of whom 7 were listed as functionaries. Twenty-four heads of families were laborers whose main work was agricultural. Further attesting to the still rural character of this particular municipality, an additional 30 persons were day workers whose services were used variously in the city and on the farm. But Aix, like many spa municipalities, differed from other cities its size because of its relatively high number of shopkeepers and artisans. Of the 34 businesses in the city by the middle of the eighteenth century, 10 were inns and

3 were pharmacies. The city could also boast at least 4 wine merchants at this time as well as several clothiers.

The quality and extent of the spa towns' civic infrastructures varied. Where there was a larger permanent population, facilities tended to be more extensive. Thus Vichy, whose early modern population was measured in hundreds of persons, was in most respects a cruder place to visit than Aix-les-Bains, whose permanent population already exceeded 1,100 by the sixteenth century. Even the smaller villages, however, typically had a church and some sort of a town hall. Similarly, all watering places possessed amenities geared toward pleasing cosmopolitan curists. Every spa town had at least some sort of restaurant or café open during the summer, and the larger municipalities often had several of each. The regular coming and going of carriages during the summer season ensured that mail service was far better and more reliable than such small cities deserved. National and even international periodicals could often be found in the spa towns too. Moreover, many municipalities featured reading rooms and book merchants.

Rooming houses of various sizes abounded in all of the principal spa municipalities, although few of these offered much in the way of luxury. With single rooms or suites and family-style meals served in a communal dining room, the typical house with rooms to let accommodated between three and five individuals or families at a time. Few rooming houses were large or well enough equipped to handle more than fifteen guests. Except for the month of July, when the spa's summer population was at its peak, a town's ten or so principal innkeepers could usually house all interested travelers. But during the peak seasons—when indigents, clerics, soldiers, and nobles all but flooded these small cities—temporary "hotels" burst open everywhere. Anyone with a spare room, or anyone whose family could be rearranged so as to create an extra room, took in weekly boarders.

How did municipal economies of the early modern period attempt to organize themselves and their resources to exploit the presence of summer visitors? In the first place, France's spa towns had no concerted plan to make money from their bathing facilities. As we have already noted, a town's mineral waters were distributed to many visitors without any charge. In addition to indigents, soldiers, and clerics, visiting functionaries and doctors could bathe for free. Gratis privileges were also extended to all residents of a spa town as well as visitors from neighboring communes.[48] But if a spa's basins and fountains seldom contributed directly to the municipal economy, this fact did not mean that spas were fundamentally profitless places.

Throughout the seventeenth and eighteenth centuries, doctors at every spa in France struggled mightily to make more money from their association with a watering place and its affluent summer population. The principal concern of any spa doctor was to increase the number of persons on whom his medical practice depended. Such dictates of professional survival were by no means conducted in a generous spirit with respect to other doctors.[49] Rather, practitioners routinely sought to poach each other's wealthier patients. The few exceptions to the competitive spirit usually involved a younger doctor showing reserve and deference to a more established physician. Or, perhaps more often, professional collegiality within a spa's medical corps was a family matter. A doctor's son would acquire medical training that eventually allowed for an interfamilial transfer of an established spa practice.

Such practical techniques as these won a measure of prosperity for many doctors, but wealthy these physicians were not. Instead, their reliance on a poorly defined system of honorary payment made it difficult for them to exploit fully the wealth that many of their patients possessed. Invalids at a spa—regardless of their wealth—paid their doctors only as much money as they felt their cures were worth. As few treatments produced results that were both dramatic and immediately recognized, most curists felt disposed to offer only a modest payment to their doctors. It was only natural, then, that doctors sought to find other ways to extract money directly from their watering places.

Their schemes involved both promotional writing and price hiking. Doctors' promotional efforts, which were usually contained within a guidebook of some sort, were not published in large numbers or widely distributed.[50] Thus Dr. Cabias, whose work is noted above, and his like-minded colleagues did not derive great profits from their literary projects. But spa doctors did garner more money for themselves by making all aspects of curing more expensive. To whatever extent their clients would permit, practitioners elaborated on the ways and means of water curing and sought to increase their honorariums accordingly. Bath chairs came into vogue at least partly for this reason, as the chairs tended to raise the tariff that a curist could be charged. Similarly, at some spas, massage and showering became medical arts that were administered at a price that was usually two to three times the cost of simply bathing.[51]

However motivated they might have been to take their watering places in speculative and entrepreneurial directions, individual spa doctors were not entirely free to make of their milieu whatever they wished. On the contrary, an administrative body was created at the state level in the later seventeenth century—the superintendence of French mineral waters—

whose responsibility it was to oversee the country's watering places and its spa physicians. The bureaucracy was in fact quite powerful, as its head was also the first physician to the French king. In each province where there were exploitable mineral springs, a state-appointed intendant was posted at a prominent spa.[52] Notwithstanding their stated responsibilities with respect to surveillance and research on the medicinal properties of spa waters, the medical intendants typically established private practices and made veritable fiefdoms of their spas. By combining their salaries with honorariums from their medical practices, these doctors secured a generous amount of both wealth and prestige. In the process, of course, they alienated all other doctors at their spas and guaranteed, with the state's authority in their column, that there would be relatively little fiscal innovation in the administration of watering places.

More like the intendants than rank and file spa doctors, most residents of a spa town had only a secondary interest in a watering place's economic production. Instead, it was their ongoing project to make what money they could out of many and sundry commercial relations with a spa's guests. Throughout the dozen or so small towns where a critical mass of wealthy visitors congregated each summer, busy and ambitious locals did as they had to do to exploit a relatively captive audience. Those who owned or rented a dwelling with extra rooms became, for the course of the summer, proprietors of rooming houses. The same persons, depending of course on the extent of their financial means, might have operated restaurants or cafés for the summer guests too. Similarly, among the more affluent, shopkeeping and carriage hiring were prosperous seasonal activities. But even locals of the most modest means benefited from the thermal economy. For them, lucrative options included domestic service, carriage driving, stable work, or any one of many seasonal jobs involved in maintaining a spa's bathing facilities.

TOWARD MODESTY AND RESPECTABILITY

The historical continuity of France's spas was only slightly affected by the events of the French Revolution's moderate phase. Aristocrats, in fact, found many spas to be convenient and familiar places to wait out the first three summers of the Revolution. Certain spas even held strategic value in this regard, as they were well situated as exit points from France. Aix-les-Bains in the Savoy was especially favored for its proximity to Piedmont and Switzerland. Throughout the early 1780s, for example, Aix had routinely hosted around 500 visitors each summer, while the summers of

1790 and 1791 saw the arrival of 740 and 750 visitors respectively.[53] Suffice it to say that these people were not spending the sort of thermal season they might have before the Revolution. Or, at least, they were not spending much money on Aix's mineral waters. A paltry 300 francs more were received into the spa's accounts in the summer of 1790 than had been received from a summer population in 1785 of 200 hundred fewer persons.[54]

The status quo at the spas appeared to change dramatically as 1792 brought an end to the moderate phase of the Revolution. The rise of the Jacobins unleashed a scathing critique against the remaining institutions of the Old Regime. The spa towns, for their long-standing association with the aristocracy and also because so many of them had sheltered wealthy emigrants, were spared none of this ideological tirade. Identified as seats of counter-revolution in many instances and otherwise implicated in the aristocratic excesses of the Old Regime, bathing facilities had to be brought within the pale of the Jacobins' political culture.[55] The privileged aristocrats, who had "always come to Vichy and its hospital for the summer months that were once so vulgarly known as the season," were now denounced as unwanted "foreigners who would no longer crowd out the soldiers and others more entitled to the facilities."[56]

Refitting the spas after a republican image was not that difficult. Basins, most of which had traditionally been known as "Royal Baths," were now rechristened as "baths of the people." By the spring of 1792 at Vichy, for example, a departmental committee was already actively creating a new administration for the spa and its hospital. To the nuns who had long been nursing in the commune's hospital, an edict was issued 15 September 1792 stipulating that they must "accept fully the decrees against wearing ecclesiastical attire."[57] The Committee of Public Safety, by the next year, had a stated goal that spas would be transformed into "hospitals consecrated for the defenders of the republic."[58] Nothing at all changed by way of the medical administration of thermal waters except that gratis cures were now even more common than before. Public fountains, of course, had never been in any way privileged or privatized, so there was little about them to be democratized. Where a spa town also had newer and more regal bathing facilities, these were commandeered for the exclusive use of veterans and wounded soldiers. Thus, at Aix-les-Bains, the elaborately marbled new thermal establishment, which had only been completed in the early 1780s, now welcomed old and wounded soldiers.[59] Thermal establishments, according to the inscriptions that now loomed over their entrances, were supposed "to strengthen the arms that would destroy tyranny."[60]

Whether or not it helped to destroy tyranny, the inscription of a new kind of politics at the spa clearly damaged the local economies where its tenets held sway. In the first place, many mineral water sources in France fell under the direct ownership of the state in this period, as all such sources belonging to communes or religious orders were ordered to transfer their proprietary rights to the nation.[61] Perhaps much more detrimental to local interests, however, was the fact that those aristocrats who remained in France through 1793 and 1794 were unlikely to be so conspicuous as to haunt their favored watering places, particularly not when regional authorities were known to make surveillance reports to the state's authorities regarding prominent or suspicious persons in residence.[62] Declining visitor statistics from these years show this hesitancy clearly enough. At Aix-les-Bains, the great season of the *émigrés,* 1791, had seen 760 summer visitors. Two years later, the town counted a mere 332 persons on holiday. Spa commerce had declined so markedly by the middle 1790s that many spa locales abandoned altogether the practice of counting their summer guests.[63]

To many contemporaries, it must certainly have seemed that spas in anything like their traditional construction would never survive the Revolution. Those who held this belief would have based their thinking on more than the political recalibration to which the spas were being subjected. Rather, local doctors and others who had long traded on the thermal economy heard the spas' death knell in the neglect and physical destruction that beset nearly every bathing facility in France. The state simply declared that the old spa was dead and that the new one had been born, but it offered neither the administrative mechanisms nor the fiscal means to provide sufficient nuance to either pronouncement. While the Terror passed and then the Directory, these "baths of the people"—and the people whose economic viability had been grossly disturbed by the fall of the thermal marketplace—waited for some word as to what the spas' future would hold. In the meantime, baths crumbled for want of maintenance or in direct response to the actions of vandalizing soldiers.

But the early years of the First Empire suggested to many observers that something of the Old Regime baths might indeed be resurrected. Under Bonaparte, some of the summer season's glories did indeed return, as did some of its old practitioners. The reunion of aristocrats and other persons of "quality" at the spas, however, was not to be easy. For beyond the political transformations that the revolutionaries had put into place, their tenure had brought to fruition important shifts in the cultural and economic sensibilities of French society. And these shifts, whose roots extended well into the world of the Old Regime, spoke directly to whatever the nineteenth-century spas would become.

In the first place, spas and their administrators had to reckon with a shift in cultural sensibilities concerning privacy, morality, and the physical organization of their bathing facilities. One telling splinter from the discourse, in opposition to basin bathing and predating the Revolution, was penned in 1786 by the Intendant of Auvergne: "I arrived at Le Mont-Dore only to be immediately struck by the dirtiness of the water and of the baths themselves as well as the indecency of these facilities where the two sexes are mixed together. What I had heard before coming here did not prepare me for the scenes that I saw. Now more than ever I believe in the necessity of executing a project that will render these facilities commodious and decent enough so that they might be called healthful."[64] But if this official correspondence suggested a heightened concern among elites with respect to hygiene and the decency of bath organization, "high" discourse hardly held a monopoly on such sensibilities. On the contrary, popular utterances expressed some of the same concerns about the indecency suggested by communal bathing. At Aix-les-Bains in the latter decades of the eighteenth century, for instance, a durable rumor among locals and visitors of all stripes had it that the spa's basin was the nocturnal home of an especially vicious race of serpents.[65] Regardless of whether this rumor had any basis in fact, it clearly showed a tension concerning the condition of the spa's pool and the sort of carnivalesque sessions that might have transpired therein. Serpents, after all, carried symbolic meaning that the rodents and debris simply did not.

Other markers of this shift in mentality were architectural, also predating the Revolution. A transformation in the principles of spa design had begun at various European watering places in the last quarter of the eighteenth century. In the main, the new architecture accentuated privacy as well as the medical nature of spa curing. At England's Bath, for instance, an elaborate bathing establishment was completed in 1778 after more than a decade of planning (fig. 4). While collective bathing was featured in the central basin of the Hot Bath, the larger pool was ringed by six private tubs. Equally new were the eight private dressing rooms at Bath's new thermal establishment. The facility was completely enclosed, and its entrances were monitored by a concierge. Beyond supervising the general goings-on of the place, the doorman was supposed to collect an admission fee from all bathers. Set high enough to segregate the bathing population according to class, the admission fee broke at least two long-standing precedents. Now, at least part of the spa's point was to make a profit for those who had built and would administer it. Moreover, the organization of the spa made concrete a certain discretion between the elite and popular classes.

Bath's new facility was not merely a matter of English prudery written in stone. On the contrary, many French aristocrats who saw the Hot Bath wanted to install its equivalents at their own spas. At Luchon, for example, a series of plans was created in the early 1780s for a thermal establishment that would have made even Bath's new spa look primitive (fig. 5). Drafted by a regional architect, one M. Bourgeois, the plans for Luchon's bathing establishment did not allow for any sort of group bath. Rather, individual bath rooms were to be the sites of all curing, and each of these was to have sufficient room for bathers to change their clothes in private. Only

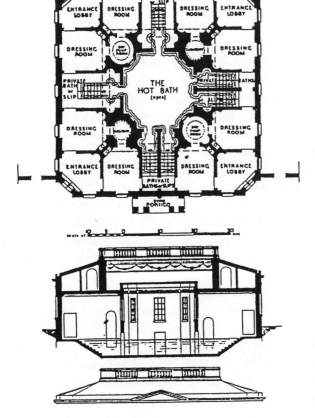

FIGURE 4 Architectural drawing showing the increased privacy featured in the interior of the Hot Bath, built in 1778 at Bath, England. Reprinted from Granville, *The Spas of England and Principal Sea-bathing Places.*

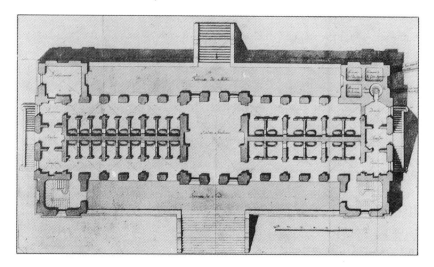

FIGURE 5 Architectural drawing for the thermal establishment at Luchon, 1784, showing an early example of individual bathing spaces. The plans were not realized. Reprinted from Institut Français d'Architecture, *Villes d'eaux en France*, 69.

the Revolution interrupted the realization of M. Bourgeois's grand plans for Luchon. The same fate befell other French plans to create spas that would match the sort of facilities that England's Bath could boast.

Still other signs of the transformation in attitude concerning spa bathing and bath design were administrative and regulatory. At Aix-les-Bains, for example, a strict set of regulations for bathing was issued in 1783.[66] These rules modified the spas' traditional paternalism concerning invalid indigents. The poor were still welcomed in all of Aix's bathing facilities, but now their presence was no longer unconditional. Before journeying to Aix, would-be bathers had to gain a "certificate of poverty" from an ecclesiastical or secular official of their commune. Upon their arrival at Aix, they then had to present themselves and their papers to the spa's chief doctor for inspection. Having satisfied the doctor as to the level of their destitution and medical necessity, indigent visitors were then admitted to the new spa.[67]

Within the thermal establishment, however, the poor still received courtesies and medical treatments equal to their paying counterparts. Rules were particularly insistent on this point. Article 9, for example, instructed the spa's medical director to ensure that indigents were treated in a "manner that no one could perceive as different in even the smallest detail from the services rendered" to paying customers. But the same article included a clause that made the aforementioned equality a more complicated matter: "At the same time that he sees to it that the rich invalids are being treated with all the order and punctuality possible, he (the medical director) must pay particular attention that the poor are served immediately after the rich, without the slightest delay."[68] Equal services indeed and in the identical facility too, but rich and poor bathers did not share the new spa at the same time. And in this mixture of paternalism and temporal segregation, the new thermal establishment spoke in yet another voice against the collective social practices of the old spas.

Ultimately, however, the resurrection of the Old Regime spa in the early 1800s was hampered by what the Revolution had done to unfetter commercial and economic development. A new and extraordinarily ambitious class of men had profited from the Revolution's tireless attacks on privilege. And these men, when they made their way through the tiny villages and modest cities that were France's spa towns, looked upon these places and saw—even in the midst of decayed and neglected baths and bathing establishments—nothing but vast potential for their own profit. Many of them were extended the right to lease spas under the First Empire by various local, regional, and national agreements. What they did with their opportunities signaled to all observers that the structures of the early modern spa belonged to a world that was lost.

— 2 —

PRODUCING LEISURE:
ECONOMICS, CLASS FORMATION,
AND THE *SÉJOUR* FOR SALE

*M*ore than anything else, the ambitious entrepreneurs who leased French spas in the early nineteenth century seemed interested in counting. For unlike the bathing establishments of the Old Regime, where bathers had come and gone with relative freedom, spas now came to be led by administrations that were obsessed with the need to monitor all activities with respect to bathing. Thus, beyond the details of their identities, bathers at a First Empire spa were tracked according to "the number of showers they took, the times at which they were treated, the houses where they lodged, and the names of the employees from whom they received medical service."[1] Visitors also were registered in a pair of accounting books kept by a spa's medical director. These ledgers noted the name, sex, and nationality of everyone who took a spa's waters.[2]

Although probably few of the spa renters derived much profit from their leases, most of which expired in the years surrounding the fall of Bonaparte, these fledgling entrepreneurs remained enchanted by what they saw as a real opportunity to make money through the spas. With the coming of the Restoration, however, the spas' protospeculators would encounter a host of compelling issues that went well beyond the question of whether or not their thermal leases would be renewed. How would bathing establishments that had been neglected or even destroyed during the years of the Revolution emerge again? Who would be the nineteenth-century spas' clients? Perhaps most pressing of all, how could spas be given a new economic organization so that they might be developed more profitably?

In their correspondence during the First Empire and the early years of the Restoration, municipal authorities and administrators at the spa towns of France began to articulate a vision of their milieu that differed fundamentally from how the spas of the Old Regime and revolutionary era had been understood. Local authorities, as they surveyed their towns and bathing establishments, seldom failed to comment that such facilities were ripe with vast "potential." A medical official in one spa municipality, for example, echoed precisely these confident sentiments in 1818 when he characterized his mineral springs as "the most precious in all of Europe in their abundance, mineralization, and temperature." Further, this contemporary stressed that his spa was liberally blessed with "beautiful routes," "a picturesque countryside," "an advantageous geographical position," and "pure air."[3]

Important features such as these had always helped spas to attract patrons beyond the invalids and indigents who would come in any case— wealthy tourists whose holiday-making was of vital importance to a spa town's economy. Now, however, enthusiastic pronouncements about one's town and bathing establishment were more than the stuff of traditional boosterism. Beginning in the Restoration, it was the rich but poorly defined terrain of the future—where dreams and desires for personal and communal profit were nourished—that caused municipal administrators to wax eloquent as to the potential of their thermal baths. In direct contrast to the unorganized exploitation of visitors that had characterized the early modern period, spa municipalities wanted to pursue a highly coordinated development program.

THE DEMOGRAPHIC AND ECONOMIC TERMS
OF EMBOURGEOISEMENT

In the main, spa renters and administrators were local doctors who were thoroughly versed in the arts of competitive business practice.[4] But from the first years of the Restoration, doctors recognized that the nature of competition at the spa was changing rapidly. No longer could the several physicians of a particular spa fight against each other for seasonal business. Competition, if anyone was to benefit from it, now had to be directed at rival thermal establishments. Speaking for many of his associates across France, one water doctor noted in a governmental report in 1818 that "everything [had] changed since 1789 for thermal establishments." Spas, this doctor warned, no longer could "be improved in stages, particular projects taking so long to complete that years [passed] before achieving the whole."[5] Competition, the organizing concept of the new thermal environment for this spa doctor and so many others, demanded that a "backward" spa make haste to match the "progress" that its rivals had already seen. Patient-poaching, in the new era of the spas, would be conducted along regional and even national lines. Thus, to a concerned contemporary in Aix-les-Bains in the neighboring Savoy, it was most frustrating that "Vichy [had] just augmented its establishment and garden; Mont-Dore, Bourbon-Lancy, Plombières, and the stations of the Pyrenees [were] all increasing their curative means and reputations with each passing day."[6]

Beyond the business acumen gained in a career of patient-poaching and other competitive practices, spa physicians were among the country's only clear "experts" in the ways and means of holiday-making. In addition to prescribing thermal cures and consulting with patients, doctors had long participated in their spas' social affairs. These various points of contact, which saw the relationship between patient and physician shift regularly to one of guest and host, had allowed spa practitioners the opportunity to observe unfettered what their clients expected from a three-week season at a bath. What did wealthy travelers need in the way of bathing facilities? What were the more common complaints of these visitors? How did such persons like to entertain themselves when they were not bathing? What sort of accommodations did guests expect? How, in the opinion of frequent travelers, did a given spa rank in comparison to others? On these and other related issues, only France's spa doctors—at least in the Restoration and earlier years of the July Monarchy—could speak with any real authority.

Even if it took some imagination for local doctors to look at their neglected spas at the outset of the Restoration and see much reason for optimism, the vast expenses that were certain to accompany improvement projects began to seem bearable enough when it became clear that many of the spas' regular visitors were willing to rejoin the thermal milieu. Indeed, upper-class bathers began to embrace spa-going in the early nineteenth century in far greater numbers than ever. At Aix-les-Bains in the Sardinian Savoy, for example, more than twice as many voyagers were counted in each year of the decade after 1810 than the 500 or so annual visitors in the 1780s.[7] More striking to the contemporaries who compared such statistics, however, was the fact that this rise in the spa's population suggested a pattern rather than a one-time increase. By 1820, Aix and many other spas were welcoming three times the number of visitors they had typically seen in the later years of the Old Regime. Scattered throughout more than two dozen notable spa towns, a visiting population of more than 31,000 persons went on vacation in each year of the 1820s.[8]

The surge in spa-going signaled to observers in the thermal locales that the social composition of their clientele surely had changed. In annual reports which dutifully noted the name, domicile, local addresses, and bathing activity of every summer visitor, administrators verified that their affluent visitors were indeed no longer almost exclusively noble in origin. This did not mean that locals failed to note with the greatest pride that some of the "more celebrated and ancient families of England, France, Italy, and Germany" had visited and taken the waters.[9] Spa authorities were simply more excited about the appearance of a class of bathers who traditionally had not visited the spas. It was with great excitement and pleasure, then, that administrators lavished attention in their annual reports upon those guests whose "families [were] not less well known but only more recently arrived in society."[10]

The spas all began keeping and publishing weekly "lists of visitors" during the early 1820s, a practice that would continue throughout the century. These lists show that the bourgeoisie was emerging in the 1820s and 1830s as a major group among spa visitors. One such list, for example, compiled by the municipal authorities of Aix-les-Bains for the first week of July 1820, notes the arrival of 126 individuals or families.[11] After declaring their names and cities of origin, nearly half of these visitors chose to add information with respect to the source of their livelihood. Of the 58 heads of families who identified the source of their livelihood, 31 labeled themselves as proprietors or landowners. There were 7 lawyers, 3 government employees, 1 book merchant, 1 architect, 1 entrepreneur, 1 merchant, and 3 priests. Only 2 persons on the list had noble titles; one was a count and the other was a countess.[12]

Similar lists from the 1830s and 1840s show the continued presence of bourgeois spa-goers clearly enough. Between the 25th and 30th of June, 1834, for example, 95 individuals or family groups arrived in Aix-les-Bains. In these five days, no fewer than 15 members of the bourgeois professions, 11 of whom were lawyers, went to the spa—as compared to only 3 persons with noble titles. But why did 33 men and heads of families refuse to offer any details as to their social identity or economic means? Reticence on matters related to one's station typically was not associated with the nobility of the Restoration or early 1830s—people with noble titles hardly hesitated to designate themselves as such. More likely, guests who failed to designate a profession or characterize themselves as landowners were members of the commercial, or middle, class of the bourgeoisie. Probably involved in manufacturing, shopkeeping, or finance, these bourgeois—considering the disdain and contempt that French elites still had for commercial enterprise compared to a career in the liberal professions or wealth that was proprietary in origin—had little reason to think that the sources of their livelihood would make a positive impression on other visitors.

The spa had become even more apparently bourgeois by the 1840s. On the 8th, 9th, and 10th of June, 1842, 40 heads of families arrived in the city of Aix-les-Bains.[13] Only 6 from this group failed to provide biographical information regarding the source of their wealth. Of the 34 who did list such information, 13 described themselves as property owners, 6 were lawyers, 6 were doctors, 4 were priests, 3 were employees of the state, and 2 were manufacturers. Only 2 nobles appeared on this list; one was a count and the other was a baron. Not even counting those who listed themselves as owners of property, nearly half of the arrivals quite clearly described themselves as bourgeois.

To the administrators of the spa towns who maintained and published visitor lists, these tallies also revealed that most spa-goers went on vacation with their families. Seventy-six of the 128 arriving "units" on Aix's 1820 list, for example, came to the spa in some configuration of a family group.[14] Husbands and wives together with their children were the most common version of the vacationing family. In several instances, however, family groups joined the spa milieu without male accompaniment. For example, 4 sets of mothers, daughters, and aunts appeared on the 1820 list. During the 1830s and 1840s, most visitors to a thriving spa continued to come as families. In those decades, when a busy spa counted 100 or more arriving units per week, 30 to 40 were coming *en famille*. Considering that many families at the spas were large—some lists from this period showed families of 10 persons or more—the great spas must have fairly teemed with parents and their children.[15]

SOCIAL AND CULTURAL EXPRESSIONS OF THE BOURGEOISIE, 1815–50

If historians have long questioned the degree to which the French bourgeoisie had a consciousness or a collective identity in the later years of the Old Regime, they have debated this issue with far less intensity with regard to the period of the Restoration and July Monarchy.[16] This is not to say, however, that scholars have viewed the nineteenth-century bourgeoisie as an homogeneous entity. On the contrary, wealthy bankers and entrepreneurs were obviously not on the same economic or social footings as the urban traders and shopkeepers who rightfully identified themselves as bourgeois. Similarly, lawyers, doctors, and other professionals clearly had lives that differed in important respects from those bourgeois who lived off incomes generated by their properties.[17]

Moreover, bourgeois "identities" varied according to gender, geography, and the different rates at which the markings of class changed. In Paris, for example, an affluent bourgeoise recognized her rightful peers by addresses, styles, and social connections that would have had hardly any meaning at all to the wife of a provincial attorney.[18] Some of the capital's cultural bounty and, indeed, a strong whiff of the pleasures of life in its public venues, filtered into the lives of bourgeois who lived in the larger regional cities. Provincial bourgeois, however, had to rely on keen powers of observation to learn how their "kind of people" were supposed to act, dress, think, and feel. Cut off from daily contact with the world of style, status, and public pleasures, these bourgeois—like Flaubert's Emma Bovary—needed some help in imagining what they wanted by way of greater social standing. But if their social desires were murkier than those of their Parisian equivalents, they still longed to participate in the nineteenth-century bourgeoisie's principle dream: to be of more importance in the future, socially speaking, than they were in the present.

Sociologists, historians, and critical theorists have battled since the nineteenth century to describe who in the past was really a "bourgeois." Without doubt, the contribution of Karl Marx's theories of the bourgeoisie have been paramount in this debate. Yet in Marx's economic and materialist scheme of class relationships and identities, it is surely true that the privilege given to social and economic factors over cultural ones has not always helped in framing a sharper image of what history's bourgeoisie has meant to its different societies. Money earned, rents collected, investments made, and the presence of an increasingly modern mode of manufacturing—these factors which contributed to France's embourgeoisement produced a materially grounded definition of the bourgeoisie, which increasingly even marxian historians have tended to abandon. Too many cultural and social attributes, which would be designations of the bourgeois by the century's end, remained very much in the making during the earlier decades of the 1800s. Even the distinctions between different ranks of the bourgeoisie, as one historian has noted recently, led contemporaries to different conclusions regarding the identifiability of who or what was bourgeois. For if an observer could say that "the bourgeoisie is too numerous [and] consist[s] of too many [diverse] elements to enable me to offer any statistics," it was possible for the same commentator to offer this contradictory qualification: "Besides . . . everyone knows what is the bourgeoisie; it represents the vast majority of the population."[19] Similarly, the language used to discuss the bourgeoisie and delineate its subsets was obfuscating and contradictory more than it ever was clarifying. Many historians have made just this point, noting, as Catherine Kudlick has recently, that "contemporaries used terms such as 'bourgeois' and 'middle class' interchangeably with phrases such as 'the intermediate classes,' 'the better-off classes,' 'the fortunate classes,' or 'the privileged persons of the capital.'"[20] For the sake of consistency as I establish how the social contours of France changed over the course of the nineteenth century, I use the term "bourgeoisie" and the subclasses organized under it—"upper," "middle," and "lower"—to designate the social group visibly on the rise in the decades prior to the 1860s, and I use the term "middle class" to specify the segment of society whose more humble means and aspirations hid the evidence of its pronounced ascendancy after 1870.

Even in the bourgeoisie's diversity, however, the several constituencies of the larger group seemed to progress over the course of the century toward the gradual identification and sharing of certain attributes.[21] Modest shopkeepers, bold entrepreneurs, members of the liberal professions, and wealthy investors all saw hard work and thrift as virtuous characteristics of their class.[22] For, as one historian of French society in the nineteenth century has written, "the first fact of life as a bourgeois was work."[23] Particularly during the Restoration and first years of the July Monarchy, the endless work of a family firm or business was an exhausting burden that husbands and wives shared.[24] Diaries from the 1830s recount how spouses "would work long hours, often until midnight, in their . . . business."[25] Again and again, contemporaries stressed that "everyone [involved in commerce] worked from 6 A.M. till 8 P.M. and went right to bed after dinner."[26] And as one historian of bourgeois families and commerce has noted, "few among [these people] did not deliberately spend most of their lives acquiring capital. Most boasted that they were the hardest workers in their factories or other enterprises—the first to arrive in the morning, the last to leave at night."[27]

Commercial activity among the French bourgeoisie tended in the nineteenth century to have a familial orientation and to be characterized by an overarching conservatism with respect to business practice.[28] In business, historians of the period have observed, it was "generally felt that the quickest road to success was the slow but sure one."[29] Rather than purchase newer and more efficient equipment, French manufacturers preferred to hold onto their outdated machines to the point of obsolescence. Self-sufficiency in matters of finance was another mark of this conservatism. Most enterprises refused to borrow money even to fund needed expansion.[30] Rather, such projects were paid for "out of company revenues and, if necessary, the pockets of the owner or his relatives or friends."[31] Typically secretive and cautious, family firms tended to table their business before a "keenly critical circle of relatives, primarily interested in the conservation of the patrimony."[32] More than the expansion of business and profits, such enterprises constituted a means "for the conveyance of individual achievement in the form of property to the next generation."[33] Within a context in which "business failures were often catastrophes that permanently ruined families," a significant measure of commercial caution and fiscal conservatism doubtlessly made a great deal of sense.[34]

This is not to argue, however, that the French economy was a "backward" or primitive beast when compared to its more entrepreneurial and mass-production-oriented English counterpart. Although such assessments of the French economy—and by extension, the French bourgeoisie—were made in the nineteenth century and continue to be made today, they neglect to value the market-oriented aspects of French production that historians such as Philippe Perrot, Leora Auslander, and Whitney Walton have so recently highlighted. French business and manufacturing were schemed to produce high-quality luxury goods. And this smaller scale, artisan orientation, far from being the only sort of "modern" production the nineteenth-century French could muster, was in fact a mode of manufacture very much driven by the keen taste for high-quality clothing, furniture, and other consumer products that the French bourgeoisie desired. In this reappraisal of the bourgeois family business and the prickly, style-conscious consumers it sold to, France's commercial and consuming classes emerge as savvy architects of a lifestyle, rather than as overcautious witnesses to a stillborn industrialization.[35]

In the bourgeois professions, as among the commercial segment of the class, careful economy seems to have been a respected virtue. Among the noted lawyers of Paris, for example, one M. Cochin was fondly described by contemporaries as being "simple in his private life, religious, even somewhat jansenist."[36] Simplicity and caution with respect to the family's economy, however, did not mean that a family or its home were supposed to "go without" the increasingly important signifiers of life as a bourgeois. In decor and other matters related to taste and lifestyle, having a "simple" piece of furniture was very likely to mean that the piece was also "elegant" and "tasteful."[37] To avoid appearing ostentatious or showy, either of which designations would have suggested the excessive adornments favored by the aristocracy but not the preference of the "bourgeois stylistic regime," consumers were given this advice by a style writer around midcentury: "It is not luxury that presided over the decoration of my abode; on the contrary, all is simple. What does the substance matter to me, provided that my eyes rest with pleasure upon some work of taste, on some product that reflects the talent or merit of an artist?"[38]

Adhering to the same call for simplicity in matters of bourgeois style and decor, a writer for the already famed *L'Illustration* applauded the French consumer's commitment to the belief that "[t]aste is superior to luxury."[39] In favoring a "simple elegance" over excess, bourgeois consumers (guided by a rising number of experts who wrote for women's magazines) were drawn to elide the concepts of taste and comfort.[40] For as one writer of a family decorative guide would write in 1825, "real good taste involves buying useful, practical, durable goods that should, above all, go together . . . what the English express in the word *comfortable.*"[41]

Although devoted to its professions and enterprises, just as its members sought a style of life whose orientation toward "simplicity" and "sober elegance" served to distinguish their world and its "things" from the styles and tastes of the Old Regime, the French bourgeoisie by no means had become deaf to the social ambitions voiced in the eighteenth century by Voltaire's Mathurin: "To dignify myself in my marriage, I am turning myself into a gentleman, and I am buying from the bailiff the flourishing office of royal receiver in the salt granaries: that's not bad. My son will be a counselor, and my daughter will raise herself to some noble family."[42] Commercial and even professional activity, while sacred to a bourgeoisie that desperately sought security and prosperity, was profane in an important social sense, too. The stigma that the monarchy and nobility traditionally had attached to commerce had diminished but had not vanished by the early nineteenth century. And within bourgeois circles, where even so-called old families dated their entrance into society only as far back as the First Empire, a collective longing for a style of living that did not depend upon work was already well developed in the 1820s.[43]

For those who could afford it, a bourgeois style of living was achieved easily enough through a combination of socially oriented investments. Successful commercial families, for example, often divested themselves at least partly from business in favor of status-rich wealth of the "proprietary" or aristocratic sort.[44] In this context, landed estates appealed to some bourgeois families not only because such properties were secure investments, but also because a high social value was still attached to the possession of these estates, even if most new owners tended to be absentee landlords.[45] Even intellectuals and artists were not always resistant to the dream of proprietary wealth. In 1837 the playwright Augustin Scribe wrote of his fond hopes to purchase "real" property in the form of a great estate. But the land, which was to cost him "almost 300,000 francs for 5,000–6,000 francs in income," was obviously not desired for its revenues.[46]

Yet living as bourgeois was not impossible for those families and individuals who were unable to acquire proprietary wealth, pay for summer-long tours of Europe, or practice the upper-bourgeois life of pleasant leisure. Education helped many commercial and professional families secure for themselves—or perpetuate through their offspring—the ways and means of a bourgeois style of living.[47] In Paris during the 1840s, for instance, fully 60 percent of the sons of lawyers, engineers, and industrialists went on to do the work that their fathers had done.[48] Education of the quicker sort, too, facilitated upper and middle bourgeois consolidation of social standing. Few cultural institutions were more important to this sort of education than the venerable etiquette book. The triumphant publishing histories of such works as the Countess de Bassanville's *Almanach du savoir-vivre: Petit code de la bonne compagnie* and *Code du cérémonial: Guide des gens du monde dans toutes les circonstances de la vie,* written and published in massive numbers after 1840 (the *Catalogue général de la librairie française* lists sixty new books of this kind in the three decades preceding 1875), testified, as one historian has observed, to "an unprecedented demand from segments of the bourgeoisie still uninitiated (since they still needed to learn) but ascending (in reality or imagination) and in headlong pursuit of signs of belonging."[49] Offering detailed notes on manners, visiting rituals, courting customs, the appropriateness of certain foods, and the like, these veritable bibles of social conduct and presentation—together with the scores of domestic novels, home manuals, and medical guides which carried similar information—were assuredly important pedagogical tools for women and men of the middle bourgeoisie who aspired to greater status and distinction.

Social manuals of this kind hardly suggested that embourgeoisement would be easy. The books quickly got to the point of their own importance as they typically addressed within the first few pages the very fears that must have compelled most people to buy them. One work in this genre explained on page 5 that civility and gentility were unmistakable markers of class. "'Good manners' were invented for the sole purpose of smoothly and confidently sorting people out, and thanks to etiquette, this sorting out happens automatically. It is like the passwords and signals invented by freemasons to keep out the uninitiated. In fact, should an ill-bred churl blunder into a fashionable salon, he will feel so constrained, so embarrassed, so ashamed of his person that he will not wish to return."[50]

If manners amounted to locked-up secrets that could be the social ruin of anyone who did not know them, etiquette manuals offered similarly dire warnings about both language and fashion: "Just a single word is enough to betray someone's origins or reveal a dubious past or present, so to the eyes of a discerning man or woman a clumsy piece of lace, a flounce, a feather, a bracelet, and especially an earring or any pretentious ornament can reveal social status or assign a particular level in the social scale."[51] When a misplaced feather could stop a social ascent, it was of no mean importance to find a good guide and read it.

Always just ahead of the bourgeoisie's own emerging identity—and deeply implicated in the construction of that identity—writers of etiquette guides were joined by a host of "experts" who authored books on everything the bourgeoisie needed to know about itself. The proliferation of "objects" that could figure or disfigure claims to social standing made it a matter of utmost importance that the right things be bought in the first place, and then that they be matched to a person or a home in obviously appropriate ways. Experts in home decor were of keen importance on this account. Professional decorators knew best how to weave comfort and simplicity—the markers of the bourgeoisie's stylistic regime—into a person's home and its accoutrements. But short of hiring the work out, guides could help the job get done correctly. Mme Pariset's *Manuel de la maîtresse de maison* of 1825, for example, offered a detailed formula on how to put a domestic interior through a successful embourgeoisement. Her advice let readers know how many paintings they needed and which kind of works were more tasteful to buy, and she offered instructions on which rooms to paint with which colors and how to secure the correct placement of furniture.[52]

Just as in matters of decor and fashion, however, where the bourgeoisie strove to distinguish itself from traditions of its aristocratic counterparts, so in the realm of leisure was it necessary to consume with care. In the decades when its identity was being set, edifying pleasures worked well to fill bourgeois leisure of the everyday, just as time spent with one's family was always appropriate and accepted. Theater, opera, and other such acquisitions and displays of culture were within easy financial reach of most bourgeois.[53] Certainly in Paris, where the social season of 1838 would feature no fewer than 884 concerts, it was not difficult to deploy the leisure of one's everyday in culturally enriching ways.[54] But rest of the longer variety—leisure of the sort that went on for a few weeks and featured some measure of travel—was not so easily rendered edifying. Society and its experts expressed the truism that "[t]o be fashionable one must enjoy leisure," but the pleasant and correct consumption of a *séjour* was not as easily achieved as a trip to the opera. Notions of a "lifestyle," though still emerging in the 1820s and 1830s, were fixed enough to indicate that holiday-making after a bourgeois fashion would necessarily invoke some of the same issues that loomed so large in everyday life. Ideas about production and consumption were first movers in the forming of bourgeois sensibilities toward vacationing. A class to which work was tantamount to respectability was not likely to seek sloth in its free time. Similarly, the everyday embracing of "simple elegance" suggested that consuming a vacation would not be to precipitate some sort of ostentatious spree. Because bourgeois articulations of good taste were "set" early and solidly as attributes of this class, the makers and takers of vacation leisure formulated sites and cultural practices that would become, first and foremost, unmistakably fashionable. In marketing the leisure that would lodge so securely in the bourgeois spa of the nineteenth century, developers echoed—just as flocks of bourgeois vacationers would come to say by their presence at spas—what a magazine for women had written in 1811: "Fashion has always been the queen of the world and nothing resists its empire."[55]

THREE MODELS OF THE DEVELOPING SPA, 1800–1850

If local doctors were among the first to quantify the coming of the bourgeoisie to the empire of the spas, these data were quickly seized by other profiteers who sought to organize themselves along entrepreneurial lines. The earliest reaction of everyone associated with the thermal economy in the Restoration was to engage in the time-honored practice of price-hiking. Prices rose throughout the spa municipalities on everything from travel expenses to food and lodging. More than anywhere else, however, the rise in prices at the spas was extreme within the bathing establishments themselves. In 1816 and after, it was not unusual for a spa's basin and other facilities to charge nearly twice what services had cost in 1815 and before. Thus, in Aix-les-Bains, 1,150 visitors spent a total of 6,221 francs on various bathing operations in 1815; the same population in 1816, however, had to spend 11,279 francs to secure roughly the same services. Only

TABLE I Populations of Spa-Goers for All of France, 1820s–1900

	1820s	1830s	1840s	1900
	31,000	38,000	90,000	800,000

two years later, 1,240 visitors spent over 17,000 francs on a number of baths that had increased only marginally since 1815.[56]

More comprehensive strategies for economic exploitation took shape this period, too. Mayors, local architects, pharmacists, and investors of all kinds rushed to form speculative alliances in France's spa towns during the third decade of the nineteenth century. While thermal entrepreneurs agreed on the richness of their future—as well as the fact that most establishments needed rebuilding before they could be profitably exploited—these ambitious individuals and parties diverged in important respects on the means by which that future ought to be achieved. Notwithstanding the variety of their initiatives, spa developers tended to approach their projects in one of three ways during the period of the Restoration and the July Monarchy.

Vichy in the 1820s represented one important model of spa development in France. Owned and administered by the French government, as were Bourbonne, Bourbon-l'Archambault, Luxeuil, Plombières, and Néris in this period, Vichy was a spa of the "French system" and rightfully expected that its proprietor would do whatever was necessary to insure its future prosperity.[57] Majestically situated on the banks of the Allier river in a valley of striking beauty, the town of nine hundred inhabitants, which had welcomed slightly fewer than 1,000 bathers every year in the 1820s, boasted a well-founded reputation for lively society in the summer season as well as waters that were highly regarded by continental doctors. The combination of Vichy's reputation and the advantages it enjoyed as a state property placed it among the premier watering places of Europe.[58]

Toward the end of the second decade of the nineteenth century, a sect of local physicians and financiers formed around the thermal establishment and began to promote an extensive renovation project there. The group's undisputed leader was one Baron Lucas, a local doctor and politician of great importance throughout the Restoration. As a spa owned by the state, Vichy's bathing establishment inevitably surrendered all of its annual profits to the government's treasury. Thus, when Lucas and his fellow entrepreneurs submitted a proposal in 1816 to the state's Council of Public Buildings calling for the remodeling of Vichy's spa, they knew they were taking advantage of the fertile if over-tilled ground of monarchical patronage.[59] In fact, the Lucas group cared about the condition of the thermal establishment—after the early modern tradition—only because its members believed that improved bathing facilities would serve to attract increased numbers of affluent persons to their locality. Those persons, whether sick or healthy, would have to consult with a doctor before taking the waters. Most of them would then be expected to follow at least a partial course of the water cure, which would mean medical consultations at regular intervals. They would need accommodations and meals for the three weeks of their thermal season, and they would be made happier and more content by the availability of entertainment and ways of recreating. Further, these guests would invariably purchase both necessities and luxuries from local merchants. What Vichy's speculative alliance wanted, then, was for the French state to invest in its municipal and regional economy.

To the displeasure of Vichy's interested parties, success in convincing the state to build a new bath translated only haltingly into a willingness on the government's part to actually complete the project. The original architectural design of 1821 for the new spa was altered repeatedly by the prefect of Allier and by various inspectors within the ministry of public works, which slowed the progress of work immeasurably. Facades and interiors were partially completed on several of the spa's buildings by the middle 1820s, but the flow of state money was meager and irregular enough to leave the whole uncompleted for more than five years. Finally, when the new spa was unveiled in 1831, together with its attached park and rooms for gaming, dancing, and reading, local sentiment had hardened in frustrated anger against the state's half-hearted patronage.[60] Vichy's entrepreneurs, as noted below, would never again overestimate the efficiency of the state's bureaus or the depths of its public works coffers.

In the Sardinian Savoy, the thermal establishment at Aix-les-Bains negotiated the 1820s and 1830s along a different and more successful path than its Bourbon rival. Directly administered by the French government until the fall of the First Empire and again after the annexation of the Savoy in 1860, Aix-les-Bains's spa was in the intervening years a possession of the Piedmont-Sardinian crown.[61] In this its administrative relationship to the state was similar to Vichy's place in the French system of spas. Like Vichy's association of developers, an alliance of spa physicians, municipal leaders, and local financiers was formed in 1816 with the goal of renovating a bathing facility that dated from the 1780s. And Aix's speculators, again like their counterparts at Vichy in the Allier, quickly sought royal patronage to pay for the spa's improvement program.[62]

But the entrepreneurs of Aix-les-Bains, led by father and son physicians Joseph and Charles Despine, harbored few illusions as to the nature of royal patronage and were wary from the outset as to the benefits of being tied to the state's coffers. Versed in the ways of royal treasuries both Sardinian and French, the Despines sensed that their sovereign's initially strong interest in his thermal spa had already waned by 1817.[63] Almost immediately, they succeeded in organizing their speculative entourage into an administrative entity, the administrative commission of the baths of Aix, and secured an arrangement such that local "entrepreneurs willingly [seized] the initiative" in the spa's fiscal management and daily administration.[64]

In 1822, the doctors Despine successfully convinced their beleaguered patron to allow the thermal establishment at Aix-les-Bains to become a quasi-public property.[65] Together with the rest of Aix's medical corps, the town mayor, a local pharmacist, and nearly one hundred other individuals, the Despines formed a governmentally insured stock company whose sole goal was the spa's restoration.[66] The corporate society formed at Aix-les-Bains garnered sufficient capital in its first offering to speedily implement most of the changes that had been deemed necessary for the spa's prosperity. Thus, by the early 1820s, while the bathing establishment was still owned by the Sardinian crown, Aix's speculators were well on their way to grafting something like capitalism onto a system of patronage that they at least nominally had to sustain.

In the later years of the decade, when more substantial work was required at and around the bathing establishment, the Despines and their group did more than simply sell additional shares in their enterprise. Seeking to meld speculative capital with state funds, the spa's corporation issued a series of pleas for patronage to the Piedmont-Sardinian king. While the royal response was not typically generous, the work on Aix's spa regularly benefited from this added source of funds. In 1830, when their counterparts at Vichy were still struggling to complete a new bathing facility and accommodate the needs of a mere 1,000 visitors, the speculators of Aix-les-Bains had successfully constructed buildings and an administrative structure that, by accommodating some 2,300 bathers each summer, had made their spa one of the more popular in Europe. And until the annexation of the Savoy in 1860, when the bathing establishment would become the property of the French Second Empire, entrepreneurialism—albeit stewarded by the state and augmented with royal resources—would continue to characterize the developmental mood and methods at Aix-les-Bains.

The majority of French spas in the nineteenth century, however, were unable to secure either the direct patronage of a Vichy or the capitalistic patronage of an Aix-les-Bains. In the first half of the century, there were over one hundred spas, out of a total of nearly 150 in France, with no economic ties to either the state, a *département,* or a commune. While some would ultimately falter and fail, the number of independent bathing places grew each year during the Restoration and July Monarchy.

Évian-les-Bains, although located in the Sardinian Savoy like Aix-les-Bains, had a history in this period that typified the experience of many independent spas in France. Ignored by the Romans in favor of the waters at nearby Amphion, Évian was only "discovered" as a curative center toward the end of the eighteenth century.[67] Seldom frequented, the scant facilities at Évian saw little of the speculative activity that so characterized the first decade of the Restoration at Vichy and Aix-les-Bains. Finally, in 1826, a Genevan entrepreneur named François Fauconnet purchased from the king of Sardinia the rights to exploit the local mineral springs. Almost immediately, Fauconnet drew together a group of anonymous investors and constituted a "Society for the Restoration of the Mineral Water Baths of Évian."[68] The speculative group quickly constructed a small bathing establishment and an attached hotel.

With only modest fiscal means, however, the enterprise faltered in its efforts to attract a a basic complement of spa physicians to practice at Évian. The Fauconnet group thus was desperately hard-pressed to build the spa's reputation as a curative center.[69] And because Évian was so lacking in social tradition or reputation, as was every spa "created" in the early nineteenth century, the Savoyard establishment and its municipality could offer decidedly few advantages to the new class of spa-goers seen at Aix and Vichy.[70] Frustrated and exhausted by his involvement in a largely unsuccessful exercise, Fauconnet retired from the corporation in 1834. Within a decade, the original group disbanded, having seen only a modest return on its initial investment.[71] Far from giving up on the potential for profit at Évian-les-Bains, however, local investors merely regrouped and bided their time until—as detailed below—circumstances would allow their aspirations to be realized.

By the early 1840s, there were annually more than 92,000 spa-goers in France—an increase of almost 300 percent since 1820. But the developmental strategies at Vichy, Aix-les-Bains, Évian, and the other spas of France, while successful in many respects, were partially impeded in these years in two important ways. First, it was still expensive and difficult to travel, as none of the French spas was served by the railroad until around midcentury. Thus to travel from Paris to Vichy in the 1840s cost around forty-two francs per person. Then, of course, one had to take a special carriage at extra expense to reach the area's spas.[72] In travel expenses alone, a family of four could expect to pay more than 200 francs to reach a spa. The total cost of a thermal holiday was obviously much higher. Including meals, wine, excursion trips, and the fees of a bathing establishment, the average spa-goer of the Restoration and July Monarchy paid between 400 and 600 francs for a three-week vacation.[73] Obviously, when a family of four had to pay between 1000 and 2000 francs to visit a spa, many would-be spa-goers of the bourgeoisie simply had to stay at home.

Perhaps more frustrating to the spa developers of France was the fact that so many French who did travel in this period went abroad to visit a watering place. Indeed, there was no spa in France that even came close to rivaling the popularity of Baden-Baden in the earlier half of the century. By 1840, that spa welcomed nearly 21,000 visitors each summer, of whom more than 5,000 were probably French.[74] Yet the great advantage that Baden, Wiesbaden, or the ever popular Spa offered French travelers was never medical in this period. Rather, it was the fact that gaming of all kinds was permitted in these foreign locales when it was no longer allowed at the spas of France. Since 1837, when the moral and political tenor of French politics turned against gaming, the casinos of France's spas had not been allowed to feature the gambling and gaming tables that had long been so celebrated at Baden and other leading European watering places. While they offered theater, dancing, billiards, and reading rooms, French casinos at spa towns lacked that amusement whose popularity with bourgeois and aristocratic spa-goers was immeasurable.[75] Until the ban on gambling was lifted, French developers could never hope to compete on an even footing with their foreign rivals. In the meantime, French developers did all that they could to emphasize the importance of medicine in the spa milieu.[76]

LEISURE, CONSUMPTION, AND IDENTITY FORMATION AFTER 1850

In French society, where domesticity and private sociability never achieved the almost cult status they knew among the bourgeoisie of Victorian England and Biedermeier Germany, the years between the fall of the July Monarchy and the century's end witnessed the emergence of an increasingly complex form of public life and the social arenas in which it could be practiced. But the apparent expansion of public space in the decades after 1850, however vast it seemed to people looking for the first time upon such creations as Paris's new boulevards, department stores, and great parks, was still somehow illusory for much of French society.[77] In the first place, many of the new venues of social life in Paris and elsewhere were class-specific by virtue of economic factors. Of course one could shop at a new department store without having to spend any money. Yet the department store was not supposed to be the sort of place where one found pleasure in just looking at objects. On the contrary, just as everything in the stores was meant to be sold, so everyone who looked was meant to be at least a potential consumer. Even more than by virtue of economics, however, many of the new locales in Paris and other French cities were rendered effectively private by a subtle but effective mixture of class-specific cultural coding.[78] These codes, whose mastery was part and parcel of the extensive "education" that stood at the heart of bourgeois identity, made it nearly impossible even for cultural craftsmen among the lower classes to perform successfully the complicated rituals which were almost immediately embedded within the city's new domains.

If anyone could enter the new Bois de Boulogne, for instance, very few visitors could organize themselves correctly enough in the difficult to master and costly categories of attire, comportment, and attitude to clearly mark off the park as their rightful domain.[79] Similarly, the scores of new cafés lining the boulevards of Baron Haussmann's Paris could sell drinks at less than exclusive prices without needing to bar their doors to the working classes. The pleasant recreation of these social spaces, even if a facade of accessibility made such amusements seem open to all social classes, was recognized as belonging to the uppper and middle bourgeoisie.

But if contemporary observers saw a bourgeois phenomenon when they heralded a new dawn of public life in French society after midcentury, it was not always clear to which bourgeoisie they were referring. For the bourgeois stratum of French society during the later years of the Second Empire and the early period of the Third Republic was no more a single, well-defined class than it had been in earlier periods. Indeed the main "subclasses" of the bourgeoisie—as consumer culture made it ever easier to buy ready-to-wear clothes, and new etiquette books appeared each year explaining precisely how to master the proliferation of accoutrements that so quickly became the easy signatures of a bourgeois lifestyle—found many of the social and cultural boundaries between their ranks becoming ever more permeable.[80]

To the various strata of the bourgeoisie, public life and the new, com-modified social spaces of French society emerged in the last four decades of the century as vitally important intersections where one could produce convincing cultural evidence in support of one's social aspirations. But to the eternal frustration of the almost-arrived, living as a bourgeois had increasingly become an extraordinarily costly and complicated business.[81] Knowing the right newspapers to read, cafés to frequent, clothing to wear, and poses to strike on the boulevards, while no doubt crucial to anyone who expected to occupy social space as a bourgeois, only began to constitute a bourgeois way of living.[82]

Among the several points where the cultural distinction of the upper bourgeoisie was made to drastically diverge from that which characterized the middle class, perhaps none had rendered imitation more difficult than the upper bourgeoisie's increasingly ambivalent relationship to the forces of economic production. Women of the upper bourgeoisie had been the first to articulate a distinctly consumptive relationship to production. Since the late 1830s, most of France's bourgeoises had had their creative energy increasingly focused on cultural rather than economic production.[83] In other words, the bourgeoise abandoned her traditional role in commercial affairs and assumed responsibility for forging the domestic sphere into a world that simultaneously opposed and supported the one in which her husband still worked.

Homes were refuges from the dictates of economic production, even while they showcased its fruits. Replete with carefully chosen and displayed symbols of domesticity, the home was a place where things were consumed.[84] Although bourgeoises typically kept scrupulous account of their expenses, they seldom hesitated to lavish great sums of money on domestic "requirements." And as places where a great deal of entertaining took place—entertaining which doubtlessly could do much to bolster a family's status and augmented the estimation in which the man was held by his business associates—homes required increasingly elaborate, sumptuous, and costly furnishings.[85] Charged with the duty of stewarding this central component of their family's cultural capital, bourgeois women necessarily became active and influential consumers. As historians have rightly suggested, it was these women whose "nonproductive" and consumptive relationship to capital helped fuel the nineteenth-century consumer revolution.[86] Obviously, women of the upper bourgeoisie had the financial means and cultural know-how to create a domestic sphere that their middling counterparts could only covet.[87] To the extent that they were able, middle-bourgeois women strove in the same period to make their homes at least suggest the ordered, easy, and opulent world of their social superiors.

If women and the domestic sphere were initially marked off by the bourgeoisie as being important in their "nonproductivity" this complicated designation was applied much more broadly in bourgeois circles in the 1860s and after.[88] Perhaps more than anything else, the dramatic recalibration of nonproduction in the bourgeois worldview—and the corresponding shift in the style in which many bourgeois endeavored to live their lives—was driven by a fundamentally changed conception of leisure. By the period of the Second Empire and throughout the Belle Époque, however, leisure increasingly was practiced by the upper bourgeoisie as a featured, pleasurable, and consumptive component of everyday identity. In effect, the conspicuous and regular performance of leisure emerged as a principal means by which one consolidated or elevated one's social standing in later nineteenth-century France. Not needing to work was perhaps the most basic of all signifiers of status. Wide-ranging and elaborate travels, like all activities that caused their practitioners to spend obviously great sums of money, were important auxiliary displays of leisure.[89] A sustained performance of leisure in the sundry social spaces of the new Paris, of course, was a recognized and well-regarded display of status, too. Inimitable by anyone without enormous means and the sensitivity to deploy those resources creatively, this all-encompassing form of leisure had emerged by the 1870s as a crucial component of bourgeois identity.[90] But if the middle bourgeoisie lacked the requisite resources to achieve either the all-encompassing leisure or the status of the upper bourgeoisie, its members—both in the cities and countryside—were nevertheless eager to strive for at least an approximation of both.

Even after the coming of the railroad, travel of any great distance remained an obvious mark of distinction in French society. Indeed, merely leaving the city for some portion of the summertime amounted to a frank statement as to one's standing in society—so much so, apparently, that Parisians in the later nineteenth century who could not manage a vacation were known to close their shutters and otherwise fake their disappearance from the city.[91] A hierarchy of socially valuable places to visit made some destinations more appealing than others. For Parisians, traveling to a relative's home in the provinces carried far less social prestige than did a full-fledged vacation, while among those upper and middle bourgeois of the provinces, a brief visit to Paris was immeasurably more worthwhile than a stay of any length in one of the regional capitals. No travel or vacation destination in the period, however, could match Vichy, Aix-les-Bains, or the other large spas in the social dividends earned by visitors.

Although the price of a thermal vacation had decreased through the 1850s and 1860s to a level easily affordable for most of the upper bourgeoisie, whose annual incomes ranged from approximately 10,000 to 30,000 francs, even basic accommodations at a watering place, which could not be secured for less than 100 francs per week, were well beyond the purse of the lower bourgeoisie.[92] For this very reason, the spas of France were rich enough in social distinction to make a thermal vacation seem like a costly but worthwhile investment for ambitious persons of the urban and rural middle bourgeoisie. Moreover, the physical structures and cultural practices of the spas of this period meshed well with the French middle class's quest for more status in society. In effect, the totality of the spa experience represented something of a living etiquette book to those Bovarys of the late Second Empire and early Third Republic who sought a closer association with the ways and means of polite society.[93] From the 1860s onward, this fact brought the French middle class, especially the provincial middle class, to the spas in search of a pleasurable place to become more bourgeois.

Spa promoters did all they could throughout the latter decades of the century to bolster the exclusive images of their cities. Such promotional works as Dr. Forestier's *Des promenades d'Aix-les-Bains,* for example, went so far as to chart the "statistical progression of Parisians" that their spas had witnessed.[94] Regardless of how they counted their populations, however, promoters could not conceal a basic fact that Parisians were only too quick to notice at the *villes d'eaux:* the majority of the spas' visitors were not wealthy families from the French capital. In fact, of 7,691 heads of families counted at Aix-les-Bains in 1875, of whom 5,805 were French, only 1,409 were Parisians. By contrast, nearly three times as many visitors to Aix came from the cities, villages, and farms of the French provinces.[95] In 1877, Jules Ferry, who was evidently eager to find some peace from the social strains of the capital, would write to his brother that it was a "fundamental joy" to discover "only ten Parisians" on vacation at Vichy in the second week of July.[96]

Just as their weekly lists of visitors showed that aristocrats still came to spas every summer, so, too, thermal entrepreneurs and developers knew, the Parisian bourgeoisie would come on holiday. And like their country cousins, of course, with these vacationers would come myriad markings of class and status. Although these visitors would venture on vacation with different expectations, aspirations, and fears, their first discoveries at any spa were always comforting enough. For the spas answered in a compelling way any concerns a bourgeois might have had about how the leisure of a vacation was to be filled.

If the bourgeoisie of the last century was consumed by a desire to produce, it is equally true that important features of that class's social identity were produced through consumption. Spas were places where visitors were consumers. They consumed as travelers. They consumed when they stayed in hotels and ate in restaurants. When they went on excursion trips and purchased clothing, they were consumers. At casinos and in other venues where they found pleasure, consuming was their main activity. But consumption at the spa was organized for an anxious bourgeoisie such that it still occurred within the context of a productive ethos. It meant a great deal, socially speaking, merely to travel, just as it could pay high social dividends to make the right friendships on a holiday. In this context, pleasure and consumption were tactics in the production of an improved social position.[97]

FROM DEVELOPMENT TO FEVER: MAKING THE *VILLES D'EAUX*

If the development of France's spas was vast in the first half of the nineteenth century compared with the more or less static situation in the early modern era, the period after 1850 was an even greater time of growth and transformation. The coming of the railroad was perhaps the single most important factor in the rapid development of the spa industry after mid-century. Rail lines were laid during the 1850s and 1860s throughout the regions in which the spas were located, making travel easier and less expensive than ever before. Most spa municipalities doubled their summer populations upon gaining a municipal rail line and train station. Aix-les-Bains, for example, hosted 4,154 visitors in 1856—three years before its rail line was built. But by 1863, three years after rail service had begun, that figure had nearly doubled.[98] The trip from Paris, guides to Aix-les-Bains advertised with some pride, was now only a fourteen-hour journey.

Throughout France, entrepreneurs and speculators of all stripes were fascinated by the enormous prosperity that rail travel had brought to the spa towns of the Second Empire. Perhaps even more, the imagination of ambitious financiers was captured by the vast physical transformation that these towns were undergoing in response to their rising summer populations. It was not simply that towns now had to build more of the same spa facilities that the period of the Restoration and the July Monarchy had created. Rather than more bathing establishments and rooming houses, the developmental challenge of the period was to bring to the spas of France the sort of pleasures and distractions that Baden and its equivalents possessed. Great hotels, elaborate casinos, lush parks, and majestic municipal buildings—the combination of these structures had given rise in the early 1850s to a new civic designation in France: the *ville d'eaux*.[99] And every spa town in the country was eager to be developed into a city of this type.

The first *ville d'eaux* to emerge in France was Plombières, one of the few spas in the country that belonged to the state's system.[100] Scenically situated in the mountains of the *département* of the Vosges, the spa saw its clientele increase steadily after the state, during the First Empire, assumed control of the thermal establishment and completed extensive renovation work there. The real rise in its fortunes, however, came with the Second Empire and the favor it found with the French emperor, Louis Napoleon. For the emperor, having consulted with his personal physician, chose Plombières as the site for his first thermal cure. In residence for more than a month during the summer of 1856, Napoleon III took a keen personal interest in the spa's future and returned on numerous occasions.

His several holidays were marked by elaborate public work projects, both at the thermal establishment and in the town itself. A completely new spa was commissioned in 1858 and finished two years later. The emperor's stay in 1858 also saw the construction of new roads—monumental boulevards by standards current in the Vosges—around and approaching the spa, as well as a new casino and cathedral. The railroad came to Plombières in 1860, complete with an impressive station to receive the town's celebrated patron. Also in that year, the state built a new civil and military hospital for indigents. The project most dear to the emperor, however, was the creation of the town's park. Napoleon III, whose interest in public space was concurrently seeing to the rebuilding of Paris and the creation of its Bois de Boulogne, personally designed the park at Plombières and followed every phase of its construction.[101]

But Plombières and the six other spas owned by the state after 1860 belied any notion of simple patronage with their labyrinthine fiscal arrangements. The French economy in the 1850s and early 1860s witnessed extraordinary growth. It was not through direct government involvement, however, that industry, foreign trade, and railway kilometrage expanded so dramatically in these years. Rather, by creating France's first investment banks, engaging in modest public spending, and encouraging extensive private speculation, the imperial government fostered a climate of economic growth.[102] This climate, where state and private interests were so intertwined, saw to the construction of the new Plombières just as surely as it did the new Paris. For as of 6 June 1857, the state effectively abandoned its proprietorship of the spa at Plombières to an anonymous investment group whose shareholders hoped to benefit both from a measure of entrepreneurial independence and from government interest. Yet, in agreeing to assume only a subsidiary role in the development of the spa for a period of eight decades, the state, nevertheless, did what it could to assure the prosperity of Plombières and its speculative sect by allowing gambling within the new casino.

At Vichy, where local speculators had learned much about the lumbering pace of the state's bureaucracy during the Restoration, there had long been a keen interest in breaking at least partly away from the state's administration. These aspirations were realized early in the period of the Second Empire, when the city's spa was leased by a public stock company in 1853 for a period of thirty-three years. The leasing company agreed to pay the state 100,000 francs annually and also to have its capital and administration prepared to complete a work project by 1858 whose estimated costs were to exceed 1,000,000 francs.[103] Vichy's proprietors were more than ready to meet this challenge, especially when they learned that Napoleon III was interested enough in their fortunes to allow Vichy's casino, like the one at Plombières, to open a room for gaming.

Completing a new thermal facility in time for the emperor's first holiday in 1861, the corporate group at Vichy indeed had impressive plans for their city's infrastructure.[104] Large compared to Plombières, Vichy had some 3000 permanent residents in 1861 and as many as seventy hotels and rooming houses.[105] Midway through the emperor's visit in 1861, Napoleon III decreed that the further aggrandizement of the spa and its community were matters of public utility. By the end of his stay, the emperor allocated substantial sums of state money, coupled with even greater commitments by private speculators, to the building of great boulevards, an enlarged park on the banks of the Allier River, a new cathedral, town hall, train station, post office, and hospital.[106] Three years later, the head of Vichy's stock company, Arthur Callou, eagerly extended his concern's lease on the spa for the privilege of being able to build a new casino. Complete with a theater that could seat 1,200 and a new ensemble of urban landmarks, Vichy, by 1866, emerged as a passable Paris-in-the-summertime. Becoming a *ville d'eaux* was immediately profitable to this spa of the French system, for within only five years the summer population of Vichy increased from 16,000 to 21,000.[107]

Beyond the pale of the French system, developers of independent spas continued to function within a less complicated fiscal and administrative context. At Le Mont-Dore, Vittel, Contrexéville, and scores of lesser-known spas, speculative groups still relied largely upon their own resources to develop both a bathing establishment and the infrastructure that constituted a *ville d'eaux*.[108] Not infrequently, however, even the developers of independent spas sought at least some measure of assistance from the empire's coffers. One M. Rousselon, for example, a leading speculator at Évian-les-Bains in the newly created *département* of the Haute-Savoie, approached the emperor in 1864 in hopes of securing "the patronage of the government."[109] Rousselon's scheme might logically have interested Napoleon III. Beyond the fact that the entrepreneur could credibly contend that the growth of Évian was obviously "in the best interests of the *département* of the Haute-Savoie," his enormous plans for the spa melded well with the emperor's own projects at Plombières and Vichy. Rousselon, according to the prospectus of his *Société Chablaisienne pour l'exploitation mobilière et immobilière des eaux minérales du Chablais,* wanted to consolidate the various springs of Versoie, Thonon, Évian, and Amphion under one corporate entity. Further, his concern would assume control over existing hotels and see to the building of new ones. Of course, the group also planned to build a new spa, casino, and public park.[110]

Short of gaining state money to underwrite his plans, Rousselon wanted the emperor to issue a declaration of public utility concerning the infrastructure of Évian.[111] In other words, "to facilitate the corporation," the entrepreneur asked that the state repave the streets of Évian, construct new civic buildings there, and "immediately establish a walk along the lakeshore."[112] Despite his affinity for such great projects, the emperor, to the immediate consternation of Rousselon, replied that he was already too engaged with the state's spas to interest himself directly in affairs at Évian or any of the other independents. What Napoleon had given Évian and the other independents already was valuable enough, for the independents were permitted to offer gambling in their casinos. This advantage was indeed important, as gambling was still forbidden at four of the state's six spas as well as at the various watering places owned and administered by *départements* and communes.

Failing to gain the emperor's fiscal favor was hardly the debilitating setback for Évian or other aspiring spas that it had been earlier in the century. Avoiding any direct patronage from the state, in fact, may have actually been a boon to the speculators whose ambitions drove Évian and the other independent spas.[113] Self-reliant and highly imaginative in matters related to capital management and business administration, the leaders of the independent spas may have prospered precisely because they came to expect so little in the way of government patronage. In organizing their spas, hotels, casinos, and water-bottling operations all under one corporation's authority, independent speculators built complete watering places that by 1870 were powerful competitors of the French system spas.[114]

Indeed some of the independent spas, like Évian, Contrexéville, and Vittel, surpassed most of their state-owned rivals in popularity during the 1870s and 1880s. By making financial and developmental decisions that did not have to filter through the state's bureaus, independent speculators were able to build their *villes d'eaux* at a pace that reflected the rapid growth of the thermal industry after 1860. For example, rail lines and train stations, whose developers recognized the central importance of easy travel, came quickly to these spas, as did the other civic improvements required of a *ville d'eaux*.[115] Independent speculators simply had no interest in doing their work in stages. On the contrary, it seemed to observers that a spa like Vittel had been raised from nothing into a full-fledged watering place in a matter of only a few years.[116] When great sums of money were concentrated in a small town that hungered for work and improvement, remarkable transformations were the rule rather than the exception.

LOCAL AND NATIONAL TENSIONS OVER SPA DEVELOPMENT: THE CASE OF AIX-LES-BAINS AFTER 1860

It was perhaps inevitable that leaders in Aix-les-Bains, who had devised a system of capitalistic patronage during the Restoration and had subsequently enjoyed great prosperity, would buck the trend toward speculative development at midcentury and later. Aix's counterparts in Vichy, after all, had decided to do under the Second Empire exactly what they had not done thirty years earlier. Vichy's developers in the earlier period had coveted the creative and quickly implemented financial and administrative schemes that had renovated Aix's bathing facilities in the 1820s, while, at the same time, their counterparts at Aix had looked fondly at the unlimited potential that ownership by the French state conferred upon Vichy's future. If that potential had been realized only haltingly in Vichy in the 1820s and 1830s, developers of Aix-les-Bains in the next generation were more than willing to believe that they might fare better, given the opportunity. When France annexed the Savoy in 1860, just such an opportunity presented itself. For in the fall of that year, proprietorship of the bathing facility at Aix was legally transferred to the French state, making Aix's spa the seventh and final thermal establishment to join the French state's system.[117]

While speculators in Plombières and Vichy exploited their spas' favorable position within the state's system, most of Aix-les-Bains's would-be profiteers clung stubbornly to a misinformed assumption about the nature of imperial patronage: that the state alone, in good speed, would plan, pay for, and build the amenities and civic facilities necessary to make the town into a *ville d'eaux*. Yet having faith in the state's commitment to

Aix did not mean that locals in the early 1860s believed that their municipality could be quickly or easily made into the type of city that Vichy
and Plombières had become. Since the Restoration, locals and visitors
alike had complained that the municipality was by and large ignoble and
uncomfortable.[118] Its streets were narrow, winding, and all but defaced
by the bland and unrepaired buildings that lined them. Lacking many
elements in municipal infrastructure characteristic of its rivals, Aix-les-
Bains, while it waited for imperial rescue, could boast only two features
beyond its thermal establishment that stood in any relief on the *ville d'eaux*
landscape.

In its Imperial Grand Hotel, the city offered accommodations that
were unsurpassed at any other French spa.[119] Finished in 1858 according
to the plans of the architect Bernard Pelligrini and with funds organized
by local entrepreneurs, the Grand Hotel was a large neoclassical structure
whose design was directly based on the famous Badischer Hof in Baden-
Baden.[120] Complete with rooftop terrace, sunlit atrium, luxurious rooms,
magnificent central balconies, well-known cuisine, and lavishly appointed
common areas, the Grand was the centerpiece of an ensemble of accommodations in Aix that included ten other hotels and more than twenty
rooming houses in 1860.[121] Until even greater hotels were built in the
Belle Époque, the Grand was a hotel known and frequented by the most
discerning travelers in Europe.

Aix's casino was its other claim to *ville d'eaux* status in this period.
Founded during the Restoration, the casino was a vitally important amusement center throughout the nineteenth century.[122] Originally housed in
the chateau of the *marquis* of Aix and equipped with a theater, library,
ballroom, game room, and billiard room, the casino was rechristened the
Grand Cercle in 1849 and furnished with a spectacular new building.[123]
Financed and administered by a local investors, the new casino was built
on a scale to match those at Baden-Baden, Wiesbaden, and Spa.[124] Beyond
its luxurious amenities, however, the casino boasted a tradition of gambling that, because the city had belonged to the kingdom of Sardinia in
the first half of the century, had not been interrupted in 1837. Indeed,
one of the conditions to the transfer of Aix's thermal establishment to
the French government in 1860 was that the casino be allowed to keep
its gaming rooms open. To this stipulation the state agreed, and from it
the city most definitely profited.

But the quality of summer visitors' life at Aix, according to most
reports from the late 1850s and early 1860s, was seriously compromised
by the absence of a public park. For if parks had once been little more than

accessories to life at a watering place, the period of the Second Empire saw them emerge as part and parcel of the *ville d'eaux* landscape. Indeed, the rising importance of such parks was underscored by no less an authority than the French minister of public works, who was charged with matters of planning and building at the spas of the French system, in an official report of 1866: "[O]ne of the most essential conditions to the life of a thermal establishment is to have situated, facing the spa, a place for invalids to promenade, take the air, and exercise in proportion to their strength." To the delight of all those who felt that Aix-les-Bains required a park, the minister was anything but abstract in assessing the importance of parks to the spas of the French system. Vichy, Plombières, Néris, Bourbon-l'Archambault, Bourbon, and Luxeuil, the minister stressed, all had this important sort of space. Among the spas under his jurisdiction, then, there was only "[t]he establishment at Aix-les-Bains . . . which was lacking in this advantage so greatly appreciated by the public."[125]

According to the minister, Aix's problem on this score, while undoubtedly ripe with social implications, had a no less crucial medical aspect. The troubling lack of a park at Aix, which "forced invalids to spend almost the entire day confined to their rooms . . . without the benefits of a distracting promenade," was, quite simply, "contrary to good health."[126] Notwithstanding the minister's genuine concern for Aix's constrained tourists, there can be little doubt that the fiscal health of the spa weighed heavily on his mind too. The possibility that travelers might abandon Aix for its want of a park, in fact, hardly seemed like pure bluster by the middle of the 1860s. The profits of the thermal establishment, which had increased dramatically in the first years after the coming of the railroad and the French administration—from 85,049 francs in 1859 to 135,096 only six years later—declined abruptly by nearly 25,000 francs in 1866.[127]

The city had been promised a park by the imperial government at the time of the annexation. By 1862, local notables had begun openly to express their concern and frustration over the fact that no progress had yet been made toward fulfilling this promise. One local pamphlet in particular, entitled *Les embellissements d'Aix-les-Bains,* encapsulated the various strains of discontent that had emerged since the annexation.[128] The author, a Savoyard aristocrat who refused to sign his tract, broadsided both the French state's and Aix's municipal leadership for dawdling on the urgent park project. Rhetorically asking where in Aix "people [could go] to see and meet each other," the author argued that it was only in the city's pitiful streets—rather than its hotels or casino—where one had to go in order to find "incontestably charming ladies" and "the most clever men of letters." This state of affairs was hardly satisfactory, as the sorry condition of Aix's thoroughfares left its promenaders with little choice but to turn endlessly around the dreary central square. Outraged that Vichy and Plombières were seeing great public work projects while Aix "destroyed itself," the pamphleteer called upon the municipal council to draft its own plans for a park and then press the French state for financing. Declaring a park to be "virtually indispensable to modern civilization," the author warned that Aix's "elegant public" was disappointed and more than mildly inconvenienced by the absence of an appropriate garden.

Whether or not such local sentiments had any influence on the state's public works ministry, the disappointing fiscal performance of Aix-les-Bains's spa in the middle 1860s was noted with grave concern by everyone involved with the administration of the state's bathing facilities. Frustrated locals at Aix-les-Bains were similarly galvanized by the important issue of their spa's declining popularity with visitors. On 20 August 1866, the prefect of the Savoy posted a decree in the name of the French minister of public works whose bold message announced that a park would soon be built in the city of Aix-les-Bains, adjacent to the state's thermal establishment.[129] But this news, if it surprised anyone at Aix-les-Bains, had not caught J. S. Revel, a local architect of some distinction, at all unprepared. Nine days later, Revel, apparently without prompting from the state, filed a report with the minister of public works in which he presented a carefully drafted set of plans for a city park.[130]

The Revel plan showed a park that was informed both by traditional French and English garden design. In the French tradition, the whole of the park was symmetrically organized to culminate in various grand vistas. From the extreme "back" of the park, for instance, one had a direct line of sight along the main thoroughfare, passing straight over two circular focal points, through the center of the Roman arch to the steps of the thermal establishment.[131] Perpendicular to this principal artery, Revel's plan showed two lesser promenades, one stretching to a café and music pavilion and the other to a pond with an island in its center. Meandering off these secondary promenades, a plethora of little paths snaked their way through a heavily foliated area surrounding the pond. Wooded, secluded, and irregularly supplied with private nooks, benches, and statuary, this portion of the park was clearly suggestive of the "natural" and romantic English garden.

Beyond its interesting combination of park styles, the Revel design offered a detailed exposition of municipal motives on the park question. Moreover, Revel's plan revealed the extent to which spa development had become an issue that local and national authorities understood in vastly different terms. This park, quite simply, was designed to be the cornerstone of a new municipal infrastructure as well as a principal seat of local pride. If the state's thermal establishment was prominently positioned at the head of the park's greatest thoroughfare, the drawing suggested that another building would ultimately have the park as its lush but symmetrically arranged "grounds." A new *hôtel de ville*, the idea for which seems to have been introduced first to national authorities in this plan and the discussions surrounding it, was to be built at the true central point of the park's "front" line. Indeed, more than 75 percent of the park's land area was to be organized as a veritable "approach" to the new town hall. Because this park would be situated in the center of town, it would necessarily destroy key streets in Aix's circulation scheme. Revel produced accompanying sketches to resolve this urban upheaval. His idea, of course, was to transform the city's winding streets into a rational and appealing network of boulevards. One of these aggrandized streets, Revel suggested, could establish a perfectly direct line of communication between the train station and the thermal spa. The "picturesque" avenue, according to Revel's estimations, would be all the more interesting, for it would have to pass directly through the new town hall, by way of a passage that "would not touch the building's upper floors."[132] And the boulevard, because of its centrality, would also be the logical place for the state to install telegraph and postal services.

Revel's discussion of the finances needed to realize this grand program showed more clearly than anything else that local authorities had decided to try to exploit their relationship to the French state. Clearly, Revel and the other leaders of Aix hoped that the French state—with its keen interest in the prosperity and profitability of the French system spas—would agree to pay for the entire park as well as the urbanist projects that were related to it. The fall of 1866 suggested that the imperial government was in fact very ready to commit its resources to the project in Aix. In November, the state issued a decree of public utility for the "acquisition and expropriation of certain lands and buildings in the city of Aix-les-Bains [for] the creation of a park adjacent to the thermal establishment."[133] But winter came to the Savoy, and so did the thermal seasons of 1867 and 1868, without Aix seeing any progress beyond the purchase of various parcels of privately held land.

Unfortunately for the local developers, Revel's design of 1866 had been dubiously received by the French minister of public works and his superiors on the emperor's state council. Obviously, what most concerned the imperial administrators was the extent to which Aix-les-Bains expected the state to shoulder the financial burden of the park. Though willing to allocate "seed" money to the park project and marshal various private resources to secure its timely realization, the state's officials saw no reason to do for Aix what they had refused to do even for the emperor's pet projects in Plombières and Vichy. Meanwhile, Aix's municipal council, holding fast to its misconceptions about imperial patronage, waited impatiently for the state to deliver a park.

The prefect of the Savoy, as an appointed official of the French state whose sympathies were expected to lie with Paris, was finally dispatched to Aix in late September 1868 to teach the city's leaders an important lesson about spa development in the imperial era. In the first of two meetings with Aix's municipal council, the prefect suggested that a *société d'actionnaires* be constituted locally to raise capital for the park. Finding no sentiment in favor of this sort of fiscal arrangement, as the park alone would hardly produce any immediate or direct profit for its would-be investors, the prefect delivered the more bitter of his two alternatives to the city of Aix in a meeting of 2 October 1868. The minutes from this meeting record that the prefect "strongly encouraged" Aix's mayor and councilmen to "vote a credit of 300,000 francs to be used in the building of a public garden." He then went on to define the park as being "attached" to the thermal establishment, which, accordingly, meant that it would be a possession of the state rather than of the city. The prefect made it clear that the imperial government's role in building the park would be at least as great as the city's. The state would pay for all earthmoving, landscaping, plantings, ponds, fences, and gates as well as for a gardener's residence. Moreover, the municipality would be spared any maintenance costs for the park for "perpetuity." On the prefect's word and that of the French minister of public works, Aix was promised a park "as comfortably established as those in the center of Paris." And for the "financial sacrifice demanded of the commune," the prefect agreed to furnish Aix-les-Bains with a "new" building for a town hall.[134]

It was not the issue of the 300,000 francs that caused Aix's municipal leaders to oppose almost unanimously the prefect's plans.[135] Neither was it the fact that the promised town hall, an existing structure that dated from the Renaissance and was to be remodeled, would not be the sort of "modern" facility that other *villes d'eaux* in the system had built.[136] Ultimately, Axois sentiment was rankled by the realization that the state, unwilling to be more than a partial and tentative patron, had made even its halting support contingent on the municipality's readiness to moderate its great aspirations for a striking civic center. Prideful locals, who rightly believed that the greatness of a spa's municipality was important to its reputation and profitability, were outraged even more by the fact that the minister of public works had no intention of allowing the Revel park to be built.

When state-financed work finally began in the summer of 1869, a park slowly emerged on a north-south line, roughly perpendicular to Revel's 1866 design. In effect, the new park, which in no way gave the city its anticipated focal point, seemed to contemporaries to be something of a random place. Lacking both a central avenue of communication and any other signs of "natural mastery" that bespoke the vaunted tradition of French gardening, the place was instead riddled with little promenades that seemed to be a collection of mere paths. Beyond its conventional use of bubbling cascades and romantic observation points, which were sparingly employed anyway, the park had no legitimate ancestor in the English garden. Its plantings, described by crestfallen officials as "minimal" and "poorly arranged," hardly sufficed to create a romantic or wild atmosphere.[137] And except for the omnipresent majestry of the Alpine foothills surrounding the city, the park offered nothing in the way of noble or dramatic vistas. The area even failed to be a secure haven for its users, as city leaders reported in the summer of 1870 that the park "was extremely difficult to police." For these reasons, "the public garden was often deserted by bathers and hardly frequented at all in the evenings."[138] Overall, the state's park, bringing neither boulevards nor any of the other urban amenities for which the city had long hoped, apparently had failed to lend the grandeur of a *ville d'eaux* to Aix-les-Bains.

By the fall of 1870, as the Prussian army prepared to surround Paris and end France's second imperial experiment, Aix's municipal leadership was seized with a collective sense of despair over its missed opportunities. Work on the park, which was abruptly halted in September 1870, had already cost the city 300,000 francs. At that juncture, the state's contribution amounted to a comparatively paltry 75,000 francs.[139] Napoleon III, after his first grand tour of the Savoy in 1860, never again returned to Aix-les-Bains. This fact, or so it seemed to many in the city after the empire's collapse, was the single explanation for Aix's mixed fortunes in the 1860s. But what most concerned Aix locals in the first years of the new decade was that their town, unlike Vichy and Plombières, was somehow a work in progress rather than a completed *ville d'eaux*.

These rival cities had been forged by a combination of enterprising civic leadership, bold financial initiatives, and an entrepreneurial self-

confidence that saw excessive state involvement as burdensome and con-
straining. Spas in the "system," like Vichy, Plombières, and Luxeuil, as
well as the greater independents, like Évian, Vittel, and Contrexéville,
were enormously profitable precisely because they took what assistance
they could get from the state but spared themselves a burdensome and
overly dependent relationship. Aix-les-Bains had known this successful
attitude too, but only in the first half of the nineteenth century, when
the spa had been under the administration of highly industrious local
notables whose ambitions had been more or less centered on the city's
bathing establishment. Subsequent to the annexation, municipal authorities and local entrepreneurs dropped the speculative posture that had long
characterized their approach to the spa business. And through the 1860s,
these one-time thermal titans, who now faced developmental challenges
in every quarter of their city and even its environs, utterly failed to recognize that they could expeditiously make their own *ville d'eaux* out of
the mysterious fiscal and administrative web that was the French state's
system.

   During the early years of the 1870s, as the Third Republic was bloodily
then begrudgingly established, Aix's crude park stood as a stark monument to the city's problematic tenure as an imperial possession. As late
as 1876, Aix's mayor denounced the state's administration of his city as
"an arbitrary regime, willing to preside over the systematic strangulation
of Aix-les-Bains." Without concerted and costly state assistance, the mayor
warned in the most dire terms he could muster that Aix's "entire enterprise
[was] doomed to an inevitable death."[140]

⟶   ⟵

Throughout the remainder of the nineteenth century, political puffery,
threats, and elaborate pleas of all kinds continued to be tactics used by
local spa developers in their relations with their counterparts at the national level. Yet by the later 1870s, developers had almost universally ceased
to expect much in the way of patronage from the state. On the contrary,
even the French state's spas had become, for all practical purposes, independent entities. Except for the spa in Aix-les-Bains, in fact, all of the
state's *villes d'eaux* were transferred by extended leases to private proprietorship in the 1870s. Within the state's many conflicting networks of political interest, monarchists and republicans alike had agreed that maintaining and upgrading spas had simply become too expensive. Thus it
was decided that the state would maintain and even increase its interest
in seeing capital concentrated and jobs created in its rural *départements,*

just as it would continue to lavish certain advantages on the towns where spas were found. But not until the later 1930s, and indeed in a concerted way only after the Second World War—when social insurance coverage came to apply to spa visits—would the state again insert itself directly and forcefully into the thermal industry.

After the Franco-Prussian war, nationalist sentiment pervaded the spas, just as it did in so many other arenas of life.[141] French curists abruptly stopped visiting German and Austro-Hungarian thermal establishments. German bathers adopted "thermal nationalism" too, quickly finding places other than Vichy, Plombières, Évian, or Aix-les-Bains in which to spend their time and money. The economic ramifications of thermal nationalism, contrary to what many observers initially expected, were anything but detrimental to the fortunes of the *villes d'eaux*. France's economy at large, spared the sharp depressionary cycle that gripped Germany into the 1880s, helped thermal nationalism become an obvious boon to those whose business it was to "sell" the vacation. With a renewed confidence in the national economy and an eagerness to boycott the spas of Germany, French bathers very quickly made their country's spas more prosperous than ever.

Almost without exception, spa towns made money during the Belle Époque. Investors in, for example, the corporations that administered five of the larger spas in this period—Vichy, Évian, Le Mont-Dore, Contrexéville, and Vittel—more than doubled their revenues in a matter of a decade or less.[142] And to the many known mineral springs in France, the three decades after 1870 added 1,200 new discoveries.[143] Although most of these new springs were never developed as spas, several new and eventually successful *villes d'eaux* were created at the end of the century. An industry that employed many thousands of service personnel and builders—who saw to the maintenance and general operation of more than three hundred bathing establishments, several hundred hotels, several scores of casinos, and a complicated array of rail facilities—thermalism created capital and

TABLE 2   Populations of Spa-Goers at Aix-les-Bains and Vichy, 1831–1913

	Aix-les-Bains	Vichy
1831	2,500	985
1861	7,317	3,741
1879	17,598	33,800
1905	27,000	71,000
1913	41,000	108,000

jobs in mammoth proportions through the fin de siècle. In the larger spa cities, it was common to find more than two-thirds of the working population employed in the thermal industry.[144] In all of France, the thermal industry gave work to at least half a million persons by 1900, a year when the industry generated more than 300,000,000 francs.[145]

Travel and a spa vacation increasingly had been made affordable to more French people than ever before. Railroad companies and spa municipalities together created all-inclusive travel packages, which made a spa vacation attainable for a broad section of the French population. Travel, meals, and casino membership included, a spa-goer at the end of the century could visit a major thermal station for three weeks and pay no more than 250 francs. More expensive vacations were always possible, as many European aristocrats were still to be found every summer at Vichy and Aix-les-Bains. But by 1900, some 800,000 people were visiting spas. And the size of the vacationing population alone suggested something that contemporaries could see signs of wherever they looked at the spas of France: in less than one century, local, regional, and national developers had turned vacationing from a more or less aristocratic occupation into one that was now enjoyed mostly by the bourgeoisie and middle class. Indeed, certain fidgety and squeamish observers had already begun to fear an eventuality that was still almost forty years away: the coming of the working classes to the *villes d'eaux.*

— 3 —

RESPECTABILITY
EMPLACED

*R*egardless of the developmental agenda pursued by a spa's interested parties in the nineteenth century, fiscal reorganization and the quest for profit were always mitigated by cultural and social concerns. Indeed, to the doctors and architects whose task it was to design and build the thermal establishments of France in the earlier decades of the century, mere money matters were always dwarfed in complexity and significance by a mountain of issues related to the *mentalité* of the times. The rejuvenation of the spas in the Restoration and July Monarchy required more than just maintenance. Spas everywhere seemed to require rather suddenly an entirely new type of interior—one that would endorse or even help to create the cultural sensibilities of an increasingly bourgeois clientele.

As noted in chapter 1, the "traditional" spa interior might be described more accurately as an exterior, as bathing in the Old Regime had been an utterly public exercise. Indeed, far from being considered indecent or indiscreet, spa bathing in the eighteenth century and before bespoke a fundamental characteristic of upper-class society in the early modern period.[1] From the organization of space to the ways in which one displayed one's body, the French aristocracy and upper bourgeoisie had endeavored to conduct their affairs as publicly as possible.[2] This set of cultural sensibilities, as French spa doctors discovered in the first years of the Restoration, did not survive the revolutionary and imperial eras.[3] Family life, private sociability, and modesty in matters related to sexuality and the body were all accorded a perceptibly heightened status by France's upper classes in the Restoration and after.[4] As the century progressed, the concept of privacy—even though the French refused to find a precise word to denote it—would inform the country's social institutions just as thoroughly as public life had under the Old Regime.[5] Commercial and professional men of the bourgeoisie, for example, increasingly turned toward a privatized form of sociability, passing much of their leisure in private societies that were vaguely political.[6] For the most part, however, bourgeois families recognized leisure as a domestic undertaking that had the family fireside at its literal and symbolic heart. Thus, when these families ventured to the spas of France in the 1820s and later, they brought with them a relatively new set of cultural calculations regarding respectability and privacy.

TOWARD A SOCIAL SEGREGATION:
SPAS AND THE CHANGING PLACE OF THE POOR

To the architects and physicians whose job it would be to design and implement a new type of spa interior, privacy and discretion were first and foremost issues that related to class. The mixing of rich and poor people in a spa town or within a thermal establishment, which had been relatively common under the Old Regime as well as during the revolutionary and imperial eras, was everywhere decried in the Restoration. Spa developers more or less suddenly began issuing warnings that the "public order and tranquility" of their municipalities was threatened by the presence of indigent visitors.[7] And wealthy visitors, who could register their complaints at most bathing places in a series of books reserved for that purpose, now felt that poor bathers tended to be unruly and disturb the "silence so essential when taking the waters."[8]

A medical director of one spa, echoing sentiments that his visitors had been recording for some time, reported in 1823 that "rich people have long complained about the poor not being isolated."[9] Local authorities in spa towns across France worried that their city's paths were "not guarded as they should be with gates and closures."[10] In reporting to the prefect of Allier in 1827, for example, municipal leaders of Bourbon-l'Archambault sought to stress that their spa's new pavilion would feature such security measures as a fence, gates, and surveillance posts.[11] Town mayors and other interested persons, anxious about protecting the reputation of their municipalities as well as their investments in a spa, increasingly decided to hire additional police officers during the summer season. The assignment of these peacekeepers, as stated by one doctor of the period, was to "expel or incarcerate the vagabonds and criminals who harass the foreign visitors."[12] A show of order of this sort, or so one developer hoped, would ensure that the "greatest possible propriety could be secured in the center of the village and on its public promenades."[13] To control this troubling cohort further, most spa towns instituted laws banning begging in the summer months.

If the presence of poor bathers caused concern in spa municipalities during the Restoration, anxieties within French bathing establishments proper were infinitely higher. Informal barriers were erected by doctors of this era to keep their thermal establishments free of indigent and even lower-class bathers. The way they did this, quite simply, was to prescribe cures for their poor patients that did not necessitate access to the principal thermal establishment.[14] The *Répertoire des malades vus à Aix-en-Savoie* of Dr. Joseph Despine, for example, which indicates that he saw approximately two hundred patients each summer through the 1820s, records precisely how a spa doctor segregated the bathing population according to class. One Count de Mutalis of Turin, who sought Dr. Despine's services on 7 July 1820, arrived at the spa in good health but with vaguely rheumatic complaints. He was given something like the doctor's standard prescription: "Baths, showers, and glasses of mineral water."[15] The point in noting the count's prescription is not medical. Rather, what is important is that he was not given any direction as to where at Aix-les-Bains to follow his cure. Like other patients of his station, the count understood that the spa's premier facility, the Royal Bathing Establishment, was open to him.

Arriving only two weeks in advance of the nobleman from Turin, a domestic servant named Jeanne Davis saw Dr. Despine about her "stomach pains and other complaints."[16] Davis was no indigent, having accompanied her mistress from Paris for a three-week stay at Aix, yet she was given an entirely different prescription than either her employer or Count de Mutalis. Davis, Dr. Despine ordered, would take her baths and cups of mineral water at the spa's century-old open bath.[17] Davis's spatially specific prescription was anything but unique. The gardener François Sadour and the valet M. Teraime, both seen by Despine in the first week of July 1820 for precisely the sort of rheumatism that bothered Count de Mutalis, were but two more of the "lesser" personages who found themselves excluded from the better facilities at the spa.[18] This segregationist strategy was a direct departure from the paternalistic treatment that indigents had received at the spas of the early modern period.

Informal efforts by French water doctors to keep indigents out of their thermal establishments were thoroughly bolstered by several administrative initiatives of the early 1820s. The first line of bureaucratic defense was the "*certificat de bonne vie et moeurs*" that all prospective indigents had to obtain.[19] Declaring an individual to be in a state of poverty, this certificate was drawn up by municipal officials of the locality in which a supposedly needy bather resided. Constituting a veritable application, the certificate was buttressed by various testimonial letters, together with a medical report, and forwarded to the prefect in whose *département* the person sought a cure. Frequently taking several months to process, these requests were regularly refused by prefects whose municipal counterparts seldom hesitated to say that too many indigents were already in residence at a given spa.[20]

For those lower-class or indigent bathers who not only passed through this bureaucratic thicket but secured a prescription from their water doctor that allowed them to enter a bathing establishment, an administrative system was designed in the middle 1820s to carefully regulate their presence in the spas.[21] Varying only slightly by *département*, this system featured a combination of interrogation and vigilant surveillance. Indigents were called individually to an introductory meeting with a spa's medical director. Subsequent to that interview, the doctor would issue an identity number and card, both of which had to be registered with the cashier and accountant of an establishment before the patient could gain entry. Attached to each identity card was a "bulletin indicating the number and nature of the various remedies the patient would be following." Patients carried identities at all times, while the treatment bulletins remained the property of the establishment's accountant. Every time patients sought entry into the thermal establishment, they each exchanged their cards for one of the twenty bath tickets accorded them by their indigent status. Entry was then duly noted on the treatment bulletins, and the patients were closely followed—by a concierge, several attendants, and the various bath givers and sedan chair carriers of the spa—for the duration of their stay in the building.[22]

By the middle of the 1820s, even this level of administrative control was deemed an inadequate means of regulating the bathing poor. "To avoid essentially miserable consequences to the good order and interests of the establishment," as one spa administrator reported in 1826, it was essential that the "concierge" and other attendants [be placed] under a redoubled obligation to ensure that no one could introduce himself there clandestinely."[23] Spa personnel at most French bathing establishments in 1826 or shortly thereafter were furnished with a simple but highly effective addition to their security system. Called a "bath number," the mechanism in question was a small card, which, working in chorus with a bath ticket, told a spa's personnel exactly who was in the building and how long they were supposed to be there.

Unlike the simple bath ticket, which was all too easily acquired, transferred, lost, or stolen, the number never left the premises of the establishment. Upon presenting a valid bath ticket to the medical director or the accountant, each bather registered and was issued a number marked with the date and time. Good for only twenty-four hours, the bath numbers clearly indicated where in the facility the bearers belonged as well as their place in the queue for treatment. At several times in the day, the attendants of a facility were issued reports as to which persons were to be treated in the rooms under their supervision. Article six of one spa's rules stressed the importance of these reports, noting that they were to "indicate the name of the person bearing each bath number, where each person was lodging, and the type of bath ticket that had been given up."[24]

Told to "keep their eyes on these reports at all times," attendants were expected to verify each person's number against their own reports before permitting anyone to enter a spa's bathing area. Having conducted this inspection and admitted the patron to her or his private bath room, the attendant was then supposed to place the bather's bath number in a box attached to the cabinet door, being careful to "lock the box with his key."[25] Surveillance within the spas continued even after an indigent was sealed in an assigned cabinet. For as one spa doctor of the period recounted, "[f]rom the center of the building, the head physician, the accountant, and the attendants [were expected to] observe every corner of the establishment."[26]

By the end of the Restoration, administrative controls and surveillance measures no longer sufficed—in the opinion of spa developers and their bourgeois visitors—to safely compartmentalize the indigent population of the spas. More than the specter of popular upheaval that was threateningly revived in the July Revolution of 1830, contemporary observers cited vague social reasons in arguing for an increased distance between the various classes of French bathers.[27] As the mayor of one spa town saw the situation, more discretion between the classes was an important demand of his market: "the persons of premier distinction who frequent our baths today wish to see adequate and separate facilities established for the less well-off malades."[28] And in a succinct corroboration of the mayor's statement, a local spa doctor reported that "delicate people of the easy classes, and of course all children, find it upsetting to share the same water with disreputable persons."[29]

With these desires so strong among French spa-goers of the upper classes, it was probably inevitable that spa developers should recognize the "utility of having baths that would be uniquely the destination of the poor."[30] Vichy was first in the hospitalization movement, beginning work on a civil hospital for the poor in 1819 and completing the project over the next decade.[31] By the middle of the 1830s, most major thermal establishments in France had built not only separate bathing facilities for indigents but also hospitals in which they could be securely lodged for the duration of their stay. Luchon's developers went so far as to build two such institutions, one for veterans and another for indigents.[32] Vichy followed the example of Luchon, opening its new hospital for veterans and soldiers in 1840.[33]

Publicly, spa developers cast themselves and their projects in the humanitarian discourse that was current in liberal and reformist circles of the period. In describing the state of one spa's indigent population, for example, a resident physician expressed concern that "despite all the efforts of the local administration to reduce the suffering of the poor, the free use of our mineral baths can not suffice to bring about the cures they seek and deserve."[34] A medical colleague at Néris-les-Bains echoed similar sentiments, declaring it to be "in the interest of humanity to make a convenient destination for the considerable number of patients who have been so little favored by fortune."[35] To another spa doctor of the period, who claimed to carry the interests of the poor in his heart, it was a "religious and humanitarian" responsibility to remedy the "increasingly unhappy condition of the class of indigents."[36] Striking a similar administrative pose, the chief physician of Bourbon-l'Archambault, in a report in 1837 that detailed a list of changes to be made in medical service to indigents, bluntly told the prefect of Allier that "humanity asks for these improvements to occur."[37]

Humanitarianism was decidedly less apparent in the architectural plans and regulatory schemes on which the spa hospitals of nineteenth-century France were based. For among themselves, developers candidly declared their goal to be "the complete isolation of services for the rich people from those designated for the indigents."[38] Poor bathers, who had traditionally taken free lodging in any of a spa town's more modest rooming houses and had been left to fill their days as they wished, would now be compartmentalized and hospitalized as a cohort. No longer under the administrative jurisdiction of a spa's medical corps only while bathing, the indigents instead were installed in something like Jeremy Bentham's panopticon.[39] Figure 6 shows the interior distribution of one spa hospital, built at Aix-les-Bains in 1829, which highlights the principal features of this type of institution.

Most important, a spa hospital's resident patients had to know that their activities were under constant administrative surveillance. To make

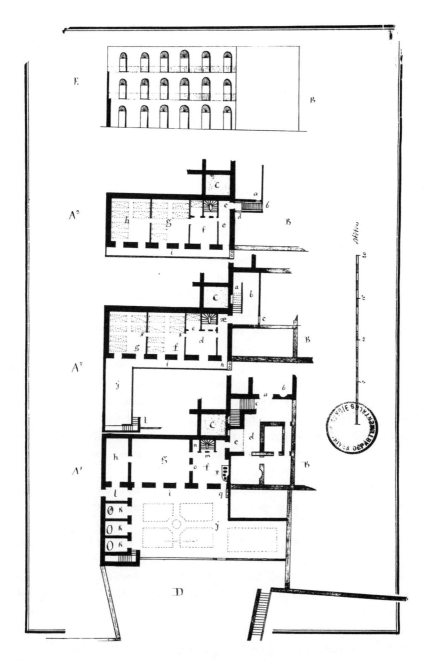

FIGURE 6   Architectural drawing for the indigent hospital at Aix-les-Bains, 1829. The individual beds and the separate floors for men and women reflect emerging ideas of privacy. The corridor labeled "k" served as the designated sight line for the hospital's administrator and the head watchman. Reprinted from Pagotto, *Le thermalisme à Aix-les-Bains au dix-neuvième siècle,* 51.

this obvious, spa administrators typically installed a day and night post (labeled "d" on fig. 6) for their accountant on the ward where the patients slept. They further bolstered this administrator's presence by installing a corridor that led from his office directly into and through the indigents' sleeping quarters. This corridor (labeled "k" on fig. 6), as the architect of Aix's hospital described on his drawing of the facility, was a "passage from one room to another that [made] it easier for the accountant to watch over the rooms."[40] The observational powers of the hospital's administration were expanded immeasurably by a design that featured individual rather than group beds.[41] And the fact that patients were typically separated according to gender served further to control the spa hospital's occupants.

If architecture left any ambiguity with respect to order and control, the posted rules of spa hospitals in the nineteenth century offered quick clarification. Indigent patients, these rules noted, were by no means free to come and go as they wished. As article 7 of Vichy's rules from 1839 stated, "the entrance will be kept closed at all times and patients shall not leave the hospital without permission." Further, patients learned soon enough, it was not within their rights to set the rhythm of their daytime activities. Vichy's indigents, for instance, were made to "arise each morning at precisely five o'clock . . . and go to bed each night in this period at eight." Similarly, the architectural gendering of the hospital interior was manifestly underscored by regulatory measures. Article 15 of Vichy's rules stated that it was "expressly forbidden for men under any circumstances to enter into the women's room." Even sociability between the two sexes was subject to strict controls, as Vichy's patients were told that "there shall be no meetings of the two sexes in the main hallway of the hospital."[42]

The rise of spa hospitals after 1830 did much to address the important issue of privacy in the thermal milieu. These facilities collected lower-class and indigent bathers, who might otherwise have lodged and sought treatment at the same places frequented by upper-class bathers, and subjected them to a combination of spatial and administrative sequestration. While there can be little doubt that needy bathers received better and more rationalized medical care in spa hospitals than they had before, the humanitarian potential of these institutions was never more than a partial justification for their presence in a spa town. To the mayors, pharmacists, doctors, and others involved in the development of French thermalism in the nineteenth century, it was common knowledge that upper-class bathers were more likely to frequent a spa where the presence of the poor had been securely confined.

To those who questioned the wisdom of investing dear capital in such an apparently profitless place as a hospital for the poor, one needed to look only at the phenomenal success of Aix-les-Bains in the years immediately following the highly publicized completion of its hospital. In 1830, the first summer after Aix's Haldimand Hospital was built, one thousand more persons visited the thermal establishment than had come the previous year, even as revolution engulfed Paris, Brussels, and other important cities from which the spa's clientele traditionally was drawn.[43] To spa developers, then, the reorganization of facilities according to class and the relatively complete compartmentalization of indigent bathers were among the more important challenges of the 1820s and 1830s.[44]

ENGENDERING MODESTY

But privacy and discretion, as these concepts were understood in the thermal milieu and other bourgeois circles of the nineteenth century, were by no means solely matters of class. During the first years of the Restoration, it was clear to spa developers that their thermal establishments had somehow become places—even when the poor were not inside—that made people feel uncomfortable. The source of this unease was not merely the fact that by 1816 most bathing establishments were regularly serving more people than they ever had before. In fact, crowding was not even among the main complaints that bathers lodged with their water doctors. More than anything else, what troubled travelers and developers alike was the apparent "indecency" and "primitive distribution" of France's bathing establishments.[45]

Collective bathing, which had already fallen into disfavor with many spa-goers of the later eighteenth century, had become by the Restoration entirely unacceptable to most visitors. Yet within virtually all of the major spas of France, bathing space continued to be collectively organized through the 1820s and into the 1830s. With large but shallow basins at their center, spas like Néris, Bagnères-de-Bigorre, and Aix-les-Bains prominently featured a recognizable version of the traditional group bath even after bathers had increasingly come to demand the "comfort and privacy" afforded by individual bath cabinets and their enclosed zinc bathtubs.[46]

In fact, wherever such comfortable and private facilities existed, their popularity all but rendered the old basin obsolete.[47] Where bath cabinets were not yet found, or where the capacity of only a few such rooms was insufficient to meet visitor demand, guests were frequently displeased. As one spa developer related in 1822, "people often complain[ed] upon their arrival, because it [was] impossible to find a proper bath in the bathing establishment."[48] These dissatisfied visitors, to the consternation of the doctors who were eager to treat them, frequently rented a bathtub in their rooming houses and paid a team of porters to deliver water from the spa's source.[49] The rise of such treatments, and the fact that they were scarcely profitable to a bathing institution, provided the spa developers with an abundantly clear example of exactly how valued private facilities had become. Developers learned and acted upon this lesson with haste, and the 1820s and 1830s witnessed a revolution in the design of France's spa interiors.

The alterations planned for Vichy's thermal facility in these years (fig. 7) were typical of the new movement in spa design. Out of an establishment that had formerly been little more than a collection of open pools, there emerged a veritable monument to private bathing.[50] The new bath was built as a quadrangle, with each segment organized around an ornamental basin. There were twenty-three individual baths surrounding each basin, amounting to forty-six bath rooms on either side of the main hallway. Each bath room was made sufficiently large so that its occupant could undress within, ending the old practice of having to change into one's bathing costume before arriving to take the waters. In the opinion of one doctor who had seen the plans for Vichy's new spa, the most important and novel feature of the establishment-in-progress was that "all the cabinets [were] completely isolated, each with its own commodious and spacious domestic style bath, the one from the other."[51]

The high level of individual privacy was further guaranteed by an overarching organizational scheme whose function was to segregate the bathing cohort by gender. According to Vichy's developers and their counterparts at other French spas, women in particular were strong advocates of gender-specific bathing facilities. Male bathers, themselves so immodest that bathing costumes had to be made a matter of regulation at Aix-les-Bains in 1832, typically conducted themselves in a manner that, according to one disgusted doctor, "regularly elicit[ed] strong complaints from foreign women." Women, in their advocacy of separate baths, may well have specified exactly why common bathing had for them become "the cause of such embarrassment."[52] But when that advocacy was echoed by the developers of France's spas, as they complained of facilities that were "impossible" or able to "provide only the crudest services thinkable," the need for gendered baths was not justified in the specific and painful terms that contemporary women might have employed.[53] Rather, as one physician explained to the speculative group from which his spa drew the capital for its improvement project, "[t]he service of men, conducted in

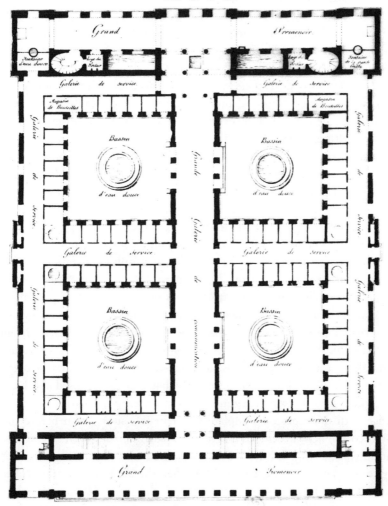

FIGURE 7   Architectural drawing for Vichy's new thermal establishment, 1830, which would make private baths and gender-specific facilities the standard that all spas in France would seek to achieve. Reprinted from Institut Français d'Architecture, *Villes d'eaux en France,* 70.

perfect isolation from that of women, [was] mandated by morality, public decency, and religion." The doctor further explained that all such measures were "applauded by the majority of women."[54] Beginning with the completion of Vichy's establishment, which served men and women on opposite sides of its main corridor, gendered facilities proliferated throughout the spas of France.

But those spa developers who, for a constellation of economic reasons, were unable to build completely new bathing establishments were faced with the difficult task of making their existing facilities conform to new cultural codes. At smaller bathing facilities, such as at Bourbon-l'Archambault in 1819, planners and builders simply placed private baths and showers where the spa's old basin had been.[55] At larger and more heavily visited establishments, however, matters were a great deal more complicated. No one felt such challenges more acutely than the investors of the speculative group at Aix-les-Bains. These entrepreneurs, in contrast to their equivalents at Vichy, had great ambitions but markedly fewer resources. Without access to the sort of public utility mandate that drove the renovation work at Vichy, Aix's entrepreneurs had sufficient capital to make only select improvements to their old facility. Developers of this spa had to prioritize their projects, always considering the extent to which a particular project would increase the establishment's reputation and profitability. Although expendable resources were dear at Aix-les-Bains throughout the 1820s and 1830s, the renovation program there strove to match the levels of discretion and privacy that Vichy was poised to achieve.

Developers at Aix had begun to alter the interior of their spa, in accordance with the repeated complaints of female visitors, even before they had incorporated themselves as a *société d'actionnaires*. The inside of Aix's bathing facility (fig. 8) included a central basin, several private pools, waiting rooms, and a main corridor. More than the basin or any other collective space in this spa, it was the hallway, which formed a semicircle behind the basin, that figured most prominently among the complaints of the female visitors in this period. Described by Aix's medical director, who claimed to speak for scores of disgruntled women, the hallway encouraged "general disorder and abuses" among male bathers. For the women who ventured into the semicircular corridor as they made their way to their assigned pools, the "inconvenient and indecent passage" was a veritable trap. Lined with men who were waiting to enter their own pools, it was evidently a "difficult and unpleasant" matter for a woman to negotiate the narrow hallway without experiencing some measure of molestation or discomfort.[56]

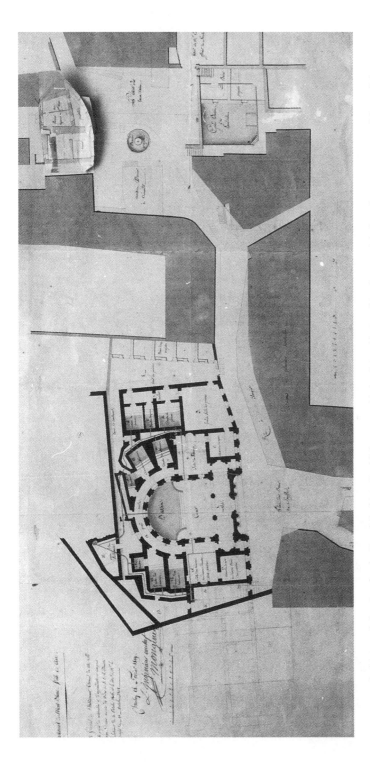

FIGURE 8   Architectural drawing for the Royal Bathing Establishment at Aix-les-Bains (designed in the 1780s) before the extensive remodeling of the 1820s. Reprinted from Leguay, *Histoire d'Aix-les-Bains et sa région: Une grande station thermale*, 150.

If this sort of contact between men and women had been accepted by both sexes when Aix's Royal Bathing Establishment was built in the 1780s, circumstances had clearly changed by the early years of the Restoration. Upon the recommendation of Aix's leading doctor, who warned that it was "an absolute necessity that prompt actions be taken to end the inconveniences" experienced inside the corridor or the establishment would risk losing a valued segment of its paying population, the spa's administration decided to install a rigid separation between the sexes in the establishment. Women would be treated on one side of the building and men on the other. At the central point of the troubling corridor, which otherwise would have continued to bring the sexes together, the administration saw fit to "establish a partition with a locking door to stop the communication between men and women."[57]

Throughout the 1820s, the developers of Aix-les-Bains considered a variety of other schemes to make their thermal establishment more modest and discreet. Domestic style bathing cabinets, complete with private dressing rooms, were constructed toward the end of the decade. The old basin, long since ignored by the spa's clients, was drained of its water and made into separate waiting rooms for men and women. By and large, however, the speculative group at Aix had insufficient capital to pay for either new facilities or extensive additions to the existing spa. What these developers were not able to do architecturally, by way of constructing a highly privatized and gendered spa to match the one that was being built at Vichy, they endeavored to do through vigilant surveillance. As developers immediately recognized, the surveillance networks established to monitor the activities of the poor in the spa were equally well suited to safeguard the propriety of "ladies and gentlemen who are visitors."[58]

A series of subtle but important modifications was made to the design of Aix's Royal Bathing Establishment and its administrative practice, in addition to the previously noted initiatives related to the poor, that secured a high degree of discretion within the institution. Immediately inside the building's main entrance, the spa's developers installed in 1829 permanent posts for both the accountant and the concierge. At a point several yards beyond these stations (labeled "m" on fig. 8) the administration posted its chief orderlies and charged them with the duty "to observe everything."[59] Were these surveillance agents to fail in their duties, powerful reinforcements were in place to protect bathers from each other. On the left side of the establishment, a door was built which gave the medical director an unencumbered view of both the establishment's entrance and the several posts of its other watchmen. And on the building's right side, the developers created a companion point of observation.[60] By the middle of the 1830s, the developers of Aix-les-Bains no longer reported that their female visitors were displeased with the spa's facilities. This welcomed quiet, according to the establishment's medical director, was attributable to architecture and administration, not to a change in the behavior of the spa's male visitors. Quite the contrary, as the chief physician stated that an acceptable level of decency had been "realized solely due to the exact policing of the establishment and the fact that its rules [were] always strictly enforced."[61]

If the movement toward more discretion in France's bathing establishments was begun by female spa-goers in search of privacy, it rapidly found medical and even legislative codification. By the early 1830s, advocates of the privatized spa could laud their facilities—and criticize those of their rivals—in the increasingly authoritative language of medicine. As a "doctor and expert in physics," one doctor with an attachment to a renovated establishment decried the traditional basins for their tendency to "collect and confine dangerous vapors." Such a mass of inexhaustible air, according to this contemporary expert, "rendered a most unsavory smell and made these baths unclean."[62] Hygiene, until recently more virtue than necessity at thermal establishments, had emerged during the Restoration as a highly regarded measure of both physical and moral salubriousness. To lack sufficient hygiene, as hapless spa developers throughout France learned in the 1830s and 1840s, meant the loss of bourgeois bathers.

Indeed, no spa in western Europe during this period could afford to have its facilities characterized as anything less than "scrupulously clean." Yet the task of representing cleanliness, healthfulness, and order was hardly an easy business for spa developers. Through a combination of architecture and administration, Vichy, Aix-les-Bains, and many other major French spas successfully showed themselves to be hygienic. For bathing facilities, being clearly classed, discreet, and private—more than the great emphasis that travel writers placed on their being "lined with white tiles and kept in a state of cleanliness and order not to be surpassed"—was a compelling articulation of hygiene to concerned contemporaries.[63] At smaller and less well established spas, however, where architectural and administrative order had not yet been so obviously installed, representing hygiene was a veritable impossibility.

Characterized by rival doctors as being "dark as dungeons" or "cells for the dead" whose walls were "cold stone and eternally sweating with the steam of the baths," the bathing establishments of small and poorly developed spas were greatly disadvantaged by their inability to build facilities that appeared to be proper, decent, and clean. Mostly, however, what compromised the fortunes of these spas—and made them such easy targets for the scathing critiques of doctors whose own spas had already been renovated to be hygienic—was their continued use of the traditional, collective bath. For when competing doctors denounced this type of bath as an "open, unseemly pond that gathered rubbish of every kind," they were clearly referring to more than the tendency of such basins to fill with litter.[64]

The open and uncontrollable pool, as it teemed with bathers of both sexes, presented a scene that was all too easily branded as being unclean and unhealthy. In the opinion of one physician-author of the 1840s, "to maintain the body in an erect posture, to exert all the muscles, and to fatigue the body by exercise during the operation of bathing, were circumstances which greatly mitigate against its good results."[65] On the other hand, virtually all medical authorities lauded the healthy practice of passively bathing in an individual bath cabinet. As one doctor wrote on this issue, "in the majority of cases, bathing in a reclining and quiescent posture is in my opinion essential."[66]

By the middle of the 1840s, the architectural and administrative principles established at Vichy and Aix-les-Bains had been matched or superseded by virtually every thermal spa in France. Highly private, thoroughly gendered, closely administered, and plainly hygienic, the new spas were ultimately not constructed by economically interested developers as much as they were by the shifting cultural sensibilities of their clientele. Spa developers seldom initiated any change in their bathing establishments without first having been prompted by visitors' complaints. Bathers of the Restoration and July Monarchy, particularly women, increasingly possessed a sense of modesty that left them ill at ease in places where their parents or grandparents might have thrived. The discomfort of these persons was by no means ignored by the speculators who had staked their economic future on the prosperity of a spa. Wherever possible, developers designed completely new spas to meet the changed specifications of their clients.

These new or renovated establishments experienced vast growth during the July Monarchy. Even before the coming of the railroad, a spa like Aix-les-Bains had increased its gross earnings by more than four times since the onset of the Restoration.[67] Yet the population of spa-goers for all of France, at least in the 1830s, had not grown to a point where developers could feel satisfied. No, there had been approximately 31,000 annual bathers in 1820, and that number had only increased by 7,000 in the early 1830s.[68] Although the new spas were making more money than their traditional counterparts ever had, and they were seeing more annual visitors, developers everywhere wanted more bathers and more profits. They understood that new facilities, administrative "advances," and surveillance systems would not achieve these goals without a good measure of additional work. Looking close to home indeed, as chapter 4 explores, doctors in particular would seize on medicine as a means of marketing the spas to the bourgeoisie.

⸺ ⸺

French spas in the first half of the nineteenth century strongly suggest that so-called Victorian mores had a Gallic manifestation well before there was an English middle-class embracing of Queen Victoria. To increase demand for vacations and profits within the burgeoning leisure industry, spa developers of the Restoration and July Monarchy had to make their bathing facilities conform to the still emerging cultural sensibilities of an affluent and largely bourgeois clientele. "Reading" the *mentalité* of French spa-goers in the 1820s and 1830s was a particularly difficult affair because the identity of France's bourgeoisie was not yet fully formed. Ideas about comfort and appropriateness, however, were clearly at the vanguard of the process of this identity formation. Wealthy vacationers, women in particular, knew well enough in the 1820s what decency was and what it was not, just as spa entrepreneurs and doctors were able to appeal to discourses which circulated well beyond their milieu—especially with respect to the rising public health movement and ideas about the working classes—to make concrete in a built environment and an attendant set of cultural practices a fairly comprehensive and bourgeois expression of respectability.

Indigent bathers had but a limited place in the particular vision that built the new spas. As a result, poor and apparently threatening people were completely removed from the principal part of the new thermal environment. Compartmentalized in hospitals which facilitated surveillance, mandated decency, and guaranteed order, poor bathers were relegated to a rational sequestration that left the main of a spa and its municipality rid of the indigent. Hospitalization actually fell short of achieving the goals that many doctors and spa promoters evidently sought. Vichy's officials took secret pride, it appears, in the fact that their hospital welcomed only sixty-five indigent visitors in all of 1852. Indeed, it happened that Vichy's administrators were accused of obstructing the availability of their mineral waters to French indigents on several occasions during the 1850s and 1860s. The problem was resolved, finally, by a series of prefectural reprimands in the 1860s and then by the prefect's decision to have his own administration rule on indigent access to Vichy's hospital.[69] Bourbon-l'Archambault, also in the Allier, witnessed the same machinations in this period as its leaders and developers in the 1860s formally asked the state's minister of interior to quit sending so many indigents to the spa's hospital.[70]

But wealthy travelers insisted upon more than the classing of the spas. Respectability was architecturally and administratively figured, too, in terms of gender. If privacy around the body, like modesty in bathing, had been all but absent from the culture of curing at Old Regime spas, the making of privacy and discretion at the spas would be precisely what doctors and developers would spend the first forty years of the nineteenth century doing. From simple partitions to individual bath rooms, private sedan chairs, and personal changing rooms, the organization of space within the spas articulated the same conceptions of respectability, modesty, and hygiene that the French bourgeoisie increasingly saw in itself.

If my analysis has revealed how an entrepreneurial sensitivity to and construction of culture and *mentalité* informed every aspect of the thermal industry's drive to make new and profitable bathing establishments, it has also suggested that politics very formally understood, beyond the issue of state patronage, had relatively little to do with the spas through midcentury. With the establishment of the Second Empire in France, however, politics of the "traditional" kind entered into every aspect of life, including the thermal milieu. One piece of legislation from 1856, in particular, had spas as its subject. Promulgated on 14 July, the law was concerned with "conditions of order and healthfulness within thermal spas." In effect, this legislation offered legal grounding for tendencies in spa design and administration that had been in place at many establishments for a quarter of a century. The state made it a matter of law that every bathing establishment in France had to conform to strict standards regarding privacy, medical administration, and hygiene. In summarizing the law, the state's reporter emphasized most of all the importance that had become attached to private and gendered interiors within the spas: "in each thermal establishment, distinct locales must be set aside, to the extent that it is possible, so that the two sexes can be treated separately."[71] Finally belonging to custom as well as law, the administrative and architectural structures of the bourgeois spa would remain constant through the nineteenth century.

— 4 —

MEDICINE AND THE RHYTHMING
OF BOURGEOIS REST

It is only the doctor who can appreciate the need for a bath.

Dr. Victor Noyer, *Lettres topographiques et médicales sur Vichy,* 1833

To visit a French spa at the end of the nineteenth century was to inhabit a distinctly bourgeois environment. In the earlier decades of the century, however, the cultural and social terms of that inhabitation were anything but plain to most spa-goers. Rather, the built environments and diverse practices that would order people's social behavior at the spas of midcentury and after were, during the Restoration and early years of the July Monarchy, almost entirely unscripted. Spas had attracted bathers for many centuries, but those earlier curists had not gone on vacation as bourgeois. Accordingly, the repertoire of practices at the Old Regime spa provided nineteenth-century visitors with only outdated examples of how to practice one's leisure in the thermal milieu.

Moreover, the very place of leisure within upper-class life had seen a drastic transformation since the latter years of the eighteenth century. Productivity had become an individual and collective attribute with which the bourgeoisie liked to identify. Under the category of lifestyle, where affluent bourgeois could enjoy a quantity of leisure that probably approximated what aristocrats of the Old Regime had known, idleness and excesses of the flesh were everywhere supplanted by a search for purposeful and orderly leisure. But if gardens, social clubs, novels, salons, natural specimen collections, and board games gave respectability and meaning to bourgeois leisure of the everyday, it remained to be seen what social and cultural justifications would gird the vacation. More to the point, what would be the cultural practices around which the bourgeois's spa visits could be organized? Certainly the retooled spa environment of the 1820s and 1830s went a long way toward tracing the contours that the bourgeois vacation would assume. But administrative practices, design principles, and promotional strategies did not in and of themselves serve to construct the cultural practices of spa-going in the period. Neither did these several features of the new spa contribute directly to the creation of a bourgeois conception of leisure. Rather, as I will show, it was medicine generally, and the science of hydrotherapy more specifically, that established one telling rhythm according to which one could "do" a spa vacation.

MEDICINE AND THE MARKETING OF THE SPA

In the 1830s, after speculative societies had formed around the thermal establishments of France, spa physicians—in many instances the very same people who invested in spas and designed their new interiors and administrations—began a literary campaign to bolster the fortunes of their bathing places.[1] Developers did not have to be entirely innovative in their campaigns, for guidebooks of one sort or another had been an established genre of travel literature at least since the later seventeenth century.[2] Doctors of the Restoration and July Monarchy, however, modified the "traditional" narrative of the guidebook just as thoroughly as they changed the built environment and administration of their bathing places. Their guides, which were written for a bourgeois audience, sought to echo in text what the spas were increasingly showing in their new interiors.[3] The result of these literary efforts, doctors hoped, would be an increased demand for the spa vacation.

Spa promoters were universally eager to advertise the fact that poor bathers were no longer treated in the same facilities as rich bathers. Dr. Constant Despine of Aix-les-Bains, like so many other developers and publicists, devoted more than a dozen pages of his 1834 guide to an elaboration of his establishment's segregationist policies for "respectable persons of poor means."[4] Authors routinely added a detailed diagram of their spa's municipality to further suggest the degree to which service for the poor had been compartmentalized. Such diagrams clearly identified the "baths of the poor" or the "indigents' hospital" as being well beyond the boundaries of the thermal establishment proper.

If guidebook writers took great pains to assure their readers that spas no longer allowed for the mixing of rich and poor bathers, their narratives were equally eager to show that respectability, propriety, and decency had become the bathing establishments' organizing principles. Many writers represented their spas as decent by detailing the scrupulous administrative apparatus that governed the baths. As this contemporary publicist endeavored to prove, disorder was simply not possible in the thermal establishment: "The bathing is regulated by a chief orderly under whom are six attendants who see that each bather takes his or her turn. . . . According to the regulations, any person desirous of making use of the showers or baths should write down his full name at the office of the administration. . . . A ticket detached from an official register will then be delivered to him at no charge. This ticket, which is altogether independent of the cards taken previously for the price of the baths or showers, is in order to ensure regularity in the arrangements."[5] Again and again, doctors utilized words like "regulation," "administration," "official," and "order" as they characterized their spas' interiors. Further, authors frequently noted that spa employees wore uniforms and identifying badges.[6] To the bourgeois readers at whom this language was directed, an explicit promise was made about the spas' propriety. No author, for example, failed to describe the provisions for gendered bathing that existed at a given spa. And most guides included a folding diagram of their facilities on which the separate quarters allotted to each sex were clearly marked.

Beyond a standard discussion of gendered bath cabinets, individual dressing rooms, and the like, guides endeavored to establish a perimeter of privacy around the larger experience of taking a water cure. Their favored way of answering all possible concerns about modesty in and around the spas was to describe in lavish detail the bath chair—that peculiar system of transportation common to so many French spas.[7] The bath or sedan chair was little more than a boxed-in seat mounted on two carrying poles. This simple mode of conveyance, which brought so many bathers from their hotels to a spa and then back again, was identified by guidebook authors as an experience that bespoke the spas' new commitment to privacy. One Dr. Chasseloup, in his guide of 1834, clearly advertised privacy in discussing the use of the bath chair: "You are enveloped in an enormous towel, like a swaddled baby, immediately after finishing with the bath. Thus completely covered, you are then put into a type of box, which is carried on two poles, and which is itself sealed from the outside with thick draping. Then you are carried directly to your lodging."[8] Thus cloaked in two layers of covering, as Dr. Chasseloup and so many of his contemporaries were eager to stress, bathers could expect to conduct their cures in proper obscurity. Drawings of the bath chair, which spa publicists featured in their guides, reinforced the rise of privacy at the spas by promising veritable anonymity to timid curists.

Ultimately, spa narratives sought to construct the thermal environment as medical and therefore rational.[9] No guide in this period was published without an elaborately detailed section on science and medicine.

Even the smaller guides devoted several pages to a chemical and physical analysis of their particular mineral waters.[10] Assessed for abundance, mineralization, purity, mode of medicinal administration, and side effects, mineral water sources—even at the height of the Romantic movement— were systematically stripped of any mystery by guidebook narratives. And if bathing at a spa had once been a notoriously unstructured affair, where cures were a random business that required little involvement with doctors, guidebooks to the new spas sought to show hydrotherapy as a serious and scientific practice.[11] Narratives of the 1830s already warned their readers that bathing at a new spa was definitely a medical affair: "[Hydrotherapy] is not always a universal panacea: to choose a spring without careful consideration, to utilize a source without taking precautions or without consulting those whose artistry is correct bathing is to commit the gravest imprudence."[12] Guides endeavored to show that mineral water was a powerful tonic to be "taken only according to the strict instructions of a doctor."[13] Spa publications also stressed that the various employees of a thermal establishment were highly trained medical technicians.

Misusing mineral waters, according to spa guides, could be medically dangerous. Young children, for example, were to be barred from the most active types of cure as well as waters with especially high mineral levels. Their organs and skin, according to most spa practitioners, were simply too feeble to withstand the often jarring effects of such treatments and tonics. Persons of extreme age, in most narratives, were likewise instructed to avoid all but the most passive cures. Women's bathing was also surrounded by certain restrictions in the narratives of spa promoters. These particular cautions, as one writer explained—in a language that reverberated widely through the French medical community and bourgeois society more generally—were mandated by the "relatively feeble constitution of women, whose organic functioning is so easily activated and in whose nature nervousness predominate[s]."[14]

But if women were told to avoid certain kinds of cures because of their physiology, hydrotherapy was also touted as a tonic with unique powers relative to their reproductive organs.[15] In France, where fears over a declining birth rate would reach great heights in the decades after midcentury, the medicinal virtues of spa waters with respect to fertility were worth stressing indeed. According to one guide, "observations which date from time immemorial attest to the stimulating and fortifying effect of [mineral water] upon the reproductive system." More to the point, this doctor wrote that he "could cite numerous examples of sterile young women whose fecundity returned because of our waters." Many women, the doctor revealed, even those who had "been married for several years without becoming a mother," found that visiting a spa invariably "increase[d] the desire to have a child." "After several baths and shower massages to [such] patients' loins and principally to [their] cervix[es]," the doctor noted that cures were usually noticed quickly enough. Somewhat less dramatically, this author promoted his waters as a tonic that would ease the "malaise and pain that often accompan[ied] menstruation or preceded it by several days."[16]

Promoters of this period also sought to show that the medicinal properties of mineral waters varied widely. As one doctor stated it, "not all sources possess the same virtues, so not all springs are equally effective for all patients."[17] In much the same way that medical diagnosis and treatment had increasingly become highly customized, spa promoters argued that only certain conditions responded well to certain kinds of water and hydrotherapy. Thus, in a guide to le Mont-Dore, whose waters were particularly effective when steamed, readers with throat and lung ailments were especially encouraged to visit. In a similar work concerning Vichy, whose waters had a unique mineralization, readers with liver disorders were offered new hope. Still, the larger spas sought to be nearly all things, medically speaking, to consumers in the thermal marketplace. Promoters of Aix-les-Bains, for instance, even as they stressed the particular effectiveness of their waters in treating rheumatic complaints, endeavored to show that their institution could cure all sorts of different ailments. Heart disease, paralysis, gout, nervousness, impotence, asthma, arthritis, consumption, bronchitis, constipation, and poor hygiene were all frequently cited as conditions that could find improvement in the waters of Aix. Rival publicists, always eager to poach curists from each other, typically denounced the curative powers of every spa but their own. Enghien, for example, was criticized in many guides for the temperature of its waters. According to its detractors, Enghien's source produced water that "was too cold for a medicinal bath without some artificial warming."[18] And because so many doctors felt that the natural integrity of a water source had to be scrupulously guaranteed, such charges were severe indeed.

If charts and lists sufficed in the 1830s to convince readers that spa cures were rational, scientific, and medically effective, guidebooks of the subsequent two decades tended to embellish their narratives with a wealth of dramatic, medical detail in an effort to articulate more compellingly the same message.[19] Mainly, guides of the later period relied on patient testimonials, which were encapsulated in "case histories," to establish the medical essence of their spas.[20] Medical narratives of this sort detailed almost every imaginable ailment and utilized patients of every age and both sexes. There is little doubt, however, that authors preferred to illustrate the medical effectiveness of their spas by citing case histories that involved women. One Dr. Forestier, for instance, in the hundred pages of case histories featured in his 1857 guide, cast women as his protagonists more than four times as often as he did men.[21] Similarly, Dr. L. Berthet, in the collection of patient biographies he included in his guide of the same era, illustrated markedly few medical conditions with male examples.[22]

In one typical guide from the middle 1850s, readers were introduced to Madame A., the "wife of a very successful French engineer." Madame's complaints of "blurred vision, shaking hands, and convulsive movements of the different muscles of the face," while "not accompanied by any real pain, [had rendered her] unable to read, work with her hands, or otherwise execute her domestic occupations." "This patient," as the narrative explained, had "endured her suffering for six years" and increasingly, because of her face's obvious "tic," avoided even important social functions. After being told by her regular physician to try hydrotherapy, Madame A. ventured to Aix-les-Bains and initiated a cure. There, following a course of increasingly powerful baths and showers, Madame A. finally managed to escape the symptoms that had plagued her for so long. As an addendum to the case of Madame A., the author noted that of the thirty-four "nervous" patients who came to his practice in the last year, nineteen saw their symptoms "improve," and fifteen were "cured" outright.[23] In effect, this practitioner claimed to have helped all of his patients.

What might explain the tendency among spa doctors and promoters to rely so heavily upon female characters in their medical case histories? Perhaps most obviously, the figure of the invalid female had a social resonance which spa promoters doubtlessly recognized and exploited. In medical literature generally, women's bodies were routinely characterized as weak and failing when compared to men. Puberty, menstruation, child birth, and menopause—each of these traumas helped medical science to conclude that women lived their entire lives as invalids. But the image of women as sick, which endured throughout the century in literatures of all kinds and in art too, was ultimately both popular and powerful because it girded a still-provisional and contested social reality: women belonged within the home, safely separated from public life and productivity.[24] It was during the course of the 1830s and 1840s, after all, when spa authors first began to detail the medical histories of so many nervous bourgeois women. This period also saw Victor Hugo create his tubercular heroine in Fantine and the noted physician Huart detail the pathology of women's reproductive systems. However else these several strands of a discourse may have functioned, they clearly sought to offer a measured and scientific explanation as to why bourgeois women were no longer routinely permitted to involve themselves in the everyday world of commerce and family enterprise.[25] Not for them the dangerous and debilitating world of material production but rather the protected domain of the home and its convalescent room. Equally suitable, as spa promoters hoped to show, was that larger place of convalescence where the productive world was not allowed to compromise the tenuous health of latently or actually ill *bourgeoises* and *demoiselles.*

It seems, however, that the spa promoters' principal incentive for writing their narratives as they did was because they expected their reading audience to be largely female. Ongoing changes in France's print culture increasingly saw women reading more frequently and widely than they ever had before. And as the many family health guides published in this period quite clearly suggest, medical literature constituted one genre which women liked and were expected to read.[26] For if a woman had traditionally acquired her expertise in the healing arts from observing the medical practices of friends and relatives, family health had more recently become a matter of codified and standardized medicine.[27] As one popular family guide of the period explained with respect to the role that mothers were to play in a family's health care, "it [was] she who [had to] dispense the medicines ordered by the doctor and see to it that his prescriptions [were] scrupulously followed." "Thus," this guide elaborated, "it [was] absolutely necessary for her to acquire some familiarity with family medicine."[28]

Women's reading in medicine, while minimal compared with that of any doctor, nonetheless afforded them a form of literacy and authority that most men of the period doubtlessly did not possess. Medical literacy, quite simply, gave women the capacity to diagnose in themselves and their families symptoms and complaints, which, if left unchecked, might have drastic and even disastrous implications.[29] Thus spa promoters, as they constructed the narrative of their case histories, did well to consider the particular audience for which their works would have the most appeal. And by adopting a narrative voice in which medical information was deployed through scores of miniature "novels," the majority of which featured female "characters," spa authors hoped to gain a level of intimacy for their texts which other narrative choices might not have encouraged.[30]

It is also likely that spa authors wrote the nervous woman into their case histories because they believed that French women might well adopt aspects of these medical biographies as important tactics in their own lives.[31] Women of the bourgeoisie, many of whom had come to have a closer relationship with their doctors than with their confessors, were not infrequently accused of wielding medicine as a means of some empowerment vis-à-vis their husbands.[32] Medically literate women could manifest, for instance, any of many vague maladies whose counter-indications ranged from sex to socializing.[33] If contemporary critics more frequently suggested that *bourgeoises* used "a good nervous condition" to free themselves of a conjugal relationship with their husbands and the burdens of motherhood, spa doctors saw good reason to think that their feminine readers might apply such conditions to justify a spa holiday.[34]

Yet male invalids, even if they were not featured in guidebook narratives to the extent that women were, did not completely escape mention in the spas' promotional literature. On the contrary, doctors warned that many male health complaints tended to be both hard to detect and potentially quite serious. Exhaustion and overwork, doctors stressed, seemed to many observers like benign symptoms in otherwise vital men. But such minor complaints, if left unchecked long enough, were liable to have severe consequences. As one doctor wrote in the early 1840s, "strong ambition and the desire for success can sometimes cause men to find only sadness and not joy."[35] This author went on to note that many features of commercial and professional life could prove to be debilitating over the long term. "How many times," the doctor queried, "have family distress, commercial failures, love, and jealousy been the root cause of mental and physical aberrations that impede the ability to think and speak clearly and decisively?"[36] Or, as another doctor wrote in the 1830s with respect to men of the "business world" engaged in "serious occupations," disastrous medical problems could result from too much "passion for success and ambition."[37] Such dire consequences for men's health, however, were thwarted easily enough, according to spa practitioners. As one doctor explained, stress and fatigue were quickly remedied by a "voyage" and the "new and purer air" and "varied promenades" that characterized a "vacation at a watering place."[38] The spa environment, this doctor and so many others promised, worked to "liberate both body and spirit."[39] In all likelihood, these warnings and advertised solutions regarding men's health were still written with a female rather than a male audience in mind. Spa doctors doubtlessly recognized a fact about many bourgeois men of this period that has been noted more recently by historians: these men's "devotion to industrial time, in which each moment brought a new acquisition, was

TABLE 3   Evolution of the Number of Water Doctors at French Spas

	Aix-les-Bains	Vichy	All Spas	All French Doctors
1830	5	—	—	—
1856	10	—	—	—
1870	—	20	400	—
1890	20	50	—	—
1913	28	—	700	25,000

such that they often surrendered seasonal vacations for work, while their wives and children went to spas."[40] Moreover, spa publicists probably understood the workings of the bourgeois family well enough to know the authority that wives and mothers wielded with respect to matters of family finance.[41] When a medically literate woman diagnosed her husband or son as being dangerously fatigued or otherwise ill, a family's economy soon expanded to pay for a stay at a spa. Men in this scenario either became holiday-makers, more often than not with their wives and children as companions, or confronted a miniature crisis within their families.

Spa guidebooks, by the last years of the July Monarchy and early period of the Second Empire, were only the more direct means of reaching thermal consumers. Increasingly, spa publicists began to utilize the testimonial and referral powers of the confraternity of French and international doctors in their relentless search for new customers. International medical conferences were a principal vehicle of this strategy, especially for doctors who had only recently graduated from a medical faculty and established themselves as specialists in mineral water therapy. Lacking sufficient money, contacts, and experience to publish guides on a grander scale, these doctors typically used conferences to highlight their research and promote their reputations. Many spa doctors published their conference papers as medical pamphlets, and these works, it was hoped, would help their authors' medical practices grow and become more profitable. To the community of spa doctors at large, conference attendance paid a clear dividend too. By associating with more "traditional" doctors whose treatment techniques and medical philosophies were not suspect in the way that hydrotherapy still was, spa physicians gained for themselves a clear measure of the professional and respectable identity that many of their colleagues now shared.

Not infrequently, doctors with no formal association to a particular spa were enlisted by that spa's medical corps to write a "disinterested" appraisal of facilities and conditions there. These unaffiliated doctors, however, were clearly asked to comment on certain spas because their high opinions had somehow been guaranteed in advance. Such was apparently the case with one Dr. H. C. Lombard's *Une cure aux bains d'Aix-en-Savoie*. Invited by Aix's medical director to visit the spa and sample its curative programs, Dr. Lombard left the Savoyard establishment as one of its great champions. He matter-of-factly dedicated his book to Aix's medical director, and he declared with certainty that no guide to the spa could ever be written to surpass the director's own *Manuel de l'étranger aux bains d'Aix*.[42]

But Dr. Lombard did not reserve his praise solely for the spa's medical director. On the contrary, his work touted the research and expertise of virtually every doctor attached to the thermal establishment. Lombard noted that one Dr. Vidal had recently published an "interesting" essay entitled "Essai sur les eaux minérales." And Vidal, Lombard described, was a veritable "font of important information and expertise on mineral waters of all types."[43] Similar comments were directed at the professional careers and published works of Drs. Guilland, Petrequin, Blanc, and Davat. Lombard and physicians like him may well have been paid to write guides that amounted to medical testimonials. Regardless, the promotional strategy in which they participated was a well-considered attempt to reach new curists through the family doctor.

Medical advertising to doctors was often far less subtle than the sort of text that Lombard authored on behalf of the doctors at Aix-les-Bains. Instead of hiding their intentions at all, most spa doctors simply admitted that family practitioners could help the spa business. Or, as these promoters more commonly described the situation, family doctors could help their patients by sending them to a bathing facility. As J. Bonjean saw it, in a work he published in 1862, "doctors and authors [had] for too long been preoccupied with writing guides and itineraries destined to furnish bathers with useful information." According to Bonjean, who was a pharmacist with unclear associations to the spa about which he wrote, "the nature of these slender volumes [had been] such that they fail[ed] to mention diverse and important points of science which must be made known to doctors." Without a thorough medical introduction to hydrotherapy and its specific applications at a given spa, Bonjean contended, family doctors "[would be] unable to choose with any certainty the right thermal destination for their patients."[44] Thus Bonjean, like so many spa doctors in this period and later, wrote his book so that it would be "favorably received by colleagues who [had] hitherto failed to appreciate the value and influence of [hydrotherapy]."[45] Once enlightened, these colleagues—

Bonjean and spa doctors everywhere hoped—would willingly send their patients on a thermal cure.[46]

Frequently, spa guides from this period printed long testimonial letters that were, either directly or indirectly, addressed to family practitioners. Aix-les-Bains's Dr. Constant Despine transcribed just such a letter, from one H. B. of London, in a guide he wrote specifically to capture yet another share of the thermal marketplace—English doctors and travelers:

> As far as my experience goes, I am greatly tempted to criticize the conduct of the English faculty, who too generally endeavor to cure rheumatism with medicine, and then, when drugs fail to do the desired work, as a last resort send their patients to the mineral baths, by which time their constitutions are considerably weakened. Let me beg of them in future to act more fairly, both towards their patients and such waters, by giving them the first chance. Let me instance a case in point. In the spring of the year 1862 my feet continued very stiff, from an attack I had had of gout and rheumatism during the previous winter. I consulted the MD I usually have recourse to in the country—whose name, by the way, ranks well in London—and he told me he thought that mineral waters would do me no good. Finding, in the course of two months, that I got no better, I applied to Dr. Weber, of Green Street, who strongly recommended me to go to Aix-la-Chapelle. As that is a mortally dull and slow place, I asked him if there were any other baths I could go to. He mentioned Aix-les-Bains, in Savoy, and there I accordingly went. It is a charming, picturesquely situated little town, and the bathing arrangements surpass those of any other place. Three weeks bathing made me as fresh on my feet as a four year old. As proof of this, about three days before my departure, I took a long walk up into the mountain above the town, in the company of two other Englishmen, one of whom had just finished a walking tour of Switzerland. Although the senior of the party by several years, I took the lead, and maintained it during the whole of our excursion.[47]

In conjunction with glowing testimonials like this one, spa promoters routinely boasted in their doctor-to-doctor advertising of those international practitioners whose patients they had already begun to counsel and treat. Thus Despine, after relating the letter of London's "H. B.," saw fit to add that "as a confirmation of what has been above stated, I am happy to note that most eminent English practitioners have recommended patients to me and I am very glad to announce the patients benefited from the waters." To add still further credence to this claim, the doctor actually named Sir Charles Locock Bart, Sir W. Ferguson, and fifteen other highly esteemed English doctors whom he counted among his champions.[48]

Despine, Bonjean, Lombard, and others who followed this promotional scheme clearly had reason to believe that their efforts were not in vain. For that matter, spa promoters and developers all over France surely saw their various enterprises as successful by midcentury. The ever growing population of French spa-goers was in itself a powerful testimonial to the work of these men. At the beginning of the Restoration—before any baths had been commodified, reconstructed, or promoted as they would be in the later 1820s and after—the total seasonal population at France's spas had been a mere 31,000 persons. By the 1840s, without the general availability of railroads, that figure had increased by approximately three times.[49] But even more important than the fact that the spas' population of visitors had grown so substantially since developers had initiated their advertising campaigns, spa speculators had managed to make their milieu into what one historian of the period has called "an obligatory stop in the daily rhythm" of the country's *grande bourgeoisie.*[50]

LEISURE REGIMES

By the Revolution of 1830 or very shortly thereafter, French bathing places began to seem like medical institutions to a degree that they never had before.[51] Along with the aspects of spa medicalization that we have already discussed, a scientific allocation of time was instituted at most spas in this period. The tradition of the three-week cure, for instance, was grounded for the first time in principles of medicine. Doctors all over France addressed the matter of the spa vacation's duration in the 1830s and 1840s. Their consensus on this issue was quite easily achieved.[52] Twenty-one days, they wrote in their guidebooks and in their research publications, were required before one could expect to experience the full and curative force of hydrotherapeutic medicine.[53]

A more significant medicalization of spa temporality also characterized the period of the early July Monarchy. That process brought time-discipline to the spa and the practice of hydrotherapeutic medicine. At larger or thoroughly renovated spas, for instance, bells were often installed to mark the passage of medical time. This way, if warm waters had somehow lulled a patient into such a state of repose as to forget a doctor's prescriptions, institutional reminders were always at hand. But bells hardly replaced the presence of orderlies in a spa's corridors or bath givers within the bathing cabinets themselves, for these administrators, as personnel rules from the period never failed to stress, were ultimately responsible for the timely circulation of patients through an establishment's facilities.

Regardless of how time-discipline was made systematic at the spas, there was little variation as to the seriousness with which doctors and other administrators applied its tenets. Spas routinely issued medical and administrative guidelines stipulating specific instructions for the duration of cures. Such rules left decidedly little room for misinterpretation on the part of bathers. Baths, for example, which were considered to be the most gentle type of cure at most establishments, seldom continued beyond one hour and fifteen minutes. More extreme forms of hydrotherapy, such as the high-pressure shower massage, hardly ever continued beyond twenty minutes.

But time-discipline applied at the spas beyond bathing procedures, too. Thus at Aix-les-Bains and many other institutions, bathers had to take great care to be on time for their cures. Reserved in advance by as much as a week, cure sessions were supposed to begin promptly according to a well-posted schedule. At tightly scheduled spas, tardiness was treated as a serious offense. First-time delinquents were warned at these establishments not to be late for curing a second time, for subsequent tardiness was punished by the patients having to "forfeit [their] medical examinations and all right[s] to the diverse medical cleansing services of the day."[54]

Spas pinned their order of operations to the dictates of a clock for many of the same reasons that factories and other "productive" sites had adopted time-discipline.[55] Efficiency was probably first among the concerns that prompted administrators in the thermal milieu to dispense their medicine in time-specific quantities. After all, the period of the Restoration saw a significant increase in the annual number of bathers at most spas. The implications of this increase for a spa's daily services were doubtlessly great. Now, Vichy and other establishments began keeping their curative centers open around the clock. But even spas that did not go to such extremes certainly recognized a compelling reason to increase their efficiency. Prices had increased enough in the period to make spa administrators eager to use their facilities in the most efficient and productive ways possible.

But the overarching desire of medical authorities to make hydrotherapy seem more rational, credible, and rigorously scientific undoubtedly outweighed the issue of efficiency in the thinking of France's bath administrators. Spa doctors found themselves constantly having to defend their favored mode of treatment. And clearly the temporal reorganization of bathing served some of the same representational purposes as individuated bathing cabinets, gendered interiors, and carefully calibrated systems of surveillance. For, like these spatial characteristics of the new spas, time-discipline subjected the experience of bathing to a rationalizing process of compartmentalization and incrementalization.

Thus practitioners, who still found it necessary in the 1850s to declare that "mineral waters [were] a serious remedy which cure[d] maladies by themselves and solely as a function of their chemical properties," often used references to time-discipline as a subtle commentary on the seriousness of hydrotherapeutic medicine.[56] In one such defense of spa medicine, a doctor warned his readers that "all newly arrived bathers had to know one thing related to the amount of time that should be spent in bathing." Too many bathers, this doctor stressed, wrongly believed "that the value of mineral water is increased by prolonging a bath."[57] On the contrary, this practitioner and his associates sought to stress, successful bathing depended on careful medical administration of mineral water. And baths, which spa physicians warned had to be "taken at precisely the temperature prescribed by the patient's doctor," were not to be wallowed in as though their waters were merely warm and pleasing.[58] In this way, the increasingly strict incrementalization of thermal medical practice, which cast the water cure and its practitioners in a serious and scientific light, was itself a form of spa promotion.

Time-discipline was hardly the only aspect of spa medicalization in this period to address hydrotherapy's credibility as a branch of medical science. Spa medicine in the 1830s and 1840s followed the larger medical community's drive toward customized diagnosis and treatment.[59] In the medical opinion of most spa doctors, who tended to follow the influential writings of Dr. Philibert Patissier, the key to the efficacy of mineral water cures was to bring a spa's water into a patient's body.[60] Through absorption of water, doctors believed, a healing measure of secretions and excretions could be achieved. The emerging science of hydrotherapy thus sought to identify and treat in isolation the ailing parts of a patient's body.

It was not only through concentrated treatments and absorption, however, that doctors endeavored to bring their tonic into the body. Rather, they focused with equal intensity on the value of the body's several orifices as conduits for the healing force of mineral water. Inhalation chambers, for instance, where curists sat with air needles inserted into their nostrils, were built at many spas in the 1830s to deliver the benefits of mineral water to the body's insides. Without question, however, the anus and the vagina were the most frequent recipients of spa doctors' orificial attention. Guidebooks from the 1830s and 1840s, like Dr. Constant Despine's *Manuel topographique et médical de l'étranger aux eaux d'Aix-en-Savoie* of 1834, described many different conditions that required a medical entrance into the anus or vagina or both. Certain ailments, the doctor noted, like indigestion, obesity, gout, infertility, amenorrhea, dysmenorrhea, and nervousness, all but required an "ascendant shower" of either the rectal or vaginal variety.[61] Yet these curative techniques and preparations were just as regularly prescribed as maintenance procedures. Thus many curists with no specific health complaints found themselves, at some point in their rest at a spa, atop or astride one of the intrusive delivery systems that Dr. Despine and so many other spa physicians defined and diagramed in their guides of the 1830s and 1840s.

The application of such cures, spa doctors of the period endeavored to stress, was a delicate science: "these [rectal and vaginal] treatments [had to be] monitored in the most exact manner, and the mixing of hot and cool water require[d] a minute graduation so that the douche was administered at a temperature well beneath that of blood."[62] Such clinical prose as this seemed to serve notice to those who still snickered at the seriousness of hydrotherapy or continued to associate thermal bathing and curing with the rowdy, communal basins of the Old Regime. Now, a diagnostic and prescriptive sensibility had assumed pride of place over what had become an essentially clinical terrain.

Bath interiors, bathing practices, and curists' bodies—these were the chief contours of the spa's clinical domain. And to doctors, who sought absolute jurisdiction over their spas as well as their patients, it was vitally important that a diagnostically informed neutrality reign over bathing.[63] Thus, as in obstetrics, surgery, and other disciplines of medical science, the practitioners of hydrotherapy objectified the bodies of their patients. In so doing, of course, they installed a modicum of propriety and modesty that facilitated even the most delicate types of examinations and treatments.

Nowhere was hydrotherapy's clinical body more in evidence than in promotional texts, written to the general reading audience, in which medical conditions related to male and female genitalia were discussed. What is significant about such texts is not their detailed treatment of genital afflictions in both males and females, but rather the fact that medical discussions of this nature are contained within works whose subject matter ranged from topography to etiquette and beyond. In referring to the side effects of certain cold water and sea bath treatments, for example, one doctor warned that patients tended to experience an "itching of the vulva."

Moreover, he noted, poorly managed cases of this sort often caused an "unnatural heaviness and weight to the uterus." Finally, the doctor advised, improperly administered vaginal injections could manifest in many patients "a throbbing with tenderness about the groin and perineum."[64]

Readers of a similar guide learned intimate details about the workings of a certain Madame V.'s reproductive system. Married for two years and "still without a family," Madame V. had recently moved to a "cold and damp house where she experienced, for the first time, acute pelvic pains and violent backaches." To these discomforts was added the cessation of her period, which she "attributed to a drive in an open carriage on a cold day." Treated initially by a midwife, whose "irrational" methods had included the "application of leeches and blisters and other things she had forgotten," Madame V. arrived at her spa with "irritability of the bladder, fullness and heat about the pelvis, her cervix pushed forward in a state of prolapsus, hard and sensitive."

Readers of the case of Madame V. were enjoined to follow her steadily improving medical condition. First, however, they had to know more about her doctor's diagnosis. Thus, the doctor explained that a "uterine catheter entered easily to a distance of about six centimeters." It was equally important that readers should see that Madame received a most rational prescription from her spa doctor. Accordingly, readers learned that Madame's doctor advised "iodine of iron before meals, a tumbler of Marlioz water at night, and daily tepid baths with the speculum." To answer those readers who might have wondered why Madame V. was not introduced to a more aggressive treatment—such as the hot or cold ascendant shower that were so routinely administered in these cases—her doctor noted that "this case was of too inflammatory a nature to support more stimulating injections."

The mini-narrative of Madame V. ended happily enough for all parties. After only eight days, Madame's "monthly epochs returned, abundant and satisfactory in color, necessitating five days of complete repose." Finally, her doctor conducted "an examination that pointed out great local improvement."[65] Specifically, Madame V.'s "cervix, less hard and voluminous, had become supple." And the patient, having taken "twelve baths and eighteen [vaginal] douches," left the spa with "her local as well as general state completely re-established."[66]

Men's sexuality and sex organs, although less prominently featured in spa literature than women's, figured into the writings of spa doctors too. For example, doctors wanted their male readers to recognize the power of hydrotherapy to combat a lack of sexual vigor and a host of other conditions related to men's genitals. If some doctors were willing to admit that "there [was] no certainty that mineral waters acted as an aphrodisiac," most spa practitioners claimed that their waters could cure male impotence. Or as one physician wrote on this issue, "it is well known that sulfurous waters in general, and, more notably the springs in Aix, augment the body's vital forces and, typically, elevate the erectability of the penis."[67] Problems with sperm production and overall sexual virility were also addressed by spa doctors in their guides. Doctors tended to consider it a serious matter, for example, if a man's ejaculate was of the "wrong" quantity or quality. Stressing that masturbation could lead to either an over- or underabundance of sperm, spa doctors routinely warned their male readers to avoid an activity that could lead to spermatorrhea. Once this or a related condition had appeared, however, doctors advised that prompt hydrotherapeutic remedies be sought.[68]

The medicalization of the spas, however, went well beyond the rise of differentiated treatments or the implementation of time-discipline. Doctors took control of the thermal milieu to such an extent that spas all across France in the 1830s made it virtually illegal for anyone to bathe without having first consulted with an accredited physician.[69] As the posted rules at one establishment summarized, "all persons who wish[ed] to use the waters, showers, or vapors [were] required to obtain a medical certificate."[70] More than just directly padding French doctors' pockets, however, required consultations went a long way toward enrolling healthy tourists in a highly regimented course of medical treatment. For, as one spa physician wrote in 1841, "a single case has not [fallen] under my observation in which careful examination could not detect a deranged state in the [body's] functions."[71]

Doctors agreed that the effectiveness of mineral water cures depended upon little more than the patient's willingness to "suspend all affairs" in favor of a "sane and regular regime."[72] That regularity, more than anything else, was based on an intensely close relationship between doctor and patient. Dr. Victor Noyer of Vichy stated the importance of this relationship clearly enough as he expressed, too, the extent to which physicians were to have authority over the lives of their patients: "In order to gain all the advantages promised by the waters, . . . the patient, when on vacation, must follow exactly whatever advice he is given by his doctor."[73] Indeed most spa-goers began each of their twenty-one days on vacation with at least a brief medical consultation. Such examinations tended to be bothersome and expensive far more than dire or unpleasant. Caricatures depicted these sessions as light-hearted meetings. One humorous rendering of "morning consultations at the thermal establishment" (fig. 9), for example, contained in a caricature and sketch album of the period, caught four different doctors in the act of prescribing expensive and elaborate treatments for such ailments as the sweats and indigestion.[74] Typically, spa-goers found during the course of their initial doctor's visit that their health was threatened by some sort of potential medical condition.

In virtually all cases, spa doctors attempted to establish a medical perimeter in which curists were to conduct themselves during their holidays. Part of the hydrotherapeutic regimen, for example, sought to monitor and minimize the level of mental activity in which patients engaged. A noted practitioner at Aix-les-Bains who wrote extensively on this issue, Dr. Auguste Forestier, advised spa-goers to "leave all thoughts of weighty matters at the door of [their] thermal establishment."[75] Worries about one's profession or business, these doctors warned, would necessarily interfere with the success of the cure. Even artists and poets were told to ignore their muses, for "passions of the soul" had to be limited too in order for hydrotherapy to achieve its potential.[76] In the same spirit, doctors routinely advised their patients to maintain a low level of social contact and fight "the great temptation . . . to join the social circle." The "risk" of too much sociability and mental activity, doctors lamented, was simply "not worth the consequences which it entailed."[77] As one especially curmudgeonly practitioner stated the situation, "I should strongly advise invalids to frequent the salon as little as possible in the evenings."[78]

Prescriptions concerning eating and drinking were part of the hydrotherapeutic regimen too.[79] Spa hotels typically boasted bountiful tables, but doctors warned their patients to avoid indulging excessively. Most doctors offered only general prescriptions in this context, usually counseling patients to "eat only light meals at regular intervals."[80] Indeed, a "well-researched and healthy diet," while not easily maintained in the face of an "appetite that [could be] overactivated by the change of air," was, in the studied opinion of the spas' medical experts, "a necessary foundation for any successful course of hydrotherapy."[81] As one practitioner stated the matter, "the importance of establishing and carrying out a suitable diet, or of initiating desirable changes in dietary habits, in connection with a course of mineral waters, cannot be over-estimated."[82] The fact that doctors could create a dietary regimen for their patients and, at least in part, oversee patient compliance was, in the opinion of spa practitioners, "one of the great advantages attending this method of treatment."[83]

Many doctors were not content to offer only general guidelines con-

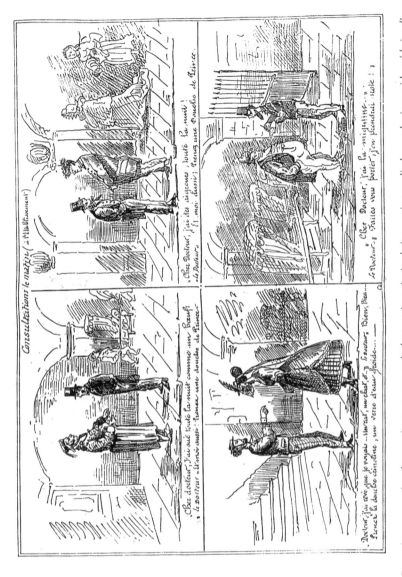

FIGURE 9 Doctoring on vacation: bourgeois spa-goers caught by a caricaturist in their morning medical consultations with *médecins d'eaux*. Reprinted from Pagotto, *Le thermalisme à Aix-les-Bains au dix-neuvième siècle*, 74.

cerning their patients' dietary regimens. Speaking for some of his more ambitious colleagues, one noted water doctor wrote that "it would certainly be an advantage . . . if the physicians were enabled to exercise more control or direction over the food supplied to, or taken by, the patients."[84] Another practitioner stipulated to his patients that "wine, if permitted at all, should always be taken in great moderation" and that "seltzer water often proves a good substitute for wine." Further, this physician noted, "it would be a wise rule for patients to abstain completely from all things brought to the table in the form of dessert."[85] In the more frank assessment of a physician at Vichy, "patients had to be forbidden from eating chocolates."[86] Another spa doctor, while characterizing his "dietary regimen" as not very "severe," nevertheless offered his patients a great deal of specific information with respect to food and drink. At Vichy, this practitioner notified patients that they should take a "breakfast at ten o'clock of two to three courses with a little red wine and water or tea or coffee for a beverage." Then, at "half-past five," patients would be offered a "fair and moderate amount of food" for their dinner.[87] At Aix-les-Bains, another doctor told patients that they should "eat sparingly of brown meats, and [eat] fresh-water fish in preference of sea fish."[88]

Exercise was also a medical matter at the spas of this period. Aix-les-Bains's Dr. Chasseloup summarized the sentiments of his profession in the 1830s on this issue, writing that "exercise of some form, either on foot or horseback, [was] absolutely essential."[89] Or, as *La grande encyclopédie* clearly stated the matter some decades later, "exercise, taken before and after [treatment], prepares and facilitates the reactionary movement from which hydrotherapeutic medicine takes its curative and reconstitutional virtues."[90] Mainly, spa doctors encouraged exercise in the form of leisurely walks through the environs of a spa town. Yet doctors also sought to impose some measure of rationality upon the promenade, so they often advised their patients to follow certain routes or to walk only at lower altitudes.[91]

Sleep, too, was a medical matter in the estimation of French water doctors. For as one physician warned, "sleep taken to excess [was] contrary to good health." Over-resting, even when on a spa vacation, was denounced by doctors as having as its only product a "weak and feeble body."[92] As in dietary prescriptions, doctors called for moderation above all else in the sleeping practices of their patients. For "moderate sleep," water doctors noted, "help[ed] the body's strength recover and made it more agile." Beyond asking patients to "go to sleep and arise at reasonable hours," doctors issued dire warnings about napping, which they took to be an injurious and even transgressive form of sleep. The afternoon nap was, in the considered opinion of one medical expert, a very "bad habit" indeed.[93]

Beyond the medicalization of these several components of spa life, doctors sought to create for patients a comprehensive regimen—a daily rhythm that organized in full nearly every hour of a patient's leisure according to the dictates of hydrotherapeutic medicine. Doctors went so far as to establish, both in their guidebooks and among the patients on whom they practiced, a daily schedule that assigned specific times for waking, eating, exercising, thermal curing, resting, walking, and going to bed.[94] Thus, as one doctor at Vichy wrote regarding his patients' mornings, "early hours are the rule here." By this, the doctor meant that "at six o'clock [in the morning], drinking and bathing commence[d] seriously."[95] Those whose prescriptions called for the drinking of mineral water were encouraged to "drink [their] water gradually [while] chatting and promenading." Then, these patients were instructed to allow an "interval of three-quarters to one hour between finishing the prescribed dose of mineral water and the morning meal."[96] Morning bathers had a slightly different order of operations to follow. After their baths, they were told to allow for "half an hour or an hour of absolute repose." Then, at approximately ten o'clock, bathers were invited to breakfast, after which their prescriptions generally called for "a lounge in the open air or a very gentle promenade."[97]

The spa afternoon, doctors noted in their guides, was a time period that was most easily "filled-up."[98] Morning water drinkers, of course, took their turn within the curative facilities of a bathing establishment. It was unusual for a round of afternoon treatments, which often included more than one type of water cure, to last any less than two hours. Preparing to bathe, waiting one's turn, curing, drying, and being carried back to one's hotel in a bath chair and then relaxing in silence for a prescribed time—the elaborate process of even simple treatments could often last the better part of an afternoon. Upon completing one's cure, spa afternoons offered a generous share of amusements and distractions. Bands and orchestras played at regular intervals throughout the day, and doctors' only advice to their patients was to not enjoy these pleasures at the expense of their prescribed walks. Rather, doctors counseled patients to promenade while they listened to such performances. This combination, doctors stressed, was the most healthful and safe way to "fill-up . . . the afternoons until the evening meal at five or six."[99] For those patients with more serious medical complaints, doctors simply prescribed isolation and quiet "during the interval between lunch and dinner." Such patients, doctors stressed, needed to "avoid all of the unnerving excitement that [came] necessarily from arranging oneself correctly for social activities."[100]

Evening, by contrast, was not thought by most physicians to be a medically "safe" time of day. Prescriptions concerning mental exercise, sociability, and diet clearly cast spa doctors as the opponents of the spa's after-dark pleasures. Casinos, balls, theatrical productions, and orchestral concerts were featured at least weekly during the summer season at most larger spas, and there can be little doubt that these distractions were frequented by many if not most patients. For these patients, after all, were, in large numbers, not in any way the desperate invalids that their daily regimens suggested. Regardless of this fact, doctors did all that they could to frighten their patients into at least a measured and moderate pursuit of evening pleasures. For, as one doctor summarized the opinion of many of his professional associates with respect to the evening pleasures at spa, "in these [amusements], with their attendant evils, invalids do join, and from them they suffer."[101]

Above all else, doctors warned, "it was always advisable to be under cover at, and for an hour or two after, sundown when the temperature falls considerably."[102] But being indoors, especially in a ballroom or a casino, was thought by doctors to be almost as dangerous as the chilled outdoors. As one doctor wrote, such facilities tended to have "poor ventilation" that was only exacerbated by "overcrowding." This "injurious atmosphere," doctors recognized, was a "consequence of the population of seasonal visitors who [knew] each other" and their understandable desire for "social entertainments, balls, dinners and theatrical . . . events."[103]

THE MEDICAL CONTOURS OF CURING

Bathing establishments proper were the seat of medical authority in the thermal milieu, and it was within these facilities that the medicalization of free time was most fully realized.[104] The nineteenth century saw hydrotherapy emerge as an increasingly well defined science with highly differentiated medical applications. Accordingly, spa doctors had an ever expanding arsenal of diagnostic, prescriptive, and therapeutic principles in which to ground their rising authority over the practice of thermal leisure. But even as the perimeter of spa medicine grew to include a host of new curative techniques, there emerged within French baths something like a standard or routine course of treatment.

Virtually every spa-goer received from her or his doctor a prescription to bathe in and drink mineral water. The former of these treatments was a perennial favorite among French spa-goers and had been for centuries. By the middle 1840s, for instance, when a large spa like Aix-les-Bains was seeing around 2,500 visitors each year, the bathing establishment was issuing more than 8,500 tickets to its private bathtubs.[105] More detailed accounting of bathing at Bourbon-l'Archambault, from records kept in the 1820s, reveals that of 111 spa visitors in the summer, only 15 did not have at least an immersion in a bathtub. The 96 persons who bathed at Bourbon in this period took a total of 1,438 baths, for an average of around 14 baths per person. Indeed, fully one-third of those who bathed at all took at least a one bath per day.[106]

If bathing at a spa had become a private and medical experience during the Restoration—individual tubs and private dressing rooms having eliminated much of the sociability and collective sensuality that had characterized the Old Regime's mode of communal bathing—such cures had hardly ceased to be pleasurable. Even spa doctors seldom failed to note that curists felt "an agreeable sense of warmth" upon entering their baths.[107] In the words of another practitioner, the "euphoria" of the patient "must never be inconvenienced in the bath by the least unpleasant impression."[108] Yet doctors wished for their patients to recognize that bathing, though it might feel pleasing to the body, was an entirely medical procedure. "It is only the doctor," wrote one physician, "who can appreciate the need for a bath and determine the duration for bathing as well as make decisions regarding temperature." No longer anything like the crude science of the Old Regime, hydrotherapeutic bathing had to be practiced with great precision, because, as doctors recognized, "a bath taken at a slightly elevated or lowered temperature [could] alter completely the intended results."[109]

Doctors stressed that the relaxing properties and comforts of the bathtub were themselves curative. An extended repose in these warm waters, doctors wrote, caused the "vital powers [to be] exalted and all the functions of the organs [to be] put into an increased state of activity.[110] The bath's capacity to raise the body's pulse and increase its rate of respiration, spa doctors argued, permitted the healing properties of spa water to penetrate the skin and attack disease or discomfort.[111] In particular, doctors tended to prescribe hydrotherapeutic baths for patients whose health was the most feeble. Severely rheumatic patients or those curists with grave conditions were often advised to bathe daily.

In addition to offering specific prescriptions as to how long a patient was to bathe, spa doctors medicalized the very practice of bathing. Thus, as one doctor described, patients were to enter a bath cabinet only when they were calm and collected, for as this doctor stressed, "it [was] dangerous to bathe when heated or perspiring."[112] To ensure medical effectiveness, doctors warned that "persons taking a whole bath should immerse themselves into the water only by slow degrees, up to the neck, having previously sponged the chest and abdomen with the bath water." After this cautious introduction of the body to the water, patients were instructed to lie calm and still. At predetermined intervals in the bathing hour, however, this repose was interrupted by the reappearance of bath attendants whose task it was to "use friction, by means of a brush or sponge," to stimulate the patient's skin. Patients were told not to relax too much when bathing, just as they were counseled to avoid sleeping immediately after curing. For fatigue, either during or after bathing, tended to "spoil the appetite, weaken the patient and put him out of humor all day."[113]

Water drinking was both the least medicalized and most common of all hydrotherapeutic practice at the nineteenth-century French spa. Spa sociability, which had once informed all facets of hydrotherapy, was relegated solely to the fountain during the 1820s. Mineral water fountains were generally situated at more than one location in a spa town, and access to them was almost always gratis. Thus, at Vichy, one could drink the waters either at the thermal establishment's elaborate and ornate *grande grille* or at any of the plainer fountains found throughout the municipality. Large groups of curists tended to congregate at certain fountains in a spa town, making these the stylish sites at which to take one's cups of water. Families drank water together, as scores of promotional sketches from this period showed, and people participated in the jovial and easy sociability for which spa society had always been famous.

But if this aspect of the spa cure was never brought fully under medical jurisdiction, it was not because doctors failed to regard water drinking as a serious cure that was well worth their expert attention. Rather, French doctors forever raged at their inability to govern their patients' conduct at mineral water fountains. In the words of one frustrated spa doctor, who believed that unsupervised curists tended to abuse their freedom at mineral water fountains, "Patients drink their water excessively, persuaded that their future relief is based on the quantity of mineral water that they consume."[114] Echoing these sentiments, another doctor wrote that "medical supervision [was] absolutely necessary." Specifically, this spa doctor warned, "Patients require advice on many points . . . as to when to drink the waters and how much to take."[115]

So spa doctors, despite the fact that it was next to impossible for them to ensure the compliance of their patients, seldom failed to issue exact prescriptions concerning water drinking. In the opinion of one doctor who wrote in the 1830s, patients were best served if they "initiate[d] their drinking with only small doses and augment[ed] these, little by little, until reach[ing] a peak of fifteen glasses per day." Around the middle of a vacation, this doctor advised his patients "to progressively reduce their water drinking."[116] Only this controlled course of therapy most doctors agreed, was likely to safeguard patients from any "dangerous accidents."[117]

Spa-goers also received from their doctors a prescription to exercise or swim in a thermal pool. At midcentury and after, in fact, pool cures had even eclipsed the vast popularity of the bathtub with doctors and patients. In 1857 at one major spa, for instance, 8,589 baths were administered to 2,361 curists, as compared with 8,934 pool treatments.[118] Such pools were hardly similar to the collective baths of the Old Regime. Rather, these facilities were always enclosed within a bathing establishment and strictly organized according to gender. Moreover, the swimming pools of the new spas were highly medicalized. Thus, as one doctor described this aspect of hydrotherapy, "the pool or swimming bath, only differ[ed] from the domestic bath in that it [was] taken in a larger body of water combined, however, with the immense benefit which the patient derive[d] from the motion and exercise allowed by the larger space."[119] Doctors sought to stress, in their descriptions of spa pools, that these were serious, medical facilities. One doctor, for instance, boasted that his pools constituted a "powerful means of alleviating many diseases."[120] More specifically, this practitioner lauded the pool for having "effected remarkable cures in cases of rickets [and] scrofula . . . as well as hysterical, uterine, and nervous disorders."[121]

Pool cures prohibited most of the wallowing in warm water that had once characterized the hydrotherapeutics of spa basins. Rather, these cures typically featured a combination of prescribed exercise and forceful showering. Figure 10, a photograph from later in the century, captures a standard swimming cure in progress. In this image, the female patient appears to be receiving physical support from a bath attendant. In the background, perched ominously at the pool's edge with a powerful hose in hand, a second attendant waits for the right moment to administer a blast of thermal water to the patient's upper body. Between and even during such brief but forceful showers, patients were shown swimming techniques as well as other sorts of exercise.[122]

These relatively passive and pleasant forms of therapy, however, were little more than a curist's introduction to the spa. Hydrotherapy routinely

FIGURE 10   Promotional photograph showing a young woman in the midst of a *piscine* cure. Ordered, controlled, and peopled by uniformed personnel, this image was proper enough to become a postcard. Reprinted from Leguay, *Histoire d'Aix-les-Bains et sa région: Une grande station thermale.*

became a punishing and even painful tonic for many bathers, especially those whose health was solid enough to weather more extreme forms of therapeutics. Cold water cures enjoyed a great vogue among the hydrotherapeutic medical community after their apparent success in French asylums and at the seaside watering places of France and England.[123] Less popular by far at spas than simple baths, cold cures were, nevertheless, routinely prescribed by spa doctors from the 1830s onward. Following the exact instructions of the German doctor Vincent Priessnitz, whose reputation as the father of cold water bathing was widespread and respected all over Europe, French doctors brought the agonies of cold water bathing to a generation of curists whose medical complaints ranged from bronchial disorders to obesity.[124]

One form of this therapy, known as the "wet sheet treatment," was employed at many of France's Alpine spas. The wet sheet bath required that a wide sheet be left in frigid water for a period of several hours. At a predetermined hour, the frosty cloth was removed from its tub and immediately wrapped around an awaiting patient. Proper technique called for many woolen blankets to then be dumped on the sheeted curist and, finally, for the entire wrap to be secured at the patient's feet and throat.

Left, in one survivor's account, "bound head and foot in a state of utter helplessness," the cold curist was liberated only after beginning to feel warm.[125] The wet sheet bath usually lasted no longer than an hour, but its critics certainly felt that amount of time was plenty to endure. Writing about his experience under the wet sheet, one patient recounted, "I could scarcely refrain from screaming out; indeed it is quite possible that I did scream."[126]

More commonly administered than the wet sheet treatment, cold water showers and baths required just as much strength and stamina to endure. Usually reserved for women whose "profuse menstruation of the constitutional origin" had rendered them uncomfortable or infertile, cold water immersions were nothing if not punishing.[127] Patients unlucky enough to get this prescription, called the Scotch Shower at most spas, after the Scottish reputation for enjoying constitutionals of the cold and wet sort, usually had to take up to fifteen minutes or more of a freezing cold bath or shower. Showering was by far the more common mode of treatment—Aix-les-Bains administered nearly 4,000 of these treatments each year of the 1820s to a bathing population of less than 2,500—and many spas installed hand-hold bars and other special facilities to accommodate the therapy.[128] Because the freezing water of these showers was routinely propelled from a height of fifteen feet or more, it reached the curists in a relentless blast that patients described as being "a liquid needle as thick as a man's arm."[129] One such curist claimed that "the whole surface of my body, even my hands and face, became very sensitive to the touch of cold water." Further, he recounted that his "nerves [had been] laid bare [and that he] left with a perfect horror of cold water, a kind of hydrophobia."[130]

Another form of French hydrotherapy introduced patients to a combination of hot and extraordinarily pressurized water. Usually administered in a small stall underneath a bathing establishment's principal facilities, where intense humidity and the stench of sulphur or alkaline vapors made it difficult for patients to breathe, these cures were both officially and popularly known as "the showers of hell."[131] While not as commonly prescribed as many other forms of hydrotherapy, these cures were hardly unknown. At Aix-les-Bains through the 1840s, each summer nearly two thousand of these treatments were performed—on a bathing population that was less than 3,000 persons.[132] Especially suited to combat skin diseases and rashes of many sorts, hot showers required great caution on the doctor's part. Too much exposure to the curative properties of the hot shower, doctors warned, could have truly painful side effects. Particularly among patients with a sensitive constitution, such scalding waters tended to blister the skin and cause it to fall off. Like the bathing cells used for cold water showering, the chambers used in these cures were equipped with hand-hold bars to help besieged patients steady themselves.

Mud baths offered some of the same sensations that patients experienced in the hot shower, but in the mud bath, a patient's movements were almost entirely constrained. Buried beneath many pounds of mud—typically heated to a temperature of more than 120 degrees and then quickly dumped upon the curist—patients were instructed to lie as still as possible.[133] The deeply heated mud invariably caused the patient an intense burning sensation. But, doctors stressed, this sense of burning disappeared quickly if the patient agreed to remain motionless. Doctors warned that "when, however, a limb [was] moved, and therefore the relative position of the mud to the skin change[d], the intense heat [was] again felt.[134] The mud used in these operations was not just any mud. Carefully collected from earthen pools that were richly penetrated by thermal waters, therapeutic mud was scientifically quantified and prescribed accordingly. Thus, depending on whether a patient's complaint was gouty or rheumatic in origin, doctors favored certain muds and avoided others.

Extreme confinement and steamed heat were other unpleasant characteristics of certain medical procedures at the spas of this period. The vapor-box bath was among the more widely prescribed and torturous of all hydrotherapeutic techniques. These baths were conducted in miniature wooden cells whose dimensions were only slightly greater than a patient's body. As one guide described it, the vapor bath was conducted within "a curious wooden box with a round hole in its moveable lid." The hole allowed the patient's neck and head to remain at liberty from the box bath. The balance of the patient's body was assaulted with a steam-curing whose extreme heat regularly surpassed 150 degrees Fahrenheit and caused an increase in body temperature of three to four degrees.[135]

Even in the writing of spa promoters, box bathing was not gently or charitably described. In one doctor's testimony, the typical vapor bath began painlessly enough: "After undressing, he steps into the wooden box and finds that he is shut in all except the head, the round hole being occupied by his neck. Immediately a valve on the level of the floor is opened, the hot vapor rises about him and he soon begins to perspire freely." But, as the doctor went on to describe, the bather was not cooled by "the perspiration, running now from his brow and trickling down his face." The heavy sweating was instead a ticklishly hot irritant that the patient, whose arms and hands were confined within the bathing case, could do little to relieve. Meanwhile, within the vapor box, the patient—as "he [felt] the steam flowing down his sides and legs"—had to endure "an extreme feeling of oppression and debility."[136] As another spa doctor described it, patients inevitably had a "subjective sense of burning in the skin" in the moments before their cure was completed.[137]

But if doctors were candid as to the unpleasantness of vapor bathing, they were by no means willing to let this form of hydrotherapeutics—or any other for that matter—fall victim to an entirely negative set of representations. For spa doctors, hygiene—just as it had informed the spatial and representational goals that spa physicians had sought to achieve in the interiors of their new buildings—had to be clearly established throughout their therapeutic realm. As this doctor and guidebook author stated plainly enough, "floors, walls, and all the apparatus used should always be kept perfectly clean." Notwithstanding the medical motives behind such hygienic impulses, however, the doctor stressed that it was what hygiene represented that made its value in the spas so great: "Not only should they be clean, but, for the sake of the impression on the patient's mind, they should always look clean. It must be owned that the sight of box vapor baths, the seats used for rectal douches, and other apparatus is often anything but pleasant; although they may in reality be clean, owing to discoloration and want of repair, they often look dirty."[138] In other words, vapor boxes and other highly medicalized examples of the new hydrotherapeutics required a certain level of maintenance with respect to patients' sensibilities. The medically justifiable discomfort associated with such cures could be borne by patients only if the entire treatment scenario was conducted within a scientific context. And that context was both easily and dramatically achieved through the representational virtues of hygiene.

Of all active hydrotherapeutic procedures developed and prescribed by spa doctors of this era—which is to exclude water drinking, simple bathing, and swimming cures—none was experienced by more patients than the so-called *douche,* or shower massage. Out of an annual total of bathing operations that already approached 20,000 at larger spas by the 1820s, shower massages accounted for nearly three-fourths of that number.[139] This ratio changed very little throughout the period of the July Monarchy. In the 1840s at Aix-les-Bains, for instance, a curist population of approximately 2,500 to 3,000 persons was administered nearly 17,000 courses of the shower massage, compared with fewer than 5,000 swimming or bathtub cures.[140] Of the 111 visitors to Bourbon-l'Archambault in one period of 1824, for example, fully 50 persons took 18 or more courses of a shower treatment.[141] Unlike cold water cures and vapor bathing, which curists experienced only occasionally during a spa holiday, the scalding water of the shower bath was a regular part of their lives—such cures were typically conducted every second or third day of a patient's stay at a spa.[142] With shower massages more than two times the price of any other form of the spa cure—a standard shower in the 1840s cost 2 francs while a private bath cost 1 franc and a piscine cure was 65 centimes—patients had invested not only a significant portion of their time but also a great deal of money following their shower cures by the time they quit their spa.[143]

The spa shower was a form of hydrotherapy that derived its purported curative force from a careful combination of mineral waters and massage. Most commonly given to patients with rheumatic symptoms, shower massages were administered in a special chair that allowed for both sitting and reclining (fig. 11). The typical cure, as one doctor described it later in the century, involved an "attendant pour[ing] water over the body from a hose, while, at the same time, [another] attendant shampoo[ed], knead[ed] and rub[bed] according to the directions given by the physician."[144] There was hardly a medical complaint imaginable for which doctors were not willing to prescribe a steady course of the shower massage,

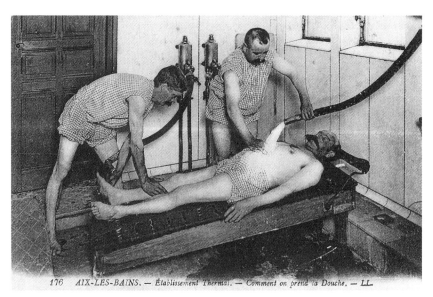

176 AIX-LES-BAINS. — Établissement Thermal. — Comment on prend la Douche. — LL.

FIGURE 11   Spa photograph showing a full-body *douche massage* in progress. Promoting spa medicine in the latter decades of the nineteenth century and the earlier years of the twentieth would see images such as this one emerge as postcards. Reprinted from Leguay, *Histoire d'Aix-les-Bains et sa région: Une grande station thermale,* 175.

provided that the patient in question was healthy enough to bear such treatment.

Perhaps no hydrotherapeutic system relied more on complicated technology and scientific administration than did these showers. Such cures depended upon a complex array of hoses and water gauges to ensure that patients received the thermal product at the correct temperature and volume. The perfect calibration of these various mechanisms, all doctors stressed, determined the degree to which the cure either succeeded or failed. In this technology, even proponents of strictly differentiated therapeutics could take solace, because the infinite gradations and combinations of temperature, types of mineral water, and force created a curative system that differed vastly according to medical conditions. To show the degree of the cure's differentiation and medicalization, guides from this period often included illustrations of bath technology. In one such illustration from the 1830s (fig. 12), for example, a guidebook's author depicted forty-four different features of the complicated water delivery system of the hot shower.

Shower massages were also highly medicalized procedures in terms of the human element of their administration. The two technicians who were directly responsible for this cure's precise delivery to the patient, while not doctors themselves, were nevertheless highly trained and regarded medical authorities at the spas. Appointed to their esteemed positions by a spa's medical corps, in conjunction with a process of training and certification that was monitored at the departmental level, "shower technicians" were recognized experts in anatomy, physiology, and disease pathology.[145] That expertise, spa doctors liked to boast, was applied directly to a patient's body through the technicians' knowing hands. As one practitioner described, it was "astonishing with what skill, what patience, tenderness and firmness the shampooing and passive movements [were] performed."[146] Many other doctors lauded the scientific touch of those who administered baths and showers under their direction, commonly characterizing these technicians as "skillful" masters whose touch was precisely "forceful" or "delicate," depending upon a patient's prescription.[147]

Yet, as many guidebooks saw them, bath "technicians" had an almost genetic calling to their craft.[148] It was true enough that technicians usually chose their line of work because that was what their parents and siblings did. And it was also true that many spas, by the middle of the century, had representatives from three generations of a family among the ranks of their technicians.[149] Hence the comments of one English doctor with respect to the locals who had tended his medical needs at French spas: "These people carry out the showering to perfection; they have inherited

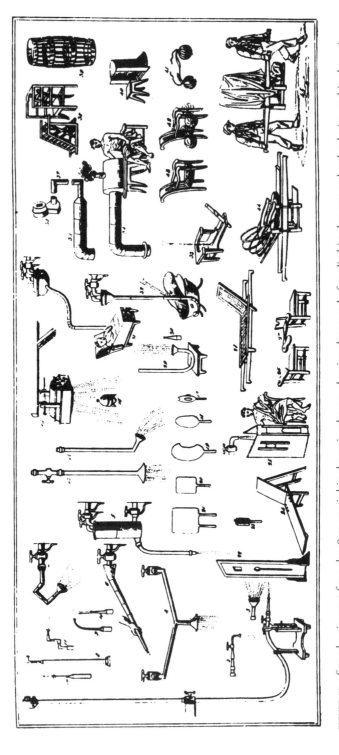

FIGURE 12 Spa advertisement from the 1830s, carried in the regional press, showing the arsenal of medical implements and technologies used in the various forms of the *douche massage*. Reprinted from Pagotto, *Le thermalisme à Aix-les-Bains au dix-neuvième siècle*, 80.

all the lightness of touch, rapidity of movement and sang-froid peculiar to their order."[150]

No combination of technology and the masseur's touch, however, could compensate for the fact that the shower massage was often an uncomfortable and even painful form of medicine. As one doctor recounted, having visited a number of French spas to study the development of hydrotherapeutics and follow a course of therapy at Aix-les-Bains, this technique stopped just short of being brutal in some of its side effects. "I myself," the doctor wrote, "experienced an extraordinarily unpleasant sensation during my first shower and immediately after it." This sensation, he hastened to add, was not present in the "initial ten or twelve minutes of the shower" during which his feet, legs and shoulders were "masterfully" and "vigorously" rubbed. By the session's end, however, the temperature and force of the shower's water had been recalibrated to an extreme degree. Simultaneously, the strong hands of his technicians had kneaded his upper and lower body to the point of an excruciating exhaustion. As a result, the doctor left his treatment breathless and in the throes of a pounding pulse and headache.

Yet his greatest discomfort still awaited the beleaguered doctor. For once he was placed within his bath chair, whose porters immediately began carrying him toward his hotel, the doctor "experienced an overwhelming sense of suffocation and an unprecedented rush of blood to the head." Feeling "flushed and powerfully oppressed," he "demanded" to be let out of his bath chair. Only when he could breath "fresh air" and gulp "several glasses of cool water" did the doctor's painful reaction to the massage begin to subside.[151] Because of his own authority as a doctor, this patient's subsequent experiences with the *douche* were vastly different. The doctor merely assigned himself a kinder course of therapy. He had, after all, enjoyed his first moments in the bath technicians' hands.

The therapeutics of spa medicine also extended to the toweling procedures employed at most thermal establishments. As one doctor described toweling, "the drying of the patient generally comprise[d] two procedures." After enveloping the patient's body in "hot linens and flannels brought straight from a gas oven," the bath attendants performed a "general and superficial drying of the body." Then, after wrapping their patient in "a fresh gown and more towels," the attendants brought all the skill and dexterity of their tender hands to bear upon the patient's body. Beyond "thoroughly" drying the patient, one attendant "rub[bed] the body with light friction" while another administered it a "deep kneading." Having completing this tandem toweling-and-more, the bath technicians terminated the cure by offering the patient's feet a gentle massage of their own.[152]

Finally, the transporting of spa patients by sedan chair, which was common at the spas until 1900, had a definite therapeutic rationale too. If patients sometimes overheated and felt too confined within their chairs, this unpleasant sensation in no way detracted from the bath chair's many advantages. Principal among its attributes, according to spa doctors, was the bath chair's proven success in preventing its occupants from becoming chilled. Sparing no effort in helping the bath chair win its war against chills, doctors routinely ordered that their patients be "wrapped in a large flannel dressing gown, then completely draped in woolen covering." To complete a temporary mummification, patients then had their "hands and feet wrapped in more toweling" before even leaving their dressing rooms. Only then, "the bath chair having been brought into the room," were patients "placed in it and its covering securely closed."[153] Bathed, shampooed, dried, and swaddled, patients were finally carried from the baths in the direction of their hotel rooms.

From the first years of the 1850s, spa administrations all over France had begun to count their seasonal population in two separate categories. The first of these, which had been the sole figure of great interest to spa authorities since the Restoration, was the number of persons who purchased admission cards to a bathing facility and followed a course of hydrotherapeutic treatment. The new statistic, however, measured the number of people who visited a spa municipality without registering to cure. More than the unpleasant fact that both numbers now needed counting, what horrified spa doctors everywhere by the middle of the 1860s was that the number of noncurists had begun to surpass at most spas the number of actual curists.[154]

The gradual and partial migration away from the spas' treatment centers obviously did not bode well for the profitability of French thermal establishments, and spa practitioners mobilized as best they could to fight it. The way they chose to compete for disinclined curists was to soften the

TABLE 4   Approximate Number of Curists to Tourists at Aix-les-Bains, 1861–1913

	1861	1880	1900	1913
Curists	4,000	6,500	10,000	11,000
Tourists	2,500	13,000	20,000	30,000

harsher medical regimes of hydrotherapy. The government of the Second Empire and the French Academy of Medicine both helped in this regard by formally stipulating in 1860 that no spa could require its patients to consult with a doctor before taking the waters.[155] Individual spa doctors and publicists did more by way of relinquishing a measure of medical control over the spa experience.[156] Aix-les-Bains's Dr. Berthet, for example, in his medical and topographical guide of 1862, cautiously denounced important aspects of the hydrotherapeutic regimen he and his colleagues had but recently established. Regarding food and drink, for instance, Berthet promised that "taking the waters imposed no dietary restrictions of any kind. . . . [P]eople [could] and should follow their own inclinations and habits."[157]

Moreover, Berthet addressed the issue of medicalized leisure, explaining that the hydrotherapeutic system was little more than a harmless form of role-playing. Berthet wrote that new curists should not be surprised "to see, from time to time, the 'sad' figure of some patient, carefully enveloped in a closed *chaise à porteurs*." But this "spectacle," Berthet noted, was illusory rather than real. For, as the doctor explained, "the young and pretty people who pass in this manner, imprisoned in toweling that shrouds a delicate body whose expiration seems imminent, should not sadden anyone." On the contrary, Berthet wrote, "these people, these immobile and mute invalids who leave the bathing establishment carried like cadavers, having grimaced and suffered through their treatments— these are the same people who appear in the evening, elegantly dressed and with fresh, happy, and healthy faces, dancing at the ball."[158]

Of the many things vacationers experienced and learned during their twenty-one days at a spa, none was more important to the bourgeoisie as a class than what hydrotherapeutics did by way of constructing a rational and ordered version of leisure practice. People with enough social aspirations and money to set out on vacation but lacking fully formed sensibilities regarding the links between leisure and social identity had very little to fear at the medicalized spas of the July Monarchy and after— not, at least, when doctors offered such a thorough charting of life on vacation. Even beyond what hydrotherapy and so many medical prescriptions concerning food, drink, sociability, and exercise suggested about the filled-up and accounted-for leisure of the spas, the regimented and medicalized vacation revealed to those who read about it or lived it that a worthy and respectable version of vacationing—a way of having a proper and bourgeois consumption of the *séjour*—had been discovered. What might have been random, where there might have been laziness—in precisely the place where time might have been wasted—there was instead erected a medical perimeter to ward off chaos and ensure the orderly expenditure of leisure. No less an authority on French society than Victor Hugo saw medicine as the skin around his leisure's onion, noting in a letter of 1843, "[U]nder the pretext of bathing in warm water and drinking sulfur, I have everyday a new, unexpected and marvelous spectacle." Accounting for the predicament that Berthet and other doctors found themselves in after 1850 is not easy, yet three reasons for the diminished place of medicalized leisure in bourgeois vacation life seem to be worth some speculation. First, it has to be understood that the statistics around bathing and vacationing are just as difficult to use as tallies of other kinds. As doctors were no longer required to see all patients who bathed, it is at least possible that the medically driven logic for accurate counting was lost. Thus there is at least some reason to think that more people cured than the spas ever counted.

But even if the statistics are accurate and do indeed show that the majority of the spas' vacationers visited without curing, this trend was gradual and by no means revealed that medicine had quickly or totally left the spa vacation. A second answer to the perceived fall of medicalized leisure is that the number of curists continued to rise at many spas, to the end of the century and well beyond. The fact that the larger visiting population went up at a much higher rate signals not that baths were abandoned to any great extent but, rather, that a new social group was increasingly coming to the spa towns on vacation. The importance and plausibility of this reading of medical leisure's re-placement in holiday life is addressed in some detail in chapter 5.

Finally, the most fulfilling explanation for the end of hydrotherapy's hold over bourgeois vacation leisure seems to be that by the middle decades of the century, a critical mass of the bourgeoisie had acquired extensive experience in the arts of leisure practice. Although still respectful of medical authority and doctors, spa-goers no longer needed doctors or medical principles to give order and purposefulness to their *séjours.* Instead of seeking a medicalized mode of leisure that implanted productivity where uncertainty might otherwise have taken root, many bourgeois vacationers went to spas in the latter half of the nineteenth century confident of who they were. The complex processes of identity formation, which spa medicine had bolstered and would continue to gird—if with less urgency—through the rest of the century, had reached by the 1850s and after a point where those "things" with which the bourgeoisie negotiated when acquiring furniture, arranging rooms, and assessing lifestyle—consumption, taste, and comfort—could be brought along on vacation.

— 5 —

SOCIAL BENEFITS

OF SPA CONSUMPTION

$\mathcal{T}$he efforts of French spa doctors in the first half of the nineteenth century and the inclinations of many bourgeois curists notwithstanding, pleasure of all kinds consistently enjoyed a place of prominence at the spa.
While medical prescriptions might have advised patients to eschew too
much sociability and other excesses, full compliance with such strictures
had never been something that spa doctors received from most vacationers—not when there remained so much to do, even at the medicalized
spas, beyond following orders and convalescing. Indeed, from the beginning of the spas' medicalization, many entrepreneurs and developers stubbornly refused to cast their lot entirely with those doctors who believed
that hydrotherapy had become the raison d'être of the thermal vacation.

In fact, beyond issuing confining prescriptions, few doctors ever attempted to tamper directly with the infrastructure of pleasures that had
existed at the spas since the Old Regime. Indeed, it was altogether common for spa doctors of the early nineteenth century to denounce pleasure
in their medical writings while investing in it under the cloak of a blind
corporate entity. So it was at Vichy during the Restoration and the early
July Monarchy that the same individual administered both the thermal
establishment and the casino. Similarly, at Aix-les-Bains, the very doctors
whose funds rebuilt the thermal establishment and whose medical guides
codified hydrotherapeutic procedures also invested heavily in the city's
gaming and entertainment houses.[1] Even though in their promotional
materials spa doctors strove to represent the spa as something other than
a pleasure center, they were unwilling to overlook any potential source
of profit. They chose, therefore, to endorse medicalization overtly while
covertly funding sites of pleasure.

The pleasure in question, however, was hardly the stuff of scandal or decadence. The bourgeoisie, which sought to culturally embellish its economic and political gains with a lifestyle that suggested "simplicity" and a "calm elegance," was not seeking in its vacations the sort of excess that was reputed to have been the order of the aristocrat's spa day during the Old Regime. Mainly, spa municipalities and their medical underwriters sought to provide curists with casinos, which, as noted in chapter 2, were able to offer gaming to their patrons only after midcentury. The paucity of gambling in the 1830s and 1840s left casinos and their spas little choice but to feature pleasures and distractions that were essentially tame and respectable. Organized dances, for instance, were held regularly in casinos, as were concerts and theatrical productions. Similarly, common areas, such as cafés, restaurants, and reading rooms, were founded and frequented at most spa casinos in the era of hydrotherapy's hegemony over the holiday.

The high cost inherent in building the casino's pleasurable and social something—that amusing adjunct to the spa's medicalization—was apparently a crucial reason why some spas and their entrepreneurial sects prospered in the July Monarchy and some did not. Doctors of the 1830s and 1840s who took the find-a-source-of-mineral-water-and-erect-a-bathing-establishment developmental approach typically did not last long in the spa business. Such was the case with the municipal developers of Châtelguyon, for example, who followed the example of Évian's investors in the earlier decades of the century. Like the Savoyard spa, Châtelguyon—whose later history was used as a model by Guy de Maupassant in his novel about the French spa, *Mont-Oriol*—created a tiny bathing establishment during the Restoration without building a casino. Accordingly, the baths of this little town languished for nearly fifty years without bringing either many bathers or much profit to the municipality. Only after Parisian developers brought capital and a casino to the place in the later 1870s did its fortunes improve enough to earn the attention of a novelist of Maupassant's stature. Casinos of this era had to be grand, just as they had to feature international performers and a host of other exciting distractions. Centers of pleasure and sociability, casinos were only the more important parts of the pleasured whole that was the *ville d'eaux* toward the century's end. As described in chapter 2, opulent hotels, theaters, lavish parks, improved civic amenities, and endless walking paths all combined to create landscape where "tasteful" vacationers could amuse themselves and seek sociability.

If hydrotherapy and pleasure traditionally had been the dual guarantees to a spa's success, with the former being more important in the first half of the nineteenth century when bourgeois identity was still so much in the making, pleasure and its obvious associations with consumption would emerge as far more important among vacationers after 1850. Maupassant showed this shift clearly enough through the scandalous dealings of the doctors and developers of the spa at Mont-Oriol. By making false claims as to the efficacy of their water, the spa's interested parties earned a necessary modicum of medical legitimacy. Having accomplished this, however, Mont-Oriol's interested parties quickly focused their attention on very different matters. And, in accordance with the wishes of their growing population of vacationers, the spa's entrepreneurs forged a municipality in which pleasure loomed large over what had once been a medical milieu. As we shall see, the social causes, cultural meanings, and historical implications of the transformation Maupassant observed were anything but simple.

Travel and vacationing would not go through a clear process of "democratization" until the government of the Popular Front guaranteed holidays to French workers in the 1936. But well before then, vacationing was being transformed into something that not just the aristocracy and bourgeoisie were thinking about or doing. Similarly, the almost hegemonic hold of the spas over French vacation life had fallen away somewhat. The seaside, alpine resorts, and tours of the provinces all found significant numbers of aficionados in the latter decades of the 1800s, just as for persons of modest means, pilgrimage to Lourdes became an extremely popular form of travel at the fin de siècle. Devotional tourism, where adventure and relaxation always held a place nearly equal to religion, brought 300,000 to Lourdes in each of the first years of the twentieth century.[2] But if the middle class boarded the pilgrim trains, it is doubtlessly true that more of them chose to follow the bourgeoisie to its favored vacation destinations. The vast growth of the spa industry in this period, more than anything else, testifies to the rise of the middle-class vacation.

Less concerned than the bourgeoisie of the earlier half of the century about how ideas of "productivity" could be made manifest in their vacations, the middle class took consumption as its leisure's mantra. Increasingly affluent and eager to achieve a higher rung on the social ladder, the middle class would find in vacationing both an overt way to announce their social arrival and a covert means of learning the cultural tactics necessary to live after a solidly bourgeois fashion. Still not frivolous or wasteful, consumption of this kind was supposed to be conspicuous but controlled. Garish displays of wealth, as detrimental for the middle class as misplaced lace or feathers had been for the bourgeoisie earlier in the century, were no ways for the merely affluent to lock class into status. Just as etiquette books and fashion manuals put so many of these socially unsure people in the possession of something like a bourgeois lifestyle, so the spas would become "living etiquette books" where a vast education could occur, all the while middle-class pupils got the keen pleasure of consuming what their rising prosperity had earned them.[3]

SPA NOVELS AS SCRIPTS FOR THE MIDDLE-CLASS VACATION

The newness of travel for most of the middle class made the publication of guidebooks a highly profitable industry throughout the latter decades of the nineteenth century. Unlike the books of the Restoration and July Monarchy, which had typically focused on the medical aspect of the spas, the guides that charged the industry after midcentury were social primers that offered invaluable information concerning the ways of bourgeois gentility and the arts of travel. Promotional writers approached their middle-class market in a variety of ways, producing books that tended to approximate manuals of etiquette. If medical testimonials all but disappeared from the guides of this era, writers hardly abandoned the elaborate narrative forms that had often characterized the case histories of spa patients. On the contrary, spa narratives became even more creative and rich as their medical content was decreased.

Spa novels, for instance, became a burgeoning genre for the first time in the years after midcentury.[4] Thermal novels, such as *Une cure au Mont-Dore, Quinze jours au Mont-Dore,* and *Jean Bonnet à Luchon,* were directly related to traditional spa promotional writing in that they were typically written by a water doctor and commissioned by a particular spa's administration.[5] Often using pseudonyms, some of the more famous spa doctors of the nineteenth century—like Aix-les-Bains's doctors Louis Berthet and Constant Despine—represented the social world of the spas as completely and comprehensibly as their intimate knowledge would allow.[6] Through characters, plots, and diverse social situations, promotional novels offered their readers a close examination of bourgeois etiquette and society on vacation.

Yet these novels were far more sophisticated than mere etiquette books, for such promotional texts always provided their clues about spa society in a subtle way, imbedded within the behavior of characters and endless examples of how one was to make use of various settings within the spa milieu. A blunt listing of matters, novelists evidently felt, would have insulted the very social ambitions that middle-class travelers hoped to realize on vacation. While they avoided offering explicit information on how to manage one's vacation, these works still shed light upon such mysteries as booking train passage, chit-chatting en route, finding a hotel, guarding one's money, clearing customs, renting a carriage, and meeting the right friends. And in the process, of course, first-time vacationers acquired the necessary skills and social confidence to master their impending voyages.

Not all spa promoters adopted the novel as their narrative form of choice. On the contrary, this period saw many spa authors apply their longstanding belief in tables and charts to the complicated business of explaining modern travel. The same was true of the national guides, like the Baedeker and Joanne series, that became popular in the era. Such works routinely contained scores of train schedules and a great deal of information concerning grades of hotels, restaurant quality, carriage rental, and the like. But even these more traditional guides exhibited many of the narrative strategies and tendencies found in spa novels.

Waxing eloquent as to the natural and physical histories of the regions and municipalities under their consideration, guides of the second half of the century tried to lend to their readers something of the traveler's sensibility and experience. Accordingly, authors gave their readers both a scientific and poetic language with which to understand their holidays. One learned much about otherwise foreign "topographies" by reading spa guides, as most books lavished a great deal of prose on carefully crafted descriptions of terrain, geology, meteorology, flora, and fauna.[7] Guides also sought to fill the more gaping holes that might have existed in their readers' knowledge of history. Specifically, authors in this genre played up whatever classical associations their spas could claim.

In discussing natural science and history, authors typically employed a style that conferred a combination of monumentality and romanticism to their subject. The forests around Contrexéville for instance, were never treated solely as a scientific matter. While most authors did explain precisely which trees and animals were commonly found in the wilderness of the Vosges, categorizing the natural features of a spa's surrounding countryside was seldom if ever done in such a way as to effectively tame those areas. On the contrary, woods and mountains were celebrated in sundry guides with poems, songs, or highly evocative prose.[8] In detailing the lovely environs of Vichy, for instance, one writer described how "independent of the pure and cool air that one breathes, the view reveals a charming countryside as the eyes behold the beautiful, rushing waters of the Sichon."[9] Similarly, guides to Aix-les-Bains, just as they used Lamartine's ode in their descriptions of the Lac du Bourget, never failed to characterize the locale's several cascades as anything but spectacular, wild, violent, and unmastered. To justify this description, writers had only to cite the tragic history of a beautiful *demoiselle* of the Restoration era, so awed by one waterfall that she allowed herself to slip and perish in its pounding waters.[10] With much the same intention and effect, guides to Vichy liked to tell the story of a romantic heroine of the region who had met her death in a local lake. From a certain "sad and arid plane," one author began, visitors could almost "feel the tragedy of a young girl who was the victim of a love that was too violent." Having lost her suitor, the "weakened and brokenhearted" girl carelessly strayed to the lake, readers are told. And there, where she "drowned tragically," the author invited his readers to contemplate the vision of "a small ensemble of trees, planted in this abandoned place to guard her memory."[11]

But even as their prose conferred a certain monumentality upon the several excursion sites and picturesque promenades within traveling distance of a *ville d'eaux,* guidebooks sought to make these wonders seem manageable and easily accessible to their inexperienced readers. In describing a promenade near Aix-les-Bains in a publication of 1876, for instance, one writer deemed it necessary to assure his readers that he would "indicate to [them] in an exact fashion which paths to follow so that [they] would not be preoccupied or confused." More than adhering to his promise, this author laboriously led his readers/followers over every "magnificent" bridge and through every "frighteningly vast" stand of trees, all the while imploring them to "step without hesitation on these picturesque paths." To make his readers still more secure on their vacation strolls, this author offered specific instructions as to what sort of clothing and shoes were best suited for such activities.[12]

Overall, the function of these books and their particular style was to infuse a thermal holiday, which had less of a medical cast for most vacationers as the century progressed, with both a purpose and a set of patterns that could be followed. If they could not openly tout the spa vacation as a means by which frustrated persons of the middle class could augment their social status, authors were at least able to construct as sacred but intelligible the natural and historical features that invariably surrounded a *ville d'eaux.* By making these various elements into destinations in their own right, guidebook authors went a long way toward answering a question that has always perplexed first-time travelers: What, exactly, does one do when one is on vacation? Perhaps even more, the elaborate narratives of the period helped to create in their readers a heightened desire to invest their dear resources in a visit to a spa.

THE DIDACTICS OF A MILIEU

If guidebooks and spa novels instructed the French middle class in the techniques of travel and the social skills of being a vacationer, the spas themselves reinforced this "learning" by being educative in their own right. The several structures of the watering place were all important learning centers for those who wanted to take pleasure in the acquisition and display of cultural capital. Residence in one of the celebrated spa hotels of this period, for instance, allowed middle-class visitors to participate in the sort of spectacular and exhibitionist social life that had come to so characterize the upper bourgeoisie. These buildings, of which a famous *ville d'eaux* might have had several by the 1880s, all but mandated that their guests live a highly public life.

Aix-les-Bains's Grand Hotel, typical of the better accommodations at France's spas, boasted a circulation scheme that saw to the exhibiting of its guests. On all four floors, the hotel's hallways wrapped around a sky-lit atrium (fig. 13). Because of this arrangement, it was virtually impossible to conduct one's daily routine without being vigilant as to one's posture, dress, mood, manners, and conversation. The hotel's entrance, like the doors to each room, was strategically positioned relative to the atrium so as to create innumerable points of observation. Guests, according to their inclination and social confidence, could thus spy on each other and make last-minute alterations in their personal "presentation" before joining the panopticonic parade of established residents.

Hotels also exhibited their guests by making their visitor registries open for public scrutiny. Curious curists, whether staying at the hotel in question or not, could learn much about the lodgers' social standings from these public sources. Dutifully noted in the ledgers were the home addresses and occupations of all guests, as well as the number of servants attending them. Guidebooks to thermal spas as well as novels about the *villes d'eaux* seldom failed to point out the important use to which hotel registries were put. As one popular guidebook noted, "the first occupation of the visitor upon establishing himself at a hotel [was] to consult the [major hotels'] lists of bathers." These lists, guidebooks never tired of explaining, "present[ed] a very real advantage to recent arrivals as they indicated the addresses and other useful information about persons with whom one might want to meet."[13]

More to the point, the registries offered interested parties the opportunity to investigate each other's social credentials—in a textual format rather than through the hotels' exhibition scheme—before actually visiting. According to spa novels from the period, whose protagonists were

FIGURE 13 Public life in a spa hotel: the atrium of Aix-les-Bains's Grand Hotel. Reprinted from Institut Français d'Architecture, *Villes d'eaux en France,* 112.

always curious about each other, social snooping was encouraged by hotel personnel—particularly when young love was at issue. The protagonist in *Le solitaire d'Aix-les-Bains,* for example, having been caught by his hotel's concierge gawking at a pretty *demoiselle,* is led by the employee to a "registry on which [he] was asked to sign [his] name and note [his] address, profession, age, and whatever other particulars [he] cared to." The knowing concierge then turns several pages in the book, finally pointing out an entry that reads, "Mademoiselle Alice, dramatic artist, twenty-two years old, born in Paris, permanent residence in Nice, just arrived in Aix-les-Bains, accompanied by one domestic and lodging at the Grand."[14] With his reconnaissance completed, the young man is left alone to devise a strategy of courtship whose ultimate result, as was so often the case in thermal novels, would be marriage.

The level of publicity provided by the registries, which had been un-
changed at many spa hotels since the 1830s, was augmented drastically in
the 1860s and 1870s by local and eventually national press coverage of this
"news." Newspapers, locally funded and oriented, were founded at most
villes d'eaux in the 1850s and 1860s. Spiced with humorous anecdotes and
heavily laden with stories about scheduled amusements, such papers as
the *Aix cosmopolite* were clearly conceived of as weekly advertisements for
their spas. A significant component of this promotional campaign always
involved the compilation and publication of hotel registries. For example,
spa developers advertised the quality of their environment by proudly noting the "persons of highest distinction" who had come on vacation. At
the same time and through the same pages, ambitious middle-class bathers—who only infrequently resided in the great palaces—could publicize
their visit and scout the long lists for people they knew or might want
to know.[15] These same curists also could revel in seeing their own names
listed on the same pages with the names of aristocrats and even royalty.

The larger *villes d'eaux* found even this form of local publicity to be
insufficient by the beginning of the Third Republic. Vichy, Aix-les-Bains,
and several other spas began publishing newspapers in Paris during the
1870s. Distributed almost exclusively through the city's major international hotels, papers like the *Gazette d'Aix-les-Bains* had virtually no content at all beyond the compiled lists of curists-in-residence.

If middle-class curists took pleasure in the knowledge that news of
their vacations might filter all the way to Paris, their first priority was
always establishing themselves within the particular society of their spa.
For most of them, no site was more useful in this regard than the spa
casino. Complete with covered promenades, regular dances, concert halls,
theaters, game rooms, reading rooms, and gardens, the casinos of the *villes
d'eaux* were vitally important instructional centers, exhibition sites, and
pleasure palaces for bourgeois society on vacation. As one observer of social
life at the spas noted, "it [was] around seven o'clock in the evening, after
the hotels had disengorged their population of visitors, when there occurred a brilliant convergence of the best society at the casino."[16]

Casinos were the undisputed hub of spa society, and their regular
constituency included couples, unescorted singles, and families.[17] Indeed,
there was nowhere else in the typical spa town to find the sort of amusements that were standard fare at a casino. Throughout the summer
months, the casinos of the *villes d'eaux* typically offered as many as four
theatrical and operatic productions each week.[18] Although these productions varied in the seriousness of their tone and were hardly unfamiliar

to most curists—a tragedy such as *Antigone* might have been offered in the same week as a comic opera such as *Le Barbier de Séville*—their captive audience more than ensured the success of their seasonal runs.

By all accounts, however, it was the casinos' regular musical entertainment and dancing that most enthralled their patrons. Concerts were daily affairs at most casinos, and many facilities offered performances in both afternoons and evenings. Formal dances were also regular events, with two balls each week probably approximating an average. The totality of these festive distractions, beyond offering a good measure of pleasure to a casino's visitors, created for them an ongoing if somewhat relentless showcase within which their social status was displayed. Just as surely as the casino entertained, it sought to organize its patrons according to the relative value of their cultural capital. Within a week's time if not before, these microcosms of polite society had subtly but tirelessly posed a series of highly revealing questions to their users: Who knew when and how to discuss politics? Who knew the more correct, artful, and current ways to dance? Who could intelligently and critically comment on theater and music? In short, one's expertise in society determined the degree to which the diversions of a casino were truly pleasant or a series of threatening and potentially embarrassing obstacles.

Initiates of the middle bourgeoisie were no doubt pleased to find that most casinos expected patrons to be at least somewhat bewildered in their new setting. To ease this confusion, casinos everywhere in the 1860s and 1870s adopted a practice of prominently posting lists of rules and regulations.[19] More than information regarding hours of service and the like, casino rules sought to define codes of behavior for people, who, presumably, were not yet in the know. Without such rules, how, for instance, would a visitor have known not to remove a newspaper from its rack in a reading room and read it on a casino's terrace? Or how might a patron have known that it was "forbidden to pick flowers or to pull branches down from trees"?[20] At Bourbon-l'Archambault, the casino's regulatory apparatus left nothing to chance, warning guests that it was "forbidden to obstruct the paths in any way or to call or to sing in the direction of the interior."[21]

Casino rules also endeavored to establish the level of formality at which the facility's society would conduct itself. Men, for example, were told explicitly which functions on which nights required their formal attire. This rule, as one of its contemporary defenders described it, helped to prevent "honorable persons . . . from presenting themselves at the casino only to be denied their pleasant evening for lacking formal attire."[22]

Even seasoned spa-goers of the upper bourgeoisie doubtlessly relied on the fashion codes from time to time, as different spas chose to set different levels of formality. Experience at Vichy's facility or its counterparts in the German empire, for example, was of little help at the ever more formal Aix-les-Bains.[23] Finally, rules defined clear parameters for the social interaction of guests. In a tone that was neither uncertain nor humorous, these rules typically forbade loud argumentation or coarse and insulting conversations.[24]

Casinos were educative in a stricter sense too, as most of them offered or could arrange for formal instruction in musical performance and social dancing. Piano lessons were routinely offered by players from a casino's orchestra, and there can be little doubt that many young bourgeois girls participated in such programs. Facility at the piano was a highly recognized sign of social distinction in bourgeois circles, and lessons were not to be ignored merely because a family was on vacation.[25] Through piano recitals, which some casinos organized for their more accomplished pupils, proud parents could exhibit their daughters' talents while they consolidated their own social status. Social dance, although characterized by one spa author as a "book that prudent mothers [did] not let their daughters read until they had reached the age of majority," was another widely recognized skill whose correct and artful utilization mattered a great deal in bourgeois circles.[26] While lessons in dance were offered to adults in spa casinos, children were clearly the principal focus of this particular pedagogy.

Guidebooks and newspapers of the larger *villes d'eaux* suggest that a significant portion of a young person's time on vacation was devoted to acquiring a polished presence on the dance floor. Dancing lessons, which were sometimes held daily, were only the more basic aspect of dance instruction. Far more colorful and important were the twice weekly children's balls that many casinos featured. These functions, where boys and girls were expected to dress as their parents would for such occasions, obviously taught much more than dance. Middle-class children could practice their conversational skills and refine their manners, as the dances typically welcomed offspring from both the upper bourgeoisie and the aristocracy.

The convergence of these different social circles at the children's ball regularly elicited humorous commentary from the writers of spa newspapers. In describing one conversation she had "overheard" at a children's ball of the middle 1880s, a writer for the *Aix bijou* allowed herself some creative license without failing to show how children of the *villes d'eaux* had internalized some of their parents' quest for status: "My father has a superb house. It is resplendent in *ardoises* [slate]" declares the first little girl. Since *ardoise* could just as well refer to unpaid bills, a misunderstanding results and the second girl counters with an even more revealing description of her family's situation: "My house is still more beautiful, as it is completely covered in mortgages."[27]

If casinos of the *villes d'eaux* were public establishments in theory, access to these institutions—like so many venues of public life in French society after midcentury—was closed in practice to anyone but relatively well connected bourgeois. To one author of a spa novel, whose protagonist expressed confusion over the difficulty he experienced in merely getting into one casino, exclusivity was part and parcel of such facilities: "I say, if everyone is admitted freely and without condition, the casino would no longer be a casino. It would be a public place. Where, then, would one go to find chosen society?"[28]

Contemporary illustrations of these buildings, contained in guides and souvenir books, tended to present them as exclusive and secure environments. In addition to offering views of opulent interiors and grand theaters, guides typically devoted a sketch or two to show the principal facades and grounds of their casinos. These sketches invariably featured a clear statement as to the sort of society that was to frequent the casinos by emphasizing that casinos were sequestered from their host municipalities by a combination of factors. Mountains, rivers, and forests were often shown to be topographical buffers between casinos and their cities. Just as commonly, however, fences, gates, and armed guards could convey much the same information. Whether or not guards really carried weapons, as many sketches suggested, it was clearly important to spa promoters that these places be perceived as secure havens, as distant from the bustle of spa towns as casino patrons were distinct from their poorer counterparts.[29]

Keeping the "wrong" people out of a spa casino, however, was hardly a military or police matter. Rather, an apparently strict bureaucratic screening, details of which were clearly posted throughout the *villes d'eaux* and carefully described in virtually every guidebook, saw more effectively to the controlling of these institutions' constituencies. Curists, in fact, had to join a casino—whose management usually reported to a profit-sensitive corporation—before they could use any of its facilities. Daily memberships were by far the most common way to join a casino. For a membership of this type, all one had to do was pay the casino's admission charge of several francs.[30]

Joining a casino for the duration of one's vacation, which only 15 to

20 percent of a spa's visiting population ever did, was, however, a significantly more complicated affair. Hopeful members had to first present letters of reference and nomination to a casino's governing body, upon whose review and recommendation all admissions depended. Merely a formality for upper bourgeois spa-goers, as were the seasonal dues of twenty-five francs per person, this presentation of credentials doubtlessly caused a certain measure of trepidation among some middle-class initiates. Notwithstanding the fact that administrative scrutiny seldom if ever barred an interested middle bourgeois from partaking in a casino's charms, there can be little doubt that such membership policies conferred status— by offering a very public validation of one's social credentials—onto those who elected to join a casino as full members.

Fashion and style requirements for women, which were never detailed on rule lists as they were for men, constituted another significant "check" on the casino's population of visitors. For if female vacationers of the period were expected to dress elegantly and correctly throughout the social spaces of the *ville d'eaux,* such expectations tended to be much higher at a spa casino. Indeed, as one contemporary commentator on fashion noted, one's dress "had to be as elegant or even more so than the attire one might have worn to promenade along the Champs-Élysées or in the Bois de Boulogne."[31] It was not enough to have evening clothing, and it was not enough to also have clothing for the afternoon. One needed clothing for the morning too, and one needed enough variations for all occasions so that duplications were kept to a minimum. Few women but those of the upper bourgeoisie could match every social function with a new and appropriate outfit. But those who could not achieve perfect stylishness still tried anyway. Spa casinos became, in the words of one contemporary writer of etiquette manuals, "an arena of combat in which few triumphs were seen." The "rivalry of style" that this author bemoaned, which sometimes became so competitive as to be openly "acerbic" and "dangerous," did more than merely create "irreconcilable enemies" among a casino's visitors.[32] In effect, the fashion wars of a casino meant that many new members, having seen for the first time the colorful field of battle, would either fire a salvo or beat a hasty retreat. In either case, these were social venues where one had to be aggressive and confident in the trading of one's cultural and social capital.

Beyond the casinos, informal checks on the social status of initiates into a spa's society abounded too. Perhaps no setting was more notorious in this regard than the hotel tables where most curists took their daily meals.[33] These tables, as one spa physician noted in his description of spa society, rendered it "impossible to keep one's identity at all secret." In an environment where "all eyes [were] open, all tongues active, and all ears avidly participating in creating a chronicle that [would] stand for a new arrival's biography," this author warned his readers that first impressions—often formed at a *table d'hôte*—tended to be neither charitable nor easily amended.[34]

Diaries and letters from the period reveal that spa-goers could indeed be ruthless in appraising each other's opening-day performance at a hotel table. Noted contemporary chroniclers like Alphonse Daudet clearly took pleasure in dissecting their table companions in letters sent home to friends. From his chair at one of Néris's tables, for example, Daudet took a scrupulously exact measure of no fewer than six women, relating in a letter exactly what was and was not correct and appealing about the innocents under his studied gaze.[35] The Goncourt brothers were equally keen observers of their dinner companions, as their journal entries from the summer of 1867 show clearly enough. For a single day in July, the brothers allocated ten lengthy paragraphs to recount the attire, food, gestures, conversations, and table manners of the "ménage of Spaniards" with whom they had taken their meals.[36]

Because the quality of one's table manners revealed more about social position and status than did clothing or other easily acquired aspects of self-presentation, it was not unusual that the taking of meals elicited, in the words of a French doctor, a "truly phrenologic inspection."[37] But suspicious members of the upper bourgeoisie were not alone in using spa tables to inspect those around them for breeding and gentility. On the contrary, middle-class vacationers, especially those from the provinces, doubtlessly seized upon these venues to continue their studies in the ways of bourgeois *politesse*. Indeed, where else could one find such a rich opportunity to improve one's manners and familiarity with certain table instruments than at a table shared by several highly seasoned practitioners of the table's high arts.[38]

But spa sociability, once one had endured the scrutiny of a hotel table and gained entry to a casino, tended to be easier and more open than what one typically would have found in everyday life. And this fact, which obviously contributed to the pleasures associated with the thermal vacation, was central to why the middle class saw a spa vacation as such a potentially profitable investment in their social fortunes. Conversation between strangers whose status was not almost precisely equivalent, which conventions of everyday society all but forbade, was very much a hallmark of life at the *villes d'eaux*.

In the common rooms of a hotel or at a casino, curists tended to gather throughout the day to take the measure of each other. Spa friendships, as countless contemporaries observed, quickly acquired an easiness and informality. Particularly in the evening, as one chronicler of spa life noted, "the intimacy between bathers expanded immeasurably; everyone treated everyone else as though their friendships were of twenty year's duration."[39] These loci of friendly sociability, so alive with conversation that one bewildered observer noted that "a stenographer [could have] more easily fulfilled his obligation in the senate," offered the middle class a valuable opportunity to join and closely study—if only for a brief time—a social circle whose more celebrated members would have been strangers and, therefore, unapproachable in the social spaces of everyday middle-class life. And even if they proved to be only fleeting, social interactions of this type obviously meant a great deal to urban and rural curists of the middle class who wished to acquire some of the social polish of the upper bourgeoisie.

THE LURE OF SOCIAL MOBILITY

Spa novels and guides encouraged their readers to see the peculiar sociability of the spas as offering the potential for tangible rewards. Encouragement in this regard, indeed, became part and parcel of why so many persons of the French middle class wished to vacation at a spa. The protagonist of one such novel, a thirty-two-year-old man who celebrates the beginning of his professional career by visiting a spa, is a strong case in point. Hopeful that his vacation will gain him valuable business alliances, the young curist works his way cautiously through a number of insignificant conversations before targeting an obviously established bourgeois. To this M. Bon-Oeil, the protagonist describes his attributes and professional qualifications with care. Then, he deliberately sets out to win the sympathy of his sharp-eyed acquaintance with a piercing declaration as to the difficulties of youth: "Oh! At the beginning everything is so difficult! We must start our lives without any real wealth!" How, the young man pleads, does one ever get beyond these painful and difficult "first pages of life"?[40] Swayed by these earnest appeals, M. Bon-Oeil offers his eager charge an important position in his manufacturing concern.

That spa sociability routinely produced such profitable results can hardly be documented. Without any doubt, however, single men on vacation, who constituted the majority group of the spa population in the 1870s and 1880s according to the thermal press from the period, seemed to embrace what many guidebooks told them: their professional and social positions could be advanced through the particular sociability characteristic of the *villes d'eaux*.[41] To market the spa vacation in this way was probably a brilliant strategy, considering that so many men of the middle class were indeed concerned about the difficulties of achieving bourgeois status in French society. Many of them had done all that they could by way of planning for future prosperity in society without being able to control the increasing costs of living as a bourgeois. Educated and without wives or children into their early and even middle thirties, this generation of young men was probably ready to accept whatever help it might receive from a chance meeting.[42] Even if one's vacation failed to net the sort of lucrative friendships that were featured in spa novels, ambitious men could still hope that their professional fortunes might improve from their vacations.

If there was any truth in the belief that one could help one's status and career by meeting the right people on vacation, so there were probably valid reasons to look for while on vacation that most precious of all commodities: love. This suggestion commonly was made by spa publicists of the period, many of whom had rightly concluded that successful marketing often involved a confluence of desires. Yet spa novels like Dr. Louis Berthet's *Le solitaire d'Aix-les-Bains* had statistical grounds on which to claim that love and a youthful subculture flourished at the *villes d'eaux*. Berthet's spa, in fact, almost always saw more unmarried visitors after 1860 than it did married couples—a marked change indeed from the familial configuration that I identified in chapter 2 as a characteristic of the spa-going population in the century's earlier decades. At Aix-les-Bains in the summer of 1870, a typical week in June brought more single women (71) than married couples, while the number of single men (161) amounted to more than half of the total number of arrivals in the same week.[43]

It would appear that many unmarried visitors to the spas of this period were not in fact unaccompanied travelers. But these were not singles accompanied by family members or religious advisers either. On the contrary, spa newspapers and other sources strongly suggest that many celibates went on vacation with their friends. Visitor lists to the major spas, for example, reveal that many persons from the same towns and cities went to the same spa for the same three-week period and stayed in the same lodging houses and hotels. When Paris was the city of origin, of course, one must question whether visitors knew each other at all before getting to their spas. But when three or four people all traveled from a provincial commune and stayed in the same local accommodations in

Vichy or Aix-les-Bains, it seems altogether likely that these individuals had planned their trips together. If indeed this was the case, it would at least begin to explain why so many *demoiselles*—whose parents were otherwise highly protective of their passages through public life—were allowed to go "alone" to a spa. These groups answered other needs of single females, too: friends, by providing ready escorts to the countless social events of the spa vacation, guaranteed each other the sort of animated but scandal-free public life that was difficult to find in the less protected and socially secure spaces of their everyday lives.[44]

Notwithstanding the many pleasures and amusements experienced by the spa's subculture of young singles, marriage patterns from this period suggest that the *villes d'eaux* were places where young people congregated not just for pleasure or to acquire added status in society but, rather, to use their spa visits in the formation of new upper- and middle-bourgeois families. By the later decades of the nineteenth century, men and women of the upper and middle bourgeoisie typically postponed marriage until they had enough capital—either through savings or a dowry—to pay for the high cost of establishing a proper household.[45] This trend toward relatively late marriage, which saw men commonly marrying in their early thirties and women in their early to middle twenties, combined with the tendency of many youths to migrate to cities, had left a generation of singles adrift from the obvious connections through which they might have once found spouses.

Men, having spent years in pursuit of an education and a career, could sometimes turn to their families for reliable help in this delicate capacity. But if a man had migrated for educational or employment purposes away from his family, he was largely alone in his search for a mate. Women, particularly in small cities or rural areas where desirable men tended to be scarce, could find themselves in an equally desperate position. To people in search of a safe but exciting social setting in which to meet potential partners, spas held out a measure of potential that may well have been unrivaled in nineteenth-century French society.

As marriage markets, the *villes d'eaux* offered anxious singles an abundant freedom from the potentially injurious associations that their families' reputations might have occasioned. In effect, spas left middle-class singles freer to reinvent themselves and search for a spouse who bolstered their refashioned identities. Stories of changed biographies were legion in the guides of the period, but true impostors were probably less frequently seen than were individuals who merely availed themselves of a unique opportunity to alter certain details of their identities.[46] Spa society could ask all the traditional questions of single women and men: What sort of family did he come from? Where did she acquire such learning? Had he been engaged to marry before? What was his occupation? Did she have to work? What amount of money did he have? How large was her dowry? But beyond the important clues that were revealed in dress, conversation, comportment, and manners, there was no way to corroborate the carefully staged "testimony" of these hopeful lovers. In any event, the average case of creative self-fashioning was hardly tantamount to a dangerous incident of social perjury. The spas, after all, as expensive, exclusive, and sophisticated social environments, virtually ensured that vacationers were at least middle class. This fact, too, must have eased the minds of concerned parents as they imagined the potential pitfalls of their daughters' or sons' thermal vacations.

To young people eager to meet each other, spas offered another important kind of freedom. In a condensed period of time and with relatively few strictures on their conduct, society on vacation allowed couples innumerable opportunities for courtship. Unlike the social universe of Paris, for example, where suitors often had to engage in deft maneuvering to place themselves at the same parties, dances, and theaters as the *demoiselles* in whom they were interested, spas offered up a full but easily negotiated set of social opportunities. Afternoon concerts at a casino, for example, usually drew the better part of a spa's population. Similarly, in the evenings, one had nowhere else to go but a spa's casino or its park. Would-be lovers could thus find each other easily and have casual meetings that, because of the fact that spa sociability was conducted in only a few highly visible venues, almost amounted to planned encounters. Perhaps of equal significance to those interested in courting, spas allowed singles to pursue each other as a full-time occupation. There was, after all, neither work nor domestic responsibility to distract one from courting activities. From breakfast until the spas' evening display of fireworks, singles could organize their passage through the day so as to be at least under each other's eyes if not always together.

Beyond the casino and its plethora of social activities, it was the spa park (fig. 14)—which virtually every *ville d'eaux* had established by the 1880s—that figured most prominently in the thermal vacation's reputation for romance. Parks, with their many meandering paths and lonely nooks, offered their users an ideal atmosphere in which to get acquainted. Away from a park's central promenades, which contemporaries regularly compared to the bustling boulevards of Paris, would-be lovers could find a socially accepted privacy whose depths encouraged their intimacy. From secluded benches or heavily foliated knolls—common features in spa parks, whose allegiance to the English garden was typically stronger than it was to the French—couples were further inspired in their budding sentiments by the orchestral concerts that routinely punctuated the later evening hours at many spa parks.

If reserved in their physical contact with each other—and no promotional sources from this period suggest that park couples engaged in anything more than an occasional caress—spa lovers could at least abandon themselves emotionally to each other. And in this relative freedom, there can be little doubt that some couples decided to cross social boundaries that in everyday society they might not have done so willingly. Thus, to men and women of the middle bourgeoisie, spa parks offered a promise of more than just romance. These places suggested the most alluring and spectacular possibility ever imagined by someone planning a vacation: love and the status of a higher-than-expected marriage might be born on vacation.

Parks, of course, suggested this possibility to their middle-class users through more than their romantic designs. Guidebook writers, even before there were many spa parks beyond the facilities that Plombières and Vichy could boast, had begun to create an image of these places as romantic. Within the lush and concealing territory of a park, according to guides, romantic love was breathlessly situated. As one writer described, parks of the *villes d'eaux* possessed a "heated air" and a "fluid magnetism that entice[d] people to pleasure, gaiety, and love."[47] To justify further their im-

FIGURE 14 Architect's sketch of the spa park at Martigny-les-Bains. Reprinted from Institut Français d'Architecture, *Villes d'eaux en France*, 31.

passioned rhetoric concerning the romance of spas and their parks, authors brought evidence to bear in the form of case histories regarding spa love. Indeed, novels like *Le solitaire d'Aix-les-Bains* offered proof—by bringing awkward, middle-class singles together and then allowing their relationship to blossom into marriage—that the spa visit promised romance to anyone who was inclined to seek it.

Shorter and more traditional guides, especially those published in pocket format, could devote no more than a few pages to the selling of this sort of desire. But even under these more constrained conditions, authors invariably wrote love into their texts by briefly relating the blissful history of some couple from "last season." In one guide to Aix-les-Bains, for example, the author characterized as romantic the spa's promenades and parks by showing young lovers in action there. And this author, eager to market his text to the segment of the thermal population that was quickly becoming a majority at the spas, used the short history of a young Italian countess and her three stubborn suitors to craft an extraordinarily direct appeal to singles of the middle bourgeoisie. For the beautiful Antonia Lovenzi, who might have accepted the affections of a brash aristocrat or an aging industrialist, chose instead to marry a young man who was but recently and modestly established in his profession.[48]

To become more attractive before society's gaze was a challenge to everyone in France who held aspirations for greater status. The selling of the spa through romantic and erotic suggestions was, therefore, hardly a unique phenomenon in later nineteenth-century French society. As Émile Zola showed clearly enough in his *Au Bonheur des dames* (1883), a novel about department-store culture in contemporary Paris, both modern merchandising and consuming were laden with erotic references.[49] Spas and department stores alike suggested to their consumers that artful consumption could actually create desire among people who were witnesses to its results. In the case of the department stores of Paris, clever and attractive purchases were supposed to confer onto their owners a convincing measure of stylishness and social appeal. Similarly, at the *villes d'eaux,* consumers found a universe where social dividends were paid according to the polish of one's presentation rather than the stubborn bulk of such credentials as one's family name or occupation. Choose the best and most lively spa, find the premier hotels, dress smartly, and act appropriately—vacationers who did these things and more believed that they were going a long way toward increasing the value of their cultural and social capital.

That vacations ended so soon after they began, causing spa-goers to fall quickly back into the tighter social orbits of their everyday lives, was no reason for eager singles or spa publicists to dwell on this inevitable denouement. Three weeks, after all, allowed ample time for interested individuals to fashion themselves as desirable and square off like so many dancers at a ball. So much time and so many opportunities, in fact, that even those who failed to find love at a spa would have balked at accusing guidebook authors of something like false advertising. On the contrary, romance and desire were everywhere at the spas—novels and guides only embellished this presence and made it more applicable to the average middle-class person's spa vacation than it probably was.

So it was that when a young middle-class man or woman returned home—which, statistically speaking, usually meant to a provincial town— it was only mildly inconvenient not to have had a suitor or romantic adventure on vacation. Who, finally, other than the individual in question or those who might have been that individual's traveling companions, knew enough of the truth to stop the returned visitor from creating his or her own vacation's history? And in the midst of tale-telling about love on vacation, yet another proverbial "couple from last summer" would be born. At the same time, of course, the tale-teller's desire to again seek romance at a spa was invariably stoked.

VISIONS OF HYDROTHERAPY AT THE CONSUMER'S SPA

Invalids seem to have loomed everywhere at the watering places of France in the latter decades of the nineteenth century, even if they figured very little in spa novels and other promotional materials. They came alone or with their vacationing families, and they were joined in pools and bath rooms by a not insignificant portion of the healthy people who danced in the casinos and took long evening strolls with new friends. But if hydro- therapy and medicine more generally continued to be ways that many spa-goers consumed their leisure, it is also clear that the medicalization of leisure had increasingly come to seem unnecessary to most vacationers. To the caricaturists and photographers whose creative work would be or- ganized into souvenir albums that visitors to the *villes d'eaux* would take home, doctoring with water became after 1860 a set of practices to be played with and scathingly critiqued.

Caricaturists of the 1860s—many of whom had gained a reputation for their satirical contributions to such politically and socially oriented journals as *Le Charivari*—lampooned the hydrotherapeutic regimen as an odd and even silly way to pass one's leisure.[50] This did not mean, however, that caricaturists failed to recognize an important relationship between the rise of medicalized leisure and the historically coincidental social and political gains of the French bourgeoisie. On the contrary, in representing and commenting upon variations of the water cure and bourgeois vacation-leisure at the spas, caricaturists established beyond any doubt that the regimented vacation was perfectly suited to the social and cultural needs of its bourgeois practitioners. Invariably, caricatures cast both the water cure and its bourgeois aficionados as absurdly excessive. Thus in one caricature from the period, which revealed the workings of the notoriously frigid Scottish shower, an enormous curtain of water falls on and all around a patient who has securely braced himself against a wall (fig. 15). Giant folds of the patient's stomach dangle nearly to his thighs, rivaled in their copiousness only by the vast garment charged with keeping at least some of this man under cover. The wiry and muscled frame of the bath attendant, in dramatic contrast to the bloated form of the patient's Gargantuan figure, is shown to be clearly in action and control here. While

PETITE DOUCHE ÉCOSSAISE.

« Que doit être la Grrrrrande, oh mon Dieu! »

FIGURE 15   A caricature from the 1860s depicting an overstuffed bourgeois gentleman as he endures an atonement in the form of a cold water shower. Reprinted from Pagotto, *Le thermalisme à Aix-les-Bains au dix-neuvième siècle, 77.*

Garçonne ..... Garçonne , ... Oh !!
Arrêtez, arrêtez , çà faisain la Grand-Croix
je vole par— ....

FIGURE 16 A Second Empire caricature of a spa-going gentleman enduring the *douche ascendante*. Reprinted from Pagotto, *Le thermalisme à Aix-les-Bains au dix-neuvième siècle*, 78.

the sober and sturdy attendant directs another blast of cold water at the heaving, fleshy buttocks and back of the curist, the latter offers a dim smile and a stuttered query. If this treatment is the so-called small Scottish shower, "what," the patient shivers, "must the grrrrrande shower be like, Oh my God?"

Similarly, the ascending shower—especially in its rectal application— was another aspect of hydrotherapeutic practice that lent itself well to humorous depictions of bathers and bathing in this period. Sketches abound from the 1860s in which a male curist is depicted floating in mid air, held up by a rush of water that is passing into the anus and out of the mouth (fig. 16). Almost hinting at the world of the carnivalesque, such caricatures seemed to suggest that the spa cure amounted to an institutionalized dressing down of the bourgeoisie.[51] More plainly, of course, caricatures of this treatment pointed out to one and all that medicalized leisure could be degrading and invasive rather than the distracting stuff of pleasure. In poking fun at the very essence of bourgeois leisure at the

DOUCHE BERTHOLET.

Par force, ou par bonne volonté!!!

« Parlez-moi d'une invention comme celle-là, si le
« malade est méchant, le Doucheur est à l'abri!»

FIGURE 17 Another sug-
gestion of the carni-
valesque: a caricaturist
of the Second Empire
captures the torturous
extremes of vapor-box
bathing. Reprinted from
Pagotto, Le thermalisme
à Aix-les-Bains au dix-
neuvième siècle, 78.

spas, these drawings and their captions asked a serious question, too. Why did such an affluent and powerful class of people fail so utterly to bring pleasure into communion with their leisure practice?

Again and again, spa caricatures endeavored to turn the carefully established medical rationale of hydrotherapy—as well as the social world of the French bourgeoisie—on its ear if not entirely upside down. Such was surely the function of the caricatures in figures 17 and 18. The first of these depicts a male patient in modified vapor box bath. The patient, held perpendicular to the ground, has only his head and arms free, sweat pouring from his brow. A strong and hardly concerned attendant looks on, holding a powerful steam hose in his hands. "This is a Chinese torture," the patient exclaims, "what are you going to do to me?" In his gentle response, the garçon makes the caricaturist's point clear enough, sending up at the same time the oversatisfied bourgeois and the science of hydrotherapeutics that organizes his holiday leisure: "Nothing at all sir . . . the pain you feel from being in this position makes you forget all of your other pains . . . you will be cured!"

FIGURE 18 Topsy-turvy at the spas: a caricature of a bather in a defenseless posture before the playful authority of two bath attendants. Reprinted from Pagotto, *Le thermalisme à Aix-les-Bains au dix-neuvième siècle*, 78.

With far less text but still more humor, the caricature in figure 18 simultaneously inverted the bourgeois world and its peculiar fascination with hydrotherapy. In this particular piece, it is a pair of bath technicians whose powerful hoses control the destiny of a male patient. Caught between the opposing forces of two streams of mineral water, the patient is suspended upside down in mid air. While his physique is not drawn to match the bloated and grotesque forms common to the genre, he is hardly spared any ridicule for having a slender frame. On the contrary, he is utterly powerless before the whims of his working-class attendants. The absurdity and humor in this scenario were doubtlessly lost on no one who had experienced the rhythms and rituals of spa hydrotherapeutics. For like this hapless bather, depicted in the throes of a curative system called "the little prince's shower," innumerable patients had found themselves in the odd position of having chosen to pass their leisure in a milieu whose principles of order took as many cues from a clinic as they did a casino.

If male curists were generally depicted as grossly obese forms in spa caricatures, females were routinely shown as skeletal and failing waifs beneath their bustled dresses. Caricatures of female patients never failed to comment on the metamorphosis in a woman's appearance that hydrother-

Douches de Princesse à la crinoline

FIGURE 19   A female patient in the midst of a cage-like hydrotherapy shower. Both the patient and her medicine suffer derision at the caricaturist's hands. Reprinted from Pagotto, *Le thermalisme à Aix-les-Bains au dix-neuvième siècle*, 74.

apy initiated. More specifically, these caricatures highlighted the difference between how women presented their bodies and how, without fashionable accoutrements, those same bodies appeared. Thus souvenir books showed sundry sketches of women, elaborately and carefully outfitted for the day, in consultation with their doctors (see lower left panel of fig. 9). In these caricatures, billowing skirts, fancy hats, heeled boots, and ornate blouses suggested that the bourgeoisie possessed sexuality, vitality, and a well-deserved social authority. But such renderings were quickly exposed as artifice when the caricaturist came to scrutinize these patients in the midst of curing or immediately afterward. Thus, one caricature from 1868 (fig. 19) shows a young girl caught in the grasp of a common hydrotherapeutic device, named in this case the "the shower of the crinolined princess." The patient is ringed, from head to toe, by a cage-like shower whose water is administered horizontally (see fig. 20 for a photograph of a similar apparatus). Steel crinolines were obviously borne with less pleasure and control than their fashionable counterpart, yet such caricatures pointed not merely to the fact that bathing could be absurdly confining and even punishing. Caricatures of this variety found their humor by dressing down hydrotherapy and undressing the bourgeoisie in one stroke. Such illustrations and their captions advised that this powerful class and the ornamented women who embodied it—just like the minutely administered principles of the water cure—had good reason to fear a complete unveiling. Because underlying the serious and studied presentation of each, when the crinolines were taken away, something of the fraud or the charlatan usually turned up.

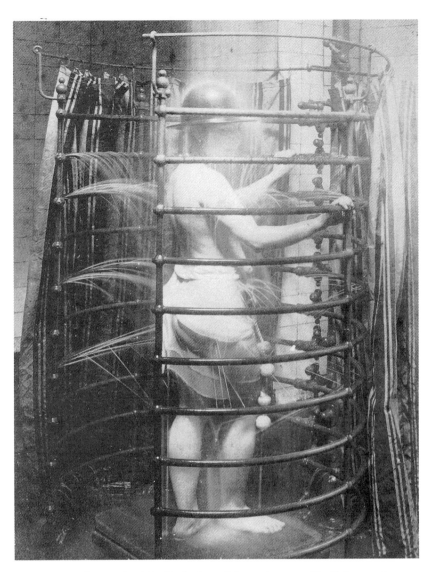

FIGURE 20 A photograph of the "circle shower" from a later era offers little room for a caricaturist's irony. Reprinted from Institut Français d'Architecture, *Villes d'eaux en France*, 186.

1 **Manière de doucher un malade qui ne donne pas de pour-boire.**

FIGURE 21 The spa regimen, as this caricaturist of the 1870s sees it, has gone far enough. Medicalized leisure is now more accurately described as *hydrothérapie sauvage*. Reprinted from Pagotto, *Le thermalisme à Aix-les-Bains au dix-neuvième siècle*, 192.

Always critical in their humorous plays, spa caricatures turned even more so after the fall of the Second Empire. Essentially, this trend saw humor replaced by a scathingly critical examination of hydrotherapy, in which doctors and their curative systems seemed menacing and even barbarous. Thus, in figure 21, the caricaturist is out to make good on what the title of his souvenir album, "The Savagery of Hydrotherapy," has promised. Accordingly, the piece exaggerates the "unpleasantries" of curing in every way possible. The bathing cell shown is dark and dank, more like a dungeon than any proper bath room. And the patient, whose crazed and pained expression suggests lunacy and torture in equal parts, has an emaciated form that hints at nothing so much as it does the life of a prison inmate. Only the bath attendant's feet appear in the image. What really matters here is the overwhelming authority of the bathing device. For this device, held as it is in the hands of an unhappy attendant, clearly has the capacity to terrorize and punish. The caption explains why the device is currently being used at its fullest and most debilitating capacity: this was "the type of shower given to patients who fail to tip."[52] Because the hydrotherapeutic table was all too easily turned to the patient's detriment, cheap patients—this image suggests—were wise to watch themselves when curing.

The same shift in spa caricature is apparent in an image of the 1880s which depicts a strikingly brutal scene in a thermal establishment (fig. 22). A bather, whose physique lacks any of the humorous and symbolic excess that earlier caricatures showed, is all but drowning in a violent therapeutic assault. Wrenched between the muscled arms and legs of two determined attendants, this patient is being flooded by at least two jets of water. His head is being held down while one attendant digs eager and apparently angry fingers into the patient's shoulders and back. Even compared to extremely critical testimony regarding the pains of hydrotherapy, this cure is excessive in every way. The caption suggests this excessiveness plainly enough, asking if "this is a bad treatment." In smaller print, beneath the primary caption, an answer to this question as well as a comment concerning the specific case is furnished. According to the spa's doctor, we learn, this is a proper treatment. Why? Because, as one of the attendants notes, the patient "is an old colonel who always acts like a tough guy during his cures."[53]

FIGURE 22 Spa medicine, as this caricature from the Third Republic suggests, has now no choice but to force its virtues onto its patients/prisoners. Reprinted from Institut Français d'Architecture, *Villes d'eaux en France.*

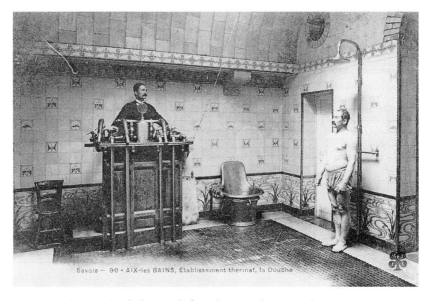

FIGURE 23 A promotional photograph from the 1890s showing a *douche* master about to administer a cold shower to his patient. Reprinted from Institut Français d'Architecture, *Villes d'eaux en France,* 209.

Hydrotherapy's grueling potential for discomfort and its tendency to disempower patients was made only more clear when guidebooks began to feature medical photographs in the 1870s and after. Indeed, the photographs shown in figures 23 and 24—both of which were widely used in guidebooks as well as hydrotherapy manuals and even as postcard images—were convincing visual evidence of how essentially medical the experience of spa curing had become. Suggesting nothing as strongly as they do an unpleasant meeting with a moment of judgement, these photographs show a severe setting in which bath attendants appear to tower over their patients. From their lofty positions of authority, the attendants seem to be on the verge of meting out punishment to their hapless patients. Sick people might need such cures, these photographs all but suggested, whereas tourists and vacationers were advised to play at things other than being invalids.[54]

Just as the medicalized rest cure was not "natural" in any sense, so its "pleasurized" counterpart was equally an historical construct with a host of complicated meanings. Among those meanings, none is more impor-

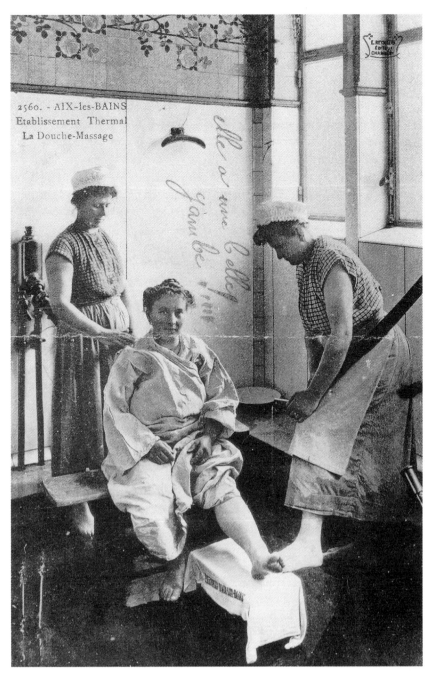

FIGURE 24 Foot bathing at Aix-les-Bains in the 1890s: a young woman accepts the curative rationale of her *douche* technicians. The inscription reads "She has a nice leg!" Reprinted from a postcard in the author's possession.

tant to an understanding of the *ville d'eaux* after 1850 than the points of contact between consumption, class anxieties, and the practice of leisure in the thermal milieu. Yet this chapter has hardly been about the new pleasures of spa-going. Instead, pleasure has been a secondary matter in an analysis of the spa that has focused on the social functions of thermal vacationing and the cultural uses of the thermal milieu's leisure locales.

One reason for this emphasis is that the story of the pleasant spa vacation has already been told, for if the middle bourgeoisie collectively agreed that spas could be used as institutional aids in the translation of class into status, such beliefs were not well served by being openly stated. Rather, as letters and postcards from the period clearly suggest, laden as they were with testaments to the fun of spa-leisure, curists saw little reason to justify their thermal vacations in terms other than those related to plea-sure. Indeed, stories of the pleasant vacation are legion in this period, as though it had been at the *villes d'eaux* where the Belle Époque had truly been good and innocent.

The primacy of pleasure at the spas of the later nineteenth century, considering that the fun of vacationing had so often been cloaked by the sometimes painful guise of hydrotherapeutics, marked a seemingly vital shift in bourgeois *mentalité* with respect to vacations. Yet this shift was more apparent than real for most spa-goers in the latter half of the century. Middle-class and provincial more than they were bourgeois or Parisian, vacationers of the era had to take their pleasures with some care. Most lacked the social acumen and cultural capital to simply do on vacation what came "naturally." Instead, they had to keep their eyes and ears open so as to absorb the right behavioral cues and clues.

Cultural advice surrounded them, but there was so much to learn. Meals often saw the unveiling of unfamiliar foods and table instruments. Similarly, endless rounds of afternoon concerts, dinners, and dances called for not only an extensive wardrobe but also the sensitivity to wear the right clothing for each occasion. To persons of the bourgeoisie, who set these standards and identified each other by their shared secrets, pleasure was very much the point of everything one did on vacation. While around the spa's tables and throughout its social venues, trying to learn by osmosis which fork to use and what hat to wear, middle-class vacationers had to practice the pleasures of bourgeois leisure until they knew enough to enjoy them unconsciously.

Spas were by no means the only sites where the bourgeoisie's cultural "wares" were simultaneously practiced, displayed, and commodified. Newspapers, magazines, novels, catalogs, and posters might all be dis-

J. J. 8403 Aix-les-Bains — Entrée de l'Etablissement Thermal

FIGURE 25   The ubiquitous *chaise-à-porteurs* and its convalescent passenger, surrounded by uninterested vacationers. Reprinted from a postcard in the author's possession.

cussed in this regard too, as these mass-produced products of the print revolution certainly contained invaluable counsel as to the ways and means of bourgeois life. Yet spas went further in reproducing the French bourgeoisie for broad consumption because leisure—that hard-to-understand matrix of time, space, and status—was at their very essence. Leisure had come to be a highly conspicuous arena for the exchange of culture's capital in the decades after midcentury when public life was enjoying such enormous social purchase and the consumer revolution was advancing. While middle-class vacationers could only hope to make a select few of the possible cultural and social "trades" at the "bourse" that was bourgeois leisure—ownership of country houses, extensive international travel, and the like being beyond their purse—they could at least try their best to do as the bourgeois did within the empire of the spas.

Far from being locales where one group merely aped the behaviors of another, however, the *villes d'eaux* explicitly promised their clients improved social fortunes that would actually endure. This promise, which curists sought to realize in several ways—by advertising their visits, learning the arts of travel, seeing to it that their children acquired the cultural capital associated with musical performance and dance, forging valuable professional alliances, and falling in love—was based on a faith in the spa's capacity to teach more than just the practice of vacation leisure. Spas and their sometimes medicalized and sometimes pleasurized leisure (fig. 25) had emerged as aspects of the cultural education that signified bourgeois status in society. To acquire a measure of that status, middle-class persons were only too willing to enroll for training—just as they did at select *lycées* and universities—at a noted *ville d'eaux*.

Epilogue

*W*ithin this book, I have tried to show that history diced finely still yields a great deal of information about the ways of the past. It is perhaps fitting, therefore, that I conclude by paying particular attention to a mere sliver from an already thin slice. In 1906, one Marie Guillaume did what nearly a million of her contemporaries did when she left her daily routine and ventured forth on vacation. It was not long after her arrival at a spa that Guillaume chose to write her friends and describe some of what she was seeing and doing. Not wishing to bother with a traditional and more time-consuming mode of correspondence, she bought mass culture's greeting and mailed postcards.[1] In one of those cards, which she addressed to several of her friends and neighbors in Bologne, Guillaume reveals a great deal about the meanings of spas and vacationing to French society at the fin de siècle.

Guillaume did not travel to Aix-les-Bains as one of the ambitious singles whose presence at the spas I chronicle in chapter 5, nor did she go there with her own family. Strictly speaking, her visit was not really a vacation at all. Rather, she went to the Savoy for the simple reason that her employers, even on their vacation, were evidently loath to manage without the domestic services that she provided. Yet her duties were relatively slight while at Aix-les-Bains, beyond accompanying Madame's sedan chair to the thermal establishment and back each morning, and she wanted her friends to know that her "burdens were indeed fewer" on vacation than they were at home.

More than this, however, Guillaume wished to convey to her friends the fact that she was enjoying the extra leisure that her employers' vacation allowed. "I took a lovely promenade on Sunday," the servant recounted, "when Madame paid for me to rent an excursion carriage through the mountains." This rare taste of luxury and natural wonder made its mark on the domestic. "It was a carriage with three horses," her friends were told, "and I have never in my whole life had a more pleasant day." Despite having to follow Madame around and do her bidding, the whole trip to

Aix seems to have pleased Guillaume a great deal. So much so, in fact, that the domestic closed her card by issuing a qualified invitation to her friends: "We return on the thirtieth in the evening," she notified her readers, "so come to the house, but not directly." But when they got together that evening in Bologne, Marie promised they would all drink coffee and that she would "tell everything about [her] travels."[2] Suffice it to say that Guillaume's coffee klatsch undoubtedly was a different kind of postmortem than what vacationers who had paid their own way and traveled for pleasure might have offered. Yet her happy report surely would have accorded with those other tellings of life on vacation in at least one crucial respect. Because if this servant found fun *en séjour,* it is safe to guess that for many French people spa leisure had become, by the last years of the Belle Époque, a "natural" set of practices whose cultural construction had been at least partly obscured by a logic of vacationing that might already have seemed transhistorical.

Posing at having fun, eagle-eyeing everything that everyone else said and did, muddling through leisure aware only of how consciously one wished to be doing something more definite and productive—a generation or more of vacationers had gone with some trepidation to Vichy and its equivalents, partly unsure of what they were to do with leisure or how to act. If the French bourgeoisie's identity formation was complete enough by midcentury so that the strict rhythming of rest that hydrotherapy had provided was needed less and less, there were still plenty of people from the middle classes who had much to study with respect to the arts of leisure.

Feeling uncomfortable and self-conscious about vacation leisure, however, was increasingly rare by the time that Guillaume went *en vacances* to Aix-les-Bains. The decade prior to the Great War saw the French middle class emerge as the majority population at the country's leisure locales and something of a style-setter with respect to the spa vacation's social tone. Indeed, as the sporting craze swept over France's spas—seeing to the building of golf courses, race tracks, pigeon shoots, *vélodromes,* and hiking paths—the spas actually became less inscribed with the markings of class and status than they had been when casinos, parks, and a sedentary gentility had governed vacationing.

The accession of the middle bourgeoisie to social prominence—at the spas if not in society more generally—was nowhere more perceptible than in the pages of thermal newspapers. Lists of curists still ran in all of these publications, but the spa press wholly abandoned its efforts to represent the milieu as highly exclusive. On the contrary, the feature stories and advertisements in these papers showed that the *villes d'eaux,* like other important "contexts" of French society and culture, had passed through a process of democratization. Travel was now something that even persons of the working classes could contemplate. Pilgrim travel, in particular, was a booming business that marketed a special sort of vacation to workers and lower bourgeoisie alike. The mysteries of a voyage, even one that spanned the entire country, were revealed to millions of French persons each year by dint of their personal experiences.

Two advertisements, both carried in a single issue of *L'Écho d'Aix-les-Bains* in the summer of 1909, speak directly to this transformation. Under the headline "How to Increase Your Height!" the first notice shows a man in a tuxedo whose body is split vertically by a ruler. By way of explaining this image, the supporting text offers a compelling pitch to anyone who ever felt slight of stature. "You can definitely grow in height by three to five centimeters in only one month," the text declares, "if you are willing to devote only five minutes each day to the *Grandisseur Desbonnet*." The inventor of this miraculous apparatus, readers learn, grew by more than "five centimeters in two months without resorting to drugs or dangerous exercise."[3] Some insecurities had vanished in France's leisure locales, while some, evidently, were merely marketed in a new key. How one looked had always been an acute concern of middle-class spa-goers during the latter decades of the nineteenth century. But for their twentieth-century counterparts, it no longer sufficed to hide one's humble self behind striking clothes and confident manners. An advertisement of this type, which probably made sense to those who might have noticed it, would have been an inconceivably brash oddity in a spa newspaper from the 1870s.

The second advertisement was written to catch the attention of middle-class parents on vacation. Beneath a drawing of a beautifully mustached man flexing his biceps, a headline calls out to all "parents seeking a career situation for their sons or daughters." Disregard the "old and overcrowded *métiers* as well as the liberal professions," parents are told, and "do not hesitate for an instant to enroll your children in Paris's new *cours d'instructeurs des écoles de culture physique*." Under the administration of one Professeur Desbonnet, noted inventor and designer of the "*grandisseur*," students learn how to establish and manage their own *écoles de culture physique*. For a mere 3,000 francs, this advertisement concludes, students receive their training as well as a "magnificent diploma and a special gold medal."[4] If such a notice hardly shows that the spas were ready to receive the influx of working-class vacationers that would come after the 1930s, it does, nevertheless, signal that the bourgeois spa, like the bourgeoisie's long nineteenth century, was almost in history's hands.

$\mathcal{N}otes$

In citing works in the notes, I have identified archival materials by the following abbreviations:

AD Allier	Archives Départementales d'Allier
ADHS	Archives Départementales de la Haute-Savoie
AD Savoie	Archives Départementales de la Savoie
AH Vichy	Archives Hospitalières de Vichy
AM Aix	Archives Municipales d'Aix-les-Bains
AMB	Archives Municipales de Brisson-Saint-Innocent
AN	Archives Nationales
ATN Aix	Archives des Thermes Nationaux d'Aix-les-Bains
BM Chambéry	Bibliothèque Municipale de Chambéry

Unless otherwise noted, all translations from French sources are my own.

INTRODUCTION

1. Spas and vacationing have also been subjected to a close historical and sociological investigation by the French, especially in the last two decades. Examples of excellent local studies of French spas, for example, include Bernard Desgranges, *Histoire des thermes de Luxeuil,* and Léon Binet, *Évian: Lieu de santé* (Paris: Plon, 1966). Recent studies of vacationing include Jean Viard, *Penser les vacances,* and André Rauch, *Vacances et pratiques corporelles.*

2. Michel de Certeau, *The Practice of Everyday Life.* A less theoretical but equally important call to the study of everyday life is Michelle Perrot, ed., *A History of Private Life: From the Fires of the Revolution to the Great War.*

3. Michael Marrus must be acknowledged for his pioneering call for the study of leisure as a social category. See his *The Emergence of Leisure* (New York: Harper and Row, 1974). The range of work produced by followers of the "new cultural history" is vast indeed. For an overview of the problematics and methods of this diverse set of approaches, see Hunt, ed., *The New Cultural History.* For specific applications of new cultural history, see Kathleen Kete, *The Beast in the Boudoir: Petkeeping in Nineteenth-Century Paris* (Berkeley and Los Angeles: University of California Press, 1994); Auslander, *Taste and Power: Furnishing Modern France;* Corbin, *The Foul and the Fragrant: Odor and the French Social Imagination;* Perrot, *Les dessus et les dessous de la bourgeoisie: Une histoire du vêtement au dix-neuvième siècle;* and Barnes, *The Making of a Social Disease: Tuberculosis in Nineteenth-Century France.*

4. For an overview of Foucault's contribution to the ongoing debates on medicine and culture, see Foucault, *Discipline and Punish: The Birth of the Prison; Naissance de la clinique; The History of Sexuality: An Introduction; Madness and Civilization: A History of Insanity in the Age of Reason;* and Rabinow, ed., *The Foucault Reader.* For work very much in the foucaultian vein, see Corbin, *Les filles de noce: Misère sexuelle et prostitution dans le dix-neuvième siècle.* See also Michelle Perrot, "The Three Ages of Industrial Discipline in Nineteenth-Century France."

5. Lecoq, *Description pittoresque de l'Auvergne: Vichy et ses environs, ou description des eaux thermales, et des sites pittoresques qui les entourent, avec quelques considerations sur l'action médicale des eaux,* 18.

6. Ibid.

7. Ibid., 21.

8. For an excellent discussion of medicalization with respect to the intellectual and social history of France, see Nye, *Crime, Madness, and Politics in Modern France: The Medical Concept of National Decline.* For a consideration of the relationship between state interests, medicine, and the law, see Harris, *Murderers and Madness: Medicine, Law, and Society in the Fin de Siècle.*

9. Harrison, "Honest Amusements: Voluntary Associations and Bourgeois Leisure."

10. A great deal of fascinating and important research has been done on the politics, pleasures, and cultural practices of everyday leisure activities and locales in nineteenth-century France. Among the better of such works are Barrows, "Nineteenth-Century Cafés: Arenas of Everyday Life"; Rearick, *Pleasures of the Belle Époque: Entertainment and Festivity in Turn-of-the-Century France;* and E. Weber, *France, Fin de Siècle* and "Gymnastics and Sports in Fin-de-Siècle France: Opium of the Classes?"

11. For an outstanding and pioneering work on leisure, class, and urbanism in one city, see Haug, *Leisure and Urbanism in Nineteenth-Century Nice.* For an excellent overview of spas and their shifting clientele in the nineteenth century, see Wallon, *La vie quotidienne dans les villes d'eaux.*

12. Published in English as *The Lure of the Sea: The Discovery of the Seaside in the Western World, 1750–1840* (Berkeley and Los Angeles: University of California Press, 1994).

13. Both Hugh Cunningham's and Robert Malcomson's works discuss the rise of the seaside holiday in nineteenth-century England. But for the most comprehensive discussion of how England's beaches were commodified for middle- and working-class consumption, see J. Walton, *The English Seaside Resort: A Social History, 1750–1914.*

14. For an insightful examination of changing attitudes and pratices of leisure in modern France, see Corbin, *L'avènement des loisirs, 1850–1960.*

15. Of the more recent and important works related to travel and narratives of the tourist, my largest debts for background information and analytical grounding are to Bruce Redford, *Venice and the Grand Tour,* and to several of the essays in Chloe Chard and Helen Langdon, eds., *Transports: Travel, Pleasure, and Imaginative Geography, 1600–1830.*

16. My insistence on the need for travel in a conception of vacation leisure is derived largely from Reason, *Man in Motion: The Psychology of Travel.* For a still helpful research aid to historical literature concerned with travel, tourism, and leisure, see Cox, *A Reference Guide to the Literature of Travel.*

17. The best and most current historical study of the Grand Tour is Black, *The British and the Grand Tour.* For a discussion that goes beyond the English case, see Towner, *The European Grand Tour, circa 1550–1840: A Study of Its Role in the History of Tourism.* For a still excellent overview of issues related to the English Grand Tour, see Mead, *The Grand*

Tour in the Eighteenth Century. Another worthwhile source on this travel and leisure experience is Lambert, ed., *Grand Tour: A Journey in the Tracks of the Age of Aristocracy*. For more contemporary discussions of research issues and techniques related to the study of elite travel in the eighteenth century, see Towner, "The Grand Tour: Sources and Methodology for the Historical Study of Tourism," and Fairburn, "The Grand Tour."

18. Parisians at Enghien, for example, would have been formally counted on the local administration's seasonal rolls as *étrangers*. Similarly, visitors to Aix-les-Bains from Chambéry—even though a mere five miles separate the two locales—were always considered to be foreigners in the eighteenth and nineteenth centuries.

19. For an interesting formulation of this conception of tourist leisure, see Schmidt, *Tourism: Sacred Sights, Secular Seer*.

20. Pilgrimage has not been sufficiently studied either in the early or late modern period as a leisure/holiday setting. A dated but still valuable summary of early modern pilgrimage in Europe, which does deal at some length with sacred travel as a form of leisure practice, is Heath, *In the Steps of the Pilgrims*. Another older work of continued importance, especially with respect to the history of pilgrimage as a veritable leisure commodity, is Watt, *Canterbury Pilgrims and Their Ways*. For France in the late modern period, the standard work on pilgrim travel is Thomas Kselman, *Miracles and Prophecies in Nineteenth-Century France* (New Brunswick: Rutgers University Press, 1983).

21. If pilgrims sometimes lacked a religious reason for their travels, guidebooks written specifically for them could help in this capacity. A discussion of these works figures into virtually all the scholarship on pilgrimage cited both above and below. For an interesting consideration of these books as historical sources, see Vaughan, "Early Guide Books as Sources of Social History."

22. The sociological and anthropological literature on the motivations for pilgrim travel is understandably vast. Beyond the works cited above, a good point of entry into this literature is Kendall, *Medieval Pilgrimage*. Other valuable works in leisure theory that specifically address pilgrim travel are V. Smith, *Hosts and Guests: The Anthropology of Tourism;* Krippendorf, *The Holiday-Makers: Understanding the Impact of Leisure and Travel;* Turner, *Image and Pilgrimage in Christian Culture;* Dupront, "Tourisme et pèlerinage, réflexions sur la psychologie collective"; Schmidt, *Tourism;* Cohen, "A Phenomenology of Tourist Experiences"; and Robinson, *A Geography of Tourism*.

23. For a still fascinating discussion of tourist travel as a phenomenon of modern mass culture, see MacCannell, *The Tourist: A New Theory of the Leisure Class*. Building on both MacCannell and the interpretive genius of Edward Said, as well as offering a feminist and postmodern invigoration of debates related to tourism and its narrations, is Caren Kaplan, *Questions of Travel: Postmodern Discourses of Displacement*.

CHAPTER ONE

1. Brockliss, "The Development of the Spa in Seventeenth-Century France," 26.

2. Pagotto, *Le thermalisme à Aix-les-Bains au dix-neuvième siècle*, 115.

3. Brockliss has rightly argued that the seventeenth-century fortunes of France's spas were ensured only when Henry III decided in the 1580s to utilize French mineral waters for a medical cure. "Development of the Spa," 23.

4. Grellety, "Une cure thermale à Vichy pendant le dix-septième siècle."

5. Brockliss, "Development of the Spa," 36.

6. Brockliss, in his far more systematic study of seventeenth-century spas, concurs

regarding the impossibility of establishing adequate estimates regarding the number of curists at French spas of the early modern period. Ibid.

7. Such statistics are available only intermittently and only for the latter half of the eighteenth century.

8. As Brockliss has shown, the seventeenth-century bathing population for France must surely have been smaller by some measure than that of the later eighteenth century. The cruder and less well developed villages around the baths, Brockliss notes, would have been impossibly hard-pressed to host more than 500 persons per summer. "Development of the Spa," 36.

9. Ibid. For an important discussion on attitudes toward poverty as well as state policies of poor relief, see Hufton, *The Poor of Eighteenth-Century France, 1750–1789.* An important analysis with a social control hypothesis is R. Schwartz, *Policing the Poor in Eighteenth-Century France.*

10. Registry of foreign drinkers of water, 1728–1753, AH Vichy, 2F.

11. The development of an "enlightened" policy of administering poor relief in the eighteenth century is thoughtfully discussed in Adams, *Bureaucrats and Beggars: French Social Policy in the Age of the Enlightenment.* For a discussion of doctor-patient relationships in the same period, which deals with aspects of the indigent experience, see Goubert, *Malades et médecine en Bretagne, 1770–1790.*

12. For a concise history of spa paternalism with respect to indigence, see Guitard, "Le prestige passé des eaux minérales," 59.

13. Brockliss, "Development of the Spa," 36.

14. Ibid., 38.

15. Ibid.

16. Ibid.

17. Ibid., 27.

18. On medicine's rise to social authority in the eighteenth century, an influential and important essay is Murphy, "Medical Culture under the Old Regime." The most valuable synthetic considerations of eighteenth-century medicine are still to be found in the work of Roy Porter. See his *The Codification of Medical Morality: Historical and Philosophical Studies of the Formalization of Western Medical Morality in the Eighteenth and Nineteenth Centuries;* the more general, transhistorical *Dictionary of the History of Medicine;* his important work on professionalization in a waning era of popular cures, *Medical Fringe and Medical Orthodoxy, 1750–1850;* and *Medicine in the Enlightenment.*

19. Clearly the eighteenth century's gradual movements toward medicalization offered a broad context in which elites could increasingly understand the logic of curing. For a discussion of medicine and society in the eighteenth century, see Lecuir, "La médicalisation de la société française dans la deuxième moitié du dix-huitième siècle en France: Aux origines des premiers traités de médecine légale." For a Paris-based discussion of similar issues, see Gelfand, *Professionalizing Modern Medicine: Paris Surgeons, Medical Science, and Institutions in the Eighteenth Century.*

20. Brockliss, "Development of the Spa," 25, 27.

21. Ibid.

22. Ibid., 29.

23. On the history of medical theory related to spa cures, see Porter, *The Medical History of Waters and Spas.*

24. Grellety, "Une cure thermale," 160.

25. Brockliss, "Development of the Spa," 31.

26. Ibid., 38.

27. Ibid., 31.

28. Grellety, "Une cure thermale," 160.

29. Ibid.

30. Ibid., 161.

31. Brockliss, "Development of the Spa," 33.

32. Léonard, *Archives du corps: La santé au dix-neuvième siècle*, 127. Scholarly debate about the extent to which eighteenth-century society witnessed a "medicalization" at all suggestive of what the nineteenth century would see continues apace. For a thorough sketch of the position which holds for an eighteenth-century medicalization, see Brockliss, *Medical Teaching at the University of Paris, 1600–1720*, and his very recent synthetic work, *The Medical World of Early Modern France*.

33. Institut Français d'Architecture, *Villes d'eaux en France*, 365.

34. Brockliss, "Development of the Spa," 32.

35. On the implications of Enlightenment science for the French social formation, see Gillispie, *Science and Polity in France at the End of the Old Regime*.

36. Néris, Luchon, Vichy, Aix-les-Bains, and scores of other mineral water sources in France employed the same open basins that had been used for centuries.

37. Calmet, *Traité historique des eaux et des bains de Plombières*, as quoted in Institut Français d'Architecture, *Villes d'eaux en France*, 336.

38. At Aix-les-Bains, for example, horses, cattle, and dogs were bathed in the spa's basin, the so-called Royal Bath, well into the July Monarchy.

39. Brockliss, "Development of the Spa," 32.

40. For a fascinating description and contemporary defense of this watering place and its curative techniques, see Spry, *A Practical Treatise on the Bath Waters*. A less rich but more culturally and socially concerned study of the facility and its important place in eighteenth-century society can be found in Barbeau, *Life and Letters at Bath in the Eighteenth Century*. A nineteenth-century moralist and medical critique of the open bath can be found in Granville, *The Spas of England and Principal Sea-Bathing Places*.

41. Spry, *Practical Treatise*, 119.

42. Barbeau, *Life and Letters*, 55.

43. Bath was also quite purposefully associated with easy sexuality. An advertising project of sorts, it seems, had carefully created this saleable image and deployed it through poetry, newspapers, and theater. For this argument in its detailed and fascinating form, see Benedict, "The Printed Resort: Erotic Consumption and the Gender of Leisure in Eighteenth-Century Spa Literature."

44. Brockliss argues for medicalization and suggests that visitors were "patients" in some modern sense of the term, just as he contends that many visitors were "willing to place (themselves) totally at the mercy of the physicians" ("Development of the Spa," 38). This seems unlikely as a general observation, precisely because medicine had so little of the rhetorical authority in the seventeenth century that it would two centuries later. Not even science had achieved much of its soon-to-occur privilege in the period under his scrutiny.

45. Brockliss himself notes how individual doctors were crucial in developing particular spas ("Development of the Spa," 29). Their role in creating a medical context at their spas ought to receive equal consideration.

46. Again, debates about the professionalization of medical practice in the eighteenth century, which argue forcefully that medical practitioners in their professional training

and curative methods suggested the presence of an essentially modern rigorousness in the Old Regime, miss the important fact that most spas of that period allowed bathers and curists to enjoy a measure of freedom which nineteenth-century doctors never would have allowed. For an important argument about elite education and professionalization, see Brockliss, *French Higher Education in the Seventeenth and Eighteenth Centuries.* For a more localist and medically specific consideration of professionalization as well as relations between doctors and patients around the period of the French Revolution, see Goubert, *Malades et médecine.* For the still standard work on medicalization as a shift in practice and epistemology which leads well into the nineteenth century, see Ramsey, *Professional and Popular Medicine in France, 1770–1830.*

47. All of the following statistics relative to the sociological and economic character of Aix-les-Bains come from Leguay, *Histoire d'Aix-les-Bains et sa région: Une grande station thermale,* 84–85.

48. On social relief for the poor of the Old Regime, see Adams, *Bureaucrats and Beggars.* For a discussion oriented toward the state's administration of a proto-"public health" movement in the era of the French Revolution, see Hannaway, "Medicine, Public Welfare, and the State in Eighteenth-Century France: The Société Royale de Médecine of Paris, 1776–1793."

49. For a thorough discussion of professional competition in the medical profession, as well as a fascinating general discussion of the process of professionalization, see Ramsey, *Professional and Popular Medicine in France, 1770–1830.*

50. For an exhaustive list of such works, see Carrère, *Catalogue raisonné des ouvrages qui ont été publiés sur les eaux minérales en général et sur celles de la France en particulier.* Doctors most definitely did engage in hydrotherapeutic research in the eighteenth century too, but their research was conducted on relatively small scale and without the guidance of professional societies. For perhaps the most famous work on spa bathing in the eighteenth century, see Raulin, *Traité analytique des eaux minérales en général, de leur propriétés et de leur usage dans les maladies.*

51. This was especially true at spas like Aix-les-Bains where, toward the end of the century, such therapeutic techniques as the *douche massage* were medically codified and widely practiced. For a thorough discussion of the medical codification of bathing and water drinking in this period, see Raulin, *Traité analytique.*

52. King Henry IV created the superintendence in May of 1605. See Wallon, *La vie quotidienne.*

53. Ibid.

54. Ibid.

55. For a fascinating discussion of political culture in the French Revolution, see Hunt, *Politics, Culture, and Class in the French Revolution.*

56. AH Vichy, 1L.

57. Ibid.

58. Jarrassé, *Les thermes romantiques: Bains et villégiatures en France de 1800 à 1850,* 24.

59. Pagotto, *Le thermalisme à Aix-les-Bains,* 38.

60. Ibid.

61. Jarrassé, *Les thermes romantiques,* 27.

62. Wallon, "Saisons de Vichy pendant la Revolution," 12.

63. Pagotto, *Le thermalisme à Aix-les-Bains,* 111.

64. Institut Français d'Architecture, *Villes d'eaux en France,* 330.

65. Leguay, *Histoire d'Aix-les-Bains,* 89.

66. Vichy instituted similar rules on 16 July 1806. For the genesis of regulatory measures at Vichy, see AH Vichy, 1L.

67. "Règlement pour les bains d'Aix de 1783," AD Savoie, 1FS 2802.

68. Ibid.

CHAPTER TWO

1. "Aperçu de la situation de l'établissement royal des bains d'Aix en Savoie présenté à S. M. le 30 juillet 1816 par Despine, Médecin inspecteur et Médecin honoraire," AD Savoie, 1FS 2803.

2. The instructions to the director of the establishment dictated that information on each bather be collected under the rubric of "qualité." Further, a note was written by all the names, indicating "s'ils sont de la classe de ceux qui doivent payer ou être reçues gratis." Ibid.

3. Ibid.

4. Doctors were also deeply concerned with issues of professionalization in this period. For a solid overview of the professional and institutional structures of nineteenth-century French medicine, see Ackerknecht, "Medical Education in Nineteenth-Century France," 15–18, and *Medicine at the Paris Hospital, 1794–1848*. See also Ramsey, *Professional and Popular Medicine*. For a worthwhile comparison to the English case, see Peterson, *The Medical Profession in Mid-Victorian London*. For a synthetic discussion of the medical community's drive to professionalize, see Larson, *The Rise of Professionalism*, chaps. 9 and 10.

5. "Rapport historico-médical sur la saison d'Aix-en-Savoie sur l'exercice de l'année 1818," AD Savoie, 1FS 2803.

6. Ibid.

7. AM Aix, I120.

8. It was standard practice at every thermal establishment in France for the resident medical inspector, who was the head practitioner of a given spa, to file a formal and exhaustive report with the Royal Academy of Medicine for each thermal season. The reports considered equally medical, administrative, surveillance, and fiscal affairs. This procedure, adopted at Aix-les-Bains under the French occupation, was followed there even after the Sardinian monarchy regained control of the Savoy and Aix's spa in the Restoration. For an interesting secondary account of the French medical inspectorate and its decline in the nineteenth century, see George Weisz, "Water Cures and Science: The French Academy of Medecine and Mineral Waters in the Nineteenth Century." The estimate of France's spa population comes from Martin-Fugier, *La vie élégante ou la formation du Tout-Paris, 1815–1848*, 120.

9. "Rapport du médecin inspecteur des bains d'Aix-en-Savoie sur l'exercice de l'année 1818," AD Savoie, 1FS 2803.

10. Ibid.

11. This was not the sum total of Aix's summer population at the time, of course, because arrivals from at least the preceding two weeks were probably still in residence. The average *séjour*, it should be remembered, was three weeks. Foreigner lists from the period are held within AD Savoie, 1FS 2804.

12. Lists from other thermal establishments suggest the same trends in the 1820s. At Bourbon-l'Archambault, for example, of 111 bathers registered during the 1824 season, only 18 appear to have been of the nobility. AD Allier, series X.

13. Ibid.

14. Similar patterns are revealed in the statistics for Vichy and Bourbon-l'Archambault. See AD Allier, series X.

15. But single or at least unaccompanied persons were hardly unknown in the spas of the period, as the *listes des étrangers* show. There are 45 single male arrivees and 7 female *solitaires*—again, out of 128—noted on Aix's 1820 list. The 1834 list shows a much more equal ratio of single males to single females, with 32 of the former and 20 of the latter, while the 1842 list shows a ratio that is again very much weighted on the male side, with 21 men as compared to only 7 women. The presence of so many unaccompanied people strongly suggests that the spas of this period held out great potential as marriage markets. It may well have been that single men went to the spas in such large numbers in hopes of finding romance and a spouse. Similarly, some women—especially those whose listings note, as they do for 4 of the 7 singles on the 1842 list, that they were of independent means, or *rentières*—probably saw the spa milieu as a place where male attention might be found. Yet statistics alone—even if they seem to show spas as the proverbial sites for matchmaking—do not tell the whole story. The biographies of the vast majority of the unaccompanied women at the spas have different nuances from those of the *rentières* of 1842. Of the 20 from 1834, for example, 4 noted that they were "*pensionnaires* at a *monastère.*" Twelve others added that they had been born under different names than they currently used. At least 16 of these 20 women, then, were apparently not in the market for marriage. Unmarried women, in point of fact, were something of a rarity at the spas. Ibid.

16. For an important if strikingly ideological summary of the heated debate concerning the existence of a bourgeoisie before the Revolution, see Soboul, "The Classical Historiography of the French Revolution and Its Critics." For a still informative and insightful discussion of the bourgeoisie before 1789, see Barber, *The Bourgeoisie in Eighteenth-Century France.*

17. These distinctions are discussed in thoughtful detail in Daumard, *Les bourgeois et la bourgeoisie en France depuis 1815.*

18. Daumard argues, however, that there were certain basic elements, of fashion, for example, that were common among the various strata of the bourgeoisie. Ibid., 31–32.

19. The prefect of the Paris police, Henri Gisquet, as quoted in Kudlick, *Cholera in Post- Revolutionary Paris: A Cultural History,* 24.

20. Ibid.

21. I am following Daumard's persuasive argument for an overarching commonality among the different "bourgeoisies" in nineteenth-century France. Daumard, *Les bourgeois et la bourgeoisie,* 261–64.

22. This orientation toward productivity, Daumard contends, was based on the bourgeoisie's faith that society would be better in the future. Ibid., 263.

23. Ibid.

24. Sharing of work was especially common with husbands and wives of smaller enterprises. Ibid., 214.

25. Bonnie Smith, *Ladies of the Leisure Class: The Bourgeoises of Northern France in the Nineteenth Century,* 37.

26. Barber, *Bourgeoisie,* 82.

27. Smith, *Ladies of the Leisure Class,* 21.

28. Landes, "French Entrepreneurship and Industrial Growth in the Nineteenth Century," 48. For a dated but still interesting history of the French economy in this period,

see Cameron, "Economic Growth and Stagnation in France, 1815–1914." For Landes's related discussion of domesticity and religion in the worldview and business sensibility of Bourgeois men in this period, see "Religion and Enterprise: The Case of the French Textile Industry," 41–86.

29. Landes, "Religion and Enterprise," 48. I hesitate to refer to these persons as businessmen for the simple reason that bourgeois women were, at least in some regions of France and in some industries, full participants in commercial activity. I shall discussed this more in chapter 5.

30. But this was by no means always the case. For a discussion of bourgeois commercial activity in the period that deals at some length with speculative activity, see Daumard, *Les bourgeois et la bourgeoisie*, 190–91.

31. Landes, "Religion and Enterprise," 47.

32. Ibid., 53.

33. B. Smith, *Ladies of the Leisure Class: The Bourgeoises of Northern France in the Nineteenth Century*, 23. Smith and Landes hardly agree on the nature of family business in nineteenth-century France. For Smith's brief summation of her differences with Landes, see pp. 22, 23, and 233 n. 9.

34. Ibid., 22.

35. On clothing manufacturing and its relationship to the bourgeois marketplace, see Philippe Perrot, *Fashioning the Bourgeoisie: A History of Clothing in the Nineteenth Century*, trans. Richard Bienvenu (Princeton: Princeton University Press, 1994), 38–60. On French manufacturing and the hand-production of consumer goods, see W. Walton, *France at the Crystal Palace: Bourgeois Taste and Artisan Manufacture in the Nineteenth Century*, 5. On the cultural politics of taste and the manufacture of French furniture, see Auslander, *Taste and Power*, 220–24.

36. Gaudry, *Histoire du barreau de Paris depuis son origine jusqu'à 1830*, 98.

37. Whitney Walton notes that such terms were "ubiquitous" and even interchangeable in describing French manufactured goods. *France at the Crystal Palace*, 27.

38. Emma Faucon, *Voyage d'une jeune fille autour de sa chambre: Nouvelle morale et instructive* (Paris: Maillet, 1860), as quoted in W. Walton, *France at the Crystal Palace*, 27.

39. *L'Illustration*, 18 January 1851, as quoted in W. Walton, *France at the Crystal Palace*, 35.

40. Auslander, *Taste and Power*, 223.

41. Ibid.

42. Voltaire, *Le droit du seigneur*, vol.6, *Oeuvres de Voltaire* (Paris, 1838), as quoted in translation in Barber, *Bourgeoisie*, 58.

43. Morazé, *Les bourgeois conquérants*, 151. On social ambitions among the different vintages of France's bourgeois families, see Daumard, *Le bourgeois et la bourgeoisie*, 166–74.

44. Landes, "Religion and Enterprise," 55.

45. Ibid.

46. Augustin Eugène Scribe, as quoted in Daumard, "The Parisian Bourgeoisie, 1815–1848," 137.

47. On the importance of education to the upper bourgeoisie, see Martin-Fugier, *La bourgeoisie*, 241–45.

48. Daumard, *Les bourgeois et la bourgeoisie*, 159.

49. P. Perrot, *Les dessus et les dessous*, 88. A sampling of these books includes Bassanville,

Almanach du savoir-vivre: Petit code de la bonne compagnie and *Code du cérémonial: Guide des gens du monded dans toutes les circonstances de la vie,* and Eugène Muller, *Petit traité de La politesse française: Code des bienséances et du savoir vivre* (Paris: Garnier, 1861).

50. P. Perrot, *Les dessus et les dessous,* 88.

51. Ibid.

52. Mme Pariset, *Manuel de la maîtresse de maison, ou lettres sur l'économie domestique,* quoted in Auslander, *Taste and Power,* 223.

53. Opera tickets were indeed affordable in the period. A box could be had at the Théâtre-Français for nine francs per night in the 1830s, while similar facilities at the Italians, one of the more celebrated and expensive houses in Paris, cost only one franc more. Martin-Fugier, *La vie élégante,* 312.

54. Ibid., 314.

55. *Journal des dames et des modes,* August 1811, as quoted in Auslander, *Taste and Power,* 224.

56. Pagotto, *Le thermalisme à Aix-les-Bains,* 114.

57. Vichy first became a state property in 1605. King Henry IV had a bathing establishment called the Maison du Roy built there. The mineral waters of Vichy were regularly exploited after that date.

58. For additional statistics concerning the curist population of Vichy, see Institut Français d'Architecture, *Villes d'eaux en France,* 29.

59. For the plans and correspondence related to building projects at Vichy under the Restoration, see AH Vichy, 1L.

60. In chapter 3, I deal specifically with the important question of interior design within the spas of this period.

61. The *médecins d'eaux* of Aix-les-Bains, with their primarily French clientele and administrative system, certainly considered their institution to be at least as French as it was Sardinian. I bring Aix in, although it was not under French jurisdiction between 1816 and 1860, because it was, before and after those dates, among the greatest spas in France. Moreover, because it was always among the very few spas in France owned by the state, its documentation is especially rich for the entire period of my study.

62. The Sardinian king had visited Aix-les-Bains in 1816 and authorized an expenditure of 12,000 livres on its thermal facilities. "Rapport de la commission administrative des bains d'Aix-en-Savoie sur l'exercice de 1817," AD Savoie, 1FS 2803.

63. The speculators of Aix-les-Bains had been unable to report to the King of Sardinia that the spa had produced a great profit in 1816, despite an increased number of visitors and a rise in the prices of all bathing operations. Work and maintenance related to the spa had simply absorbed more money than anyone had anticipated. It was not, however, with any eagerness that the doctors and administrators of Aix made this report to their sovereign. On the contrary, they did everything possible to cast the spa's fiscal situation in the best possible light, hoping to garner still more royal revenues for the coming years. Various of Aix's local speculators, especially Drs. Joseph and Charles Despine, actually went so far as to "pad" the spa's yearly accounts. Together, the two doctors put more than 1,000 francs into the bathing establishment's till to offset the shorter term insolvencies of 1817. ATN Aix, livre 26.

64. Ibid.

65. The spa at Aix-les-Bains required a great deal of patience from these fledgling entrepreneurs. Due to ongoing work projects, the high cost of administration, and, as the administrators would later claim, the insalubrious reputation from which the municipality

suffered on account of its uncontrolled population of transient indigents, the bathing facility lost money throughout this period. The deficit at the thermal establishment amounted to more than 10,000 livres by 1821.

66. With the goal of "furnishing a sum of 50,000 livres for the completion of the thermal establishment," the *société* was organized on a basis of one hundred shares, each of which sold for five hundred livres. Each *action* was guaranteed an annual return of 5 percent by the Sardinian government, and the administrative commission of the thermal establishment was authorized to direct all aspects of the *société*. Every member of the commission purchased at least one five-hundred-livre action, and the senior Dr. Despine bought two. Dr. Charles Despine bought six shares in his name, investing 3,000 livres in the enterprise. His brother, the second son of Dr. Joseph Despine, bought one share. The rest of the medical community at Aix-les-Bains took interest in the *société* too. Drs. Vidal, Dronchat, Dardel, Guilland, Perrier, and Desmaison were all among the first investors in the venture. "Acte social de la compagnie d'actionnaires pour l'améliorations des bains d'Aix-en-Savoie," AD Savoie, 1FS 2801.

67. For an outstanding account of Évian's stunted development during the later eighteenth century, see Beaurepaire, *Histoire et description des sources minérales d'Évian, d'Amphion, et du Chablais.*

68. For a brief history of this speculative group's leader and his interest in Évian, see Bougy, *Évian et ses environs.*

69. Later in the century, when Évian's developers finally found a successful strategy to exploit their mineral water sources, their efforts were furthered by a quorum of ambitious spa doctors. Probably no *médecin d'eaux* of the later period was more prolific in matters of research and publication than Évian's Dr. Jean-François Chiais. In a mere decade, the busy practitioner's work included *Les eaux d'Évian dans l'arthritisme, la neurasthénie, la goutte; Neurasthénie et goutte: Leur traitement par les eaux d'Évian; L'action réductrice des eaux d'Évian sur l'acide urique et les corps voisins; Les conditions de traitement d'Évian-les-Bains; La goutte à Évian- les-Bains;* and *L'eau d'Évian.*

70. For archival letters and reports detailing the debate among Évian's speculators over the need for casino facilities, see ADHS, 4M 231.

71. Institut Français d'Architecture, *Villes d'eaux en France,* 318, 319.

72. Martin-Fugier, *La bourgeoisie,* 120.

73. Ibid.

74. Ibid.

75. Ibid., 121.

76. I discuss this medical emphasis in detail in chapter 4.

77. While there was much that indeed was new about Paris's social spaces after midcentury, I do not wish to suggest that the city's geography—or that of the spas which I will treat below—was a complete departure from what had been there before the Second Empire. Obviously, even though my line of argument is far more concerned with ruptures and changes, I do believe that a great many important continuities existed throughout the century with respect to social space and public life. But the combined efforts of Napoleon III, his prefect of the Seine, Baron Haussmann, and scores of wealthy speculators, did indeed rebuild and physically alter the landscape of Paris in a period of less than two decades. By cutting swaths of enormous boulevards through the city, which facilitated communication in the affluent western districts, created controlled vistas of imperial grandeur, and disentangled the traditional quarters of work and revolution, the makers of the new Paris created a spectacular array of new social spaces for the practice of public life.

The standard work on the Haussmannization of Paris is still Pinkney, *Napoleon III and the Rebuilding of Paris*. For a useful discussion of class and the new city, see Clark, *The Painting of Modern Life: Paris and the Art of Manet and His Followers*.

78. A marked proliferation of police surveillance and repression also characterized the period of the Second Empire in France, particularly the decade of the 1850s. The imperial regime passed a variety of strict laws—against the press, group assemblies, political discussions, immoral acts, and seditious speech—whose impact on public life was vast indeed. Tens of thousands of public settings were actively monitored by governmental spies, and huge numbers of these same were closed for "security reasons." For a fascinating treatment of imperial surveillance and the oppositional practices it engendered in that most French of institutions—the café—see Barrows, "Nineteenth-Century Cafés." For accounts of this repression more generally, see Merriman, *The Agony of the Republic;* Margadant, *French Peasants in Revolt;* and Agulhon, *The Republic in the Village*.

79. For a discussion of fashion, comportment, and class in the Bois de Boulogne, see P. Perrot, *Fashioning the Bourgeoisie*, 308–10.

80. On consumer culture, its relationship to economic change, and gender, see Furlough, *Consumer Cooperation in France: The Politics of Consumption*. On furniture as an ever changing mode for signing the bourgeoisie, see Auslander, *Taste and Power*.

81. On gentility as well as the rising costs of bourgeois life, see Davidoff, *The Best Circles: Women and Society in Victorian Britain*.

82. On the ways that fashion determined bourgeois identity and the bourgeoisie determined fashion, see P. Perrot, *Fashioning the Bourgeoisie*.

83. For an interesting examination of women's displacement from economic to cultural "activity," see B. Smith, *Ladies of the Leisure Class*. For two interesting treatments of the English case that retain much importance for the French scene in more or less the same period, see Davidoff and Hall, *Family Fortunes: Men and Women of the English Middle Class, 1750–1850*, as well as Gillis, "The Cultural Production of Family Identities in Nineteenth-Century Britain."

84. On the links between consumer culture and domesticity, see Auslander, "The Gendering of Consumer Practices in Nineteenth-Century France."

85. Daumard writes, with respect to the bourgeoises of this period and the homes created by them, that "[m]any wives had a decisive effect on the careers of their husbands." *Les bourgeois et la bourgeoisie* 213.

86. For a good summary of women's part in the nineteenth-century consumer revolution, see B. Smith, *Changing Lives: Women in European History since 1700*, 327–30.

87. On the differences in domestic interiors between the upper and middle bourgeoisie, see Daumard, *Les bourgeois et la bourgeoisie*, 111–15.

88. Leora Auslander has been especially influential in broadening the current debate about gender and consumer culture. See in particular her essay, "Gendering of Consumer Practices," 79–113.

89. A still important discussion of the social uses of leisure is Veblen, *Theory of the Leisure Class: An Economic Study of Institutions*. A more contemporary and theoretically challenging work that deals with many of the same issues is Pierre Bourdieu, *Distinction: A Social Critique of the Judgement of Taste* (Cambridge: Harvard University Press, 1984).

90. My uses of the concept of a creative and artful deployment of leisure follows Pierre Bourdieu.

91. Eugen Weber notes that many middle bourgeois and of the latter three decades of the nineteenth century actually faked *séjours*. By closing their shades and sneaking into

their homes through rear entrances, these persons tried to convince their neighbors that they were away on holiday. *France, Fin de siècle,* 190.

92. Daumard, *Les bourgeois et la bourgeoisie,* 103–5.

93. I thank Leif Brown for his insightful discussions of various nineteenth-century American social spaces which he has characterized as "etiquette books." In particular, I acknowledge his paper "Golden Gate Park as Etiquette Book, 1870–1900," unpublished.

94. Forestier, *Des promenades d'Aix-les-Bains ou le nouveau guide pratique, médical, et pittoresque,* 34.

95. Ibid.

96. *Lettres de Jules Ferry, 1846–1893.*

97. Yet the medical pole of the spa experience, as we shall see in the next chapters, did even more by way of grafting to leisure an ordered measure of the bourgeoisie's productive ethos. Because even at the fin de siècle, when proportionally fewer spa visitors took medical cures than had been the case in the earlier half the century, there remained at the heart of the thermal vacation at least some medical rationale. One cured, or one's ailing family members took the waters, or one simply saw sick people while one waited to take a seat for dinner or board an excursion boat. Whatever the case might have been, the spa vacation sustained an unmissable association with the forces of science and productivity.

98. AM Aix, I120.

99. Vast sums of money were also expended on the creation of railroads to serve the spas of this period. My focus in this section of the chapter, however, does not permit any extended discussion of rail development. It is my belief that the history of railroads, while interesting in the sense that they facilitated the process of getting to a spa and made travel less expensive, is not central to the issues of this chapter.

100. Before the nationalization of its waters by imperial decree on 12 June 1811, Plombières's spa had been a communal possession. Of the 150 thermal establishments in France in 1857, only 6 belonged to the state; 10 belonged to *départements* and 20 to communes. The rest were owned by private parties. Institut Français d'Architecture, *Villes d'eaux en France,* 31, 336.

101. From 1857, when he first called for the park and allocated 110,000 francs for the work, Napoleon III followed the park's progress very closely. Armand Wallon, in his *La vie quotidienne dans les villes d'eaux,* mentions that contemporaries felt that Baron Haussmann himself had been consulted for the park's design. The prefect, apparently, was instrumental in bringing a musical *kiosque* and meandering stream to the park.

102. Wright, *France in Modern Times,* 162–63. For more information on the economic relationship between the state and private interests in the "liberal" phase of the Second Empire, see Pinkney, *Napoleon III.*

103. Wallon has more details about the leasing arrangements between the imperial government and the concern of Lebobe, Calloue, et Cie. See *La vie quotidienne,* 40–42.

104. Institut Français d'Architecture, *Villes d'eaux en France,* 358. At the end of 1860, as Wallon notes, the four doctors of the emperor, Andral, Jobert de Lamballe, le baron Larrey, and Conneau, decided that their patient had had enough of Plombières's water. To remedy his "distressing anemia" and generally poor health, the imperial doctors sent their charge to Vichy. *La vie quotidienne,* 62.

105. Institut Français d'Architecture, *Villes d'eaux en France,* 64.

106. Ibid., 28, 29, 31, 358.

107. The growth of its resident population was extremely high in these five years too:

from 3,741 in 1861 to 5,666 in 1866. Construction trades, medicine, and general service were all booming enterprises at and around the spa. Institut Français d'Architecture, *Villes d'eaux en France,* 29.

108. For a fascinating history of one of the most successful independent spas of this period, written by a family member of the great Dr. Bouloumie, whose speculative endeavors almost single-handedly created the *ville d'eaux* of Vittel, see Bouloumie, *Histoire de Vittel.*

109. The meeting between Rousselon and Napoleon III is alluded to in a letter of 7 October 1864 that the French minister of agriculture, commerce, and public works sent to Rousselon. AN, F14 8279.

110. Ibid. For additional details concerning this proposal, see AD Haute-Savoie, 5M 122.

111. For a thorough discussion of public utility decrees and their political applications during the period, see Tamara Whited, "A Question Almost Political: Reforesting and Reclaiming Alpine France, 1860–1882," *Proceedings of the 1992 Annual Meeting of the Western Society for French History* (Riverside, CA: University of California, Riverside, 1993). For relevant archival materials on public utility decrees with respect to the spas of France in this period, see AN, F14 8259 and F14 8268.

112. Prospectus of the *Société Chablaisienne,* AN, F14 8279. For additional archival materials related to the developmental history of Évian in the period, see especially AD Haute-Savoie, 5M 113.

113. For other archival information on the thermal establishment at Évian-les-Bains, as well as an administrative history of the decision to bottle and market mineral water from the sources, see AD Haute-Savoie, M5 5 4.1

114. For a contemporary discussion of spa development at Vittel, see Patezon, *Guide aux eaux minérales de Vittel.* A similar study for another successful independent spa of the period is Debout, *Guide médical à Contrexéville* and, by the same author, *Thirty-Five Years at Contrexéville.*

115. See Haug, *Leisure and Urbanism,* for a thoughtful discussion of the importance of railroads to the development of leisure locales.

116. For Vittel's "official" history, in which the spa's development is painted as an almost overnight occurrence, see Bouloumie, *Histoire de Vittel.*

117. Ninety-six percent of the Savoy voted on 22 and 23 April 1860 for the annexation. Of the 1091 electors at Aix-les-Bains who were asked if they wanted to be annexed to France, only 13 responded in the negative. The plebiscite, like so many others conducted by the French emperor and other European statesmen of this period, was resoundingly successful, at least in part, because it was "arranged." Beyond the issue of how strong sentiments really were in favor of annexation, there was no doubt that the issue of reattachment to France was decided well before the plebiscite. In a meeting between Count Cavour and a representative of Napoleon III held at Turin on 24 March 1860, the two states agreed to the transfer of the Savoy and Nice. The annexations were a repayment to Napoleon for the help he had given to the Sardinians in the war against Austria. For more information on the plebiscite at Aix-les-Bains and the particular arrangements of the annexation, see Leguay, *Histoire d'Aix-les-Bains,* 106–10. For a general discussion of plebiscites in this period, particularly as they were used by the Second Empire, see Zeldin, *The Political System of Napoleon III.* A good administrative summary of the law that declared Aix-les-Bains's thermal establishment to be a work of public utility can be found in "Suppléments de crédit," a report filed by the French minister of agriculture, commerce, and public works for 1864, AN, F14 8261.

118. The weekly meetings of the administrative commission at Aix-les-Bains saw a great deal of discussion about the need for better walking paths, a public park, reading rooms, theaters, etc. The medical directors' annual reports, both to state officials in Turin and Paris, were equally concerned with public space. See AD Savoie, 1FS 2803, and ATN Aix, livre 26.

119. The Grand Hotel was built by a set of financial arrangements that were all too familiar to Aix's counterparts in the "French System." Underwritten by the Sardinian Prime Minister, Count Cavour, a local *société d'actionnaires* was constituted to pay for the facility in 1854.

120. Built by one Friedrich Weinbrenner in 1809, the Badischer Hof was a standard of hotel design for the first half of the nineteenth century and beyond. Institut Français d'Architecture, *Villes d'eaux en France*, 112.

121. Leguay, *Histoire d'Aix-les-Bains*, 224. The rise of hotels in the Belle Époque was dramatic at Aix-les-Bains: there were thirty-one in 1875 and seventy-three in 1921. The number of private *pensions* saw proportional decreases in the same period.

122. For the history of the founding of the casino, see "Acte de formation de la Société du cercle, 20 April 1824," AD Savoie, BC 51. For a fascinating history of the facility throughout the nineteenth and twentieth centuries, see also Frieh, *Le grand cercle d'Aix-les-Bains: Histoire d'un casino.* This work is particularly rich for its vast utilization of archival sources, many of which are reproduced in full or at least cited at great length. (Mme Frieh has a personal collection of guidebooks, regulations, photocopied archival materials, postcards, newspapers, photographs, and medical papers related to Aix-les-Bains, its casino, and its thermal establishment. Because of her graciousness and knowledge, I was able to draw liberally on this collection and find my way more easily through holdings in Aix, Chambéry, Brisson-Saint-Innocent, and Annecy. She is a vitally important source of information on the history of French thermalism since 1800.)

123. For the financial and administrative history of the casino, see Frieh, *Le grand cercle.*

124. The enterprising speculators who built Aix's casino were among the first locals to plumb the depths of the state's commitment to the city after the annexation. As early as the spring of 1863, these entrepreneurs filed a report with the French minister of agriculture asking that the government accord an annual sum of 10,000 francs to the casino. This allocation, according to the casino's representatives, was needed to support the requisite maintenance of the building. Traditionally paid for out of the *société*'s budget, maintenance more or less suddenly seemed like an onerous responsibility for the casino to bear, especially when, as the report notes "there was an incontestable solidarity between the prosperity of the casino and that of the thermal establishment." The *actionnaires* minced no words as they finished their argument for state subsidization, declaring that "if one of these establishments is in any way allowed to decline, the other will too, and the state, as the proprietor of the baths, must necessarily have a great interest in assisting . . . the casino." See report of 25 March 1863, AN, F14 8260.

125. AN, F14 8262.

126. Ibid.

127. And, as the five final years of the 1860s would show, the fiscal disappointment of 1866 was the beginning of a trend rather than some aberration. In the summer of 1870—August and September having seen far less business due to the Franco-Prussian War—receipts were only 98,509 francs. The summer before, however, they were at almost the same figure as they had been in the first summer after the annexation—before the establishment had even been completed. AM Aix, I120.

128. *Les embellissements d'Aix-les-Bains.* The author wanted to be anonymous, signing his work only as "un baigneur." He was, in fact, one Comte de Quinsonas. All the following quotations from this pamphlet are taken from pp. 23, 24, 30, 31.

129. An original of this publication is contained within AN, F14 8262.

130. AN, F14 8260. The architect, who had been retained by the French government since 1860 to work exclusively on matters pertaining to the thermal establishment, made it clear in his report that the municipal council of Aix had ordered his study and readily endorsed its results.

131. The plans for the park at Aix-les-Bains are contained in a report filed by the French minister of public works, 6 August 1879, AN, F14 8260. Because these plans are both huge and fragile, I was unable to arrange for their reproduction. Thus my complicated and perhaps meaningless use of terms like "front" and "back" in describing the park. By "back" I mean the end of the park that faces in the direction of the municipality and the thermal establishment. By "front" I mean the end of the park that looks out and away from the civic center.

132. This summary of the Revel plan is taken from a report entitled "Copie des notes concernant les réclamations de la ville d'Aix à l'état." The report is not dated, but it is attached to an administrative cover letter whose vital information is the following: 7 April 1876, Versailles, AN, F14 8260.

133. This public utility decree is mentioned in an 11 December 1866 letter from the minister of public works to the ministre président le conseil d'état. AN, F14 8262.

134. The minutes from the prefect's 28 September and 2 October 1868 meetings with Aix's municipal council are quoted liberally in "Copie des notes concernant les réclamations de la ville d'Aix à l'état." AN, F14 8260. The full text of this meeting, in addition to a vast trove of correspondence relating to the park project, is available at AM, Aix.

135. Only because the prefect "insiste très vivement pour l'acceptation du projet du gouvernement . . . que après un troisième vote seulement à la même séance qu'il a obtenu la majorité d'une voisé." Ibid.

136. Municipal leaders had wanted a "modern" building, constructed in the imperial style, that would facilitate Aix's transformation into a great capital among the *villes d'eaux.* The chateau of the Marquis, which became Aix's *hôtel de ville* in this period and continues in that capacity to the present, had housed Aix's first casino from 1824–49.

137. My description of this park is distilled from contemporaries' comments, contained within "Plan général de l'alimentation de l'établissement thermal et du parc annexe à cet établissement," "Copie des notes concernant les réclamations de la ville d'Aix à l'état," and the 16 November 1878 meeting of the Conseil municipal of Aix-les-Bains. AN, F14 8260. For matters specifically pertaining to the financial arrangements between Aix-les-Bains and the French government on the building of the park, see AN, F14 8261 and F14 8262.

138. AN, F14 8260.

139. The budget for the park was 75,000 francs; in point of fact, the imperial government only spent 70,242. AN, F14 8262. For a good administrative summary of the state's financial dealings with Aix in this period, see in the same carton a report dated 20 April 1876.

140. Municipal Council meeting at Aix-les-Bains, 7 April 1876, AN, F14 8260.

141. For a good summary of thermal nationalism from the French point of view, see Wallon, *La vie quotidienne,* 93–97. See also E. Weber, *France, Fin de Siècle,* especially his chapter entitled "Curism and Tourism."

142. Wallon, *La vie quotidienne,* 119.

143. Weisz, "Water Cures and Science," 397.

144. Leguay, *Histoire d'Aix-les-Bains,* 212.

145. Wallon, *La vie quotidienne,* 118. Wallon estimates, based on official reports from the period, that some 325,000 of the larger cohort of 800,000 summer visitors came to the *villes d'eaux* without bothering to take the waters.

CHAPTER THREE

1. Privacy utterly lacked the moral and medical meanings that it would acquire in the first years of the nineteenth century. Instead, this was a society whose courtly customs expressed a certain contempt for closed doors and the whisperings they concealed. The intellectual tenor of the age reflected the same sentiments that the spa basins did. Rousseau and his advocacy of transparent, unmasked relationships, between not only individuals but also citizens and their governors, reinforced and politicized the concept of public life. Indeed, the permeability of public and private life, as the French Revolution would make clear enough, was in the eighteenth century a social credo if not a political one. Rousseau's *The Social Contract* makes a variety of explicit references to the politics of public life. His instructions to the Polish government, published as *The Government of Poland* in 1770, are an even more direct superimposition of politics onto public life. In this treatise, Rousseau calls for public games, festivals, ceremonies, etc., all to be played out in support of a particular polity. For a path-breaking discussion of the public nature of life in the French Revolution, see Hunt, *Politics, Culture, and Class.* See also Hunt's essay, "The Unstable Boundaries of the French Revolution," 16–29.

2. At Bath in England, for example, private dinners, parties, and dances were strictly outlawed for most of the eighteenth century. Beau Nash, director of the bathing establishment and a veritable social chairman at Bath in this period, posted a list of eleven rules that governed social interaction. These rules told visitors to conduct their social exercises in the public rooms of the "Pump Room" or ballroom. For a sympathetic but good contemporary biography of Richard "Beau" Nash, see Goldsmith, *The Life of Richard Nash of Bath.* For a general treatment of English spas in the eighteenth century and later, see Addison, *English Spas.* For an account of Bath in the eighteenth century that links its social practices to the architecture of the period, see Gadd, *Georgian Summer: Bath in the Eighteenth Century.*

3. Even more than under the Old Regime, the ideology of the French Revolution endeavored to enforce the permeability of public and private life. Particularly in the more radical phase of the Revolution, privacy came to be seen as a counter-revolutionary impulse. To be of the nation was to make one's life a public and transparent project. Doubtlessly, as Lynn Hunt has contended, the excesses of the French Revolution did much to reconfigure society along more private lines. That the Revolution created rather than accelerated a tendency toward private life, however, is a far more complicated matter.

4. Even at the French court, where, particularly after the coronation of Charles X, no effort was spared in trying to resuscitate the luster of Old Regime society, a more bourgeois pattern of sociability, which emphasized familial privacy over public display, was practiced in the 1820s. Many social functions at court were made so exclusive that hardly anyone but family members was included. Through much of the eighteenth century, gaming and dancing had brought the French court to a festive assemblage no less than three nights each week. Participation in this revelry was considered nothing short of a duty for the

nobles in residence at Versailles and Paris. Before the French Revolution, the frequency of such soirees was reduced to a weekly occurrence, and the population in attendance declined too. Bonaparte maintained the custom as did Louis XVIII. Charles X was far less taken with this form of court sociability, and he went a long way toward abandoning it in 1826. From then until the July Revolution, the soirees were held no more than three times each year. Beyond the royal family, guests were limited to visiting sovereigns, high officials, and the king's most intimate circle. As historian Anne Martin-Fugier has noted, "to be invited to one of these small parties was a mark of extreme favor because one would be sharing the privacy of the royal family." For a thorough discussion of social practices among the privileged classes in the Restoration, see Martin-Fugier, *La bourgeoisie.*

5. Much more than had been the case in the eighteenth century, upper-class homes of the early nineteenth century accentuated privacy. Working areas of the home were split off from the rooms in which the family actually lived. Similarly, rooms for congregating, ceremony, and entertaining, like the parlor and dining room, were discreetly situated at some distance from bedrooms and bathrooms. Moderately private but highly specialized sites within some homes, like libraries, billiard rooms, studies, and offices, offered refuge when even one's own family was too public. For an insightful discussion of domestic space in this period, see Michelle Perrot, "At Home," in *History of Private Life.* For the best work on the gendering of domestic space in the homes of the Restoration era and the 1830s, see Roger-Henri Guerrand's essay "Private Spaces," in *History of Private Life.* For fascinating and related literature concerned with the home as a vital element in bourgeois identity and expression, see Davidoff and Hall, *Family Fortunes;* B. Smith, *Ladies of the Leisure Class;* and Gillis, "Cultural Production."

6. For a discussion of the bourgeois sociability and *cercles* of this period, see Agulhon, *Le cercle dans la France bourgeoise: Étude d'une mutation de sociabilité.*

7. This complaint was so worded in sundry reports made by *médecins d'eaux* of this period to their speculative, administrative, and governmental colleagues. This citation comes from AD Savoie, 1FS 2803.

8. Ibid.

9. "Rapport médical sur la saison des bains d'Aix-en-Savoie, 1823," AD Savoie, 1FS 2803.

10. Ibid. This specific phrase comes from "Rapport historico-médical sur la saison d'Aix-en-Savoie, 1819."

11. Report to the prefect of Allier, 8 August 1827, AD Allier, series X.

12. "Rapport du médecin inspecteur des bains d'Aix-en-Savoie sur l'exercice de l'année 1818," AD Savoie, 1FS 2803.

13. "Rapport historico-médical sur la saison d'Aix-en-Savoie, 1819," AD Savoie, 1FS 2803.

14. Not all poor visitors were subject to these barriers. Those who either paid for their treatments or simply sought a reduction in the tariff were spared segregationist prescriptions.

15. Drs. Joseph and Charles Despine, *"Répertoire des malades vus à Aix-en-Savoie en 1820,"* AMB, uncataloged medical registries.

16. Ibid.

17. Ibid. This prescription apparently both pleased and irritated Jeanne Davis. The domestic took to the open bath with such gusto that she stayed in longer than she ought to have. Despine had to do a follow-up consultation with her and noted that "she spent too much time in the hot bath—contracted a rash."

18. Ibid.

19. Article 12 of the "Règlement pour la police intérieure des bains d'Aix-en-Savoie, 1826," AD Savoie, 1FS 2801.

20. Prefects were forever stalling this review of indigent credentials. Wherever possible, they would claim that the spas of their *département* were full and that needy bathers ought to be sent to another *département*. Jean-Marie Ginaldin, a wounded veteran of the Brigade of the Savoy, spent six frustrating months in a bureaucratic tangle whose effect was too keep him from taking a spa cure. A resident of Chambéry, the retired officer first inquired about a gratis cure at Aix-les-Bains some four months prior to the opening of the thermal season. Informing the intendant-general of the Savoy that he served two decades in the Sardinian army and had been "gravely indisposed," Ginaldin presented materials that supported his character, poverty, and medical necessity. His dossier grew throughout the spring as further letters and testimonials added to its bulk. Still, his wish "to be admitted without tariff to the thermal baths at Aix, in hopes of regaining [his] health and resuming [his] military service" languished under perpetual review. What finally brought action on his application was the letter he addressed directly to the king of Sardinia. Within two weeks of that plea, Lieutenant Ginaldin was himself flooded with official correspondence. The commandant of the Brigade of the Savoy, the intendant-general of the Savoy, and the president of the administrative commission at Aix all sent him letters of acceptance in early July. Sacred papers in hand, the lieutenant arrived directly at Aix to begin his treatment. AD Savoie, 1FS 2822.

21. Many indigents arrived at a spa bearing a medical report that was detailed and convincing enough to gain them access to an establishment's better facilities.

22. "Règlement pour la police intérieure des bains d'Aix-en-Savoie, 1826," AD Savoie, 1FS 2801. For more details on indigence at Aix-les-Bains in this period, see AD Savoie, 1FS 2822. Specifically, note the case of Joseph Machet, April 1840. These security measures were widely publicized at Aix-les-Bains. The rules of the establishment were posted at the bathing facility and other places in the community.

23. Justification given by spa administrators at Aix-les-Bains for the "Règlement pour la police intérieure des bains d'Aix-en-Savoie, 1826," AD Savoie, 1FS 2801.

24. Ibid., article 6. For the only example of one of these reports that I have been able to find, see the list of *numéro d'ordres* for 20 July 1840. AD Savoie, 1FS 2801.

25. Ibid.

26. This surveillance directive comes from the 1829 report of the medical director of the thermal establishment at Aix-les-Bains. AD Savoie, 1FS 2803.

27. For a still valuable discussion of upper-class perceptions of the urban poor in this period, see Louis Chevalier, *Laboring Class and Dangerous Classes* (New York: Fertig, 1973). The best work on the interventionist policies of the French state vis-à-vis the working-class family is Lynch, *Family, Class, and Ideology in Early Industrial France: Social Policy and the Working-Class Family, 1825–1848*. For the seminal statement on the issues of power, space, administration, and surveillance in the social institutions of early nineteenth-century France, see Foucault, *Discipline and Punish*. For an insightful history of the control of prostitution in this period which is sympathetic to Foucault, see Corbin, *Les filles de noce*. For a discussion of these issues, beyond Lynch's superior work, which relates to the working-class family, see Jacques Donzelot, *The Policing of Families* (New York: Pantheon, 1979). For a seminal essay on discipline and power in the nineteenth-century workplace, see Michelle Perrot, "Three Ages of Industrial Discipline."

28. Letter of 25 July 1822 from J. Degaillon, Mayor of Aix-les-Bains, AD Savoie, 1FS 2804.

29. "Rapport médical sur les bains d'Aix-en-Savoie pour l'année 1829," AD Savoie, 1FS 2803.

30. "Extrait des registres des délibérations de la commission administrative des bains d'Aix, 4 mars 1824," AD Savoie, 1FS 2804.

31. Barthès, *Guide pratique des malades aux eaux de Vichy,* 30.

32. Wallon, *La vie quotidienne,* 197.

33. Barthès, *Guide pratique,* 30.

34. Letter of 28 August 1828 from the administrative commission of Aix-les-Bains to the king of Sardinia, ATN Aix, livre 26.

35. AN, F14 8278.

36. Letter of 28 August 1828 from the administrative commission of Aix-les-Bains to the king of Sardinia, ATN Aix, livre 26.

37. Report of 21 August 1837, AD Allier, series X.

38. Ibid.

39. I am following Michel Foucault in this understanding of the panopticon. For Foucault's extensive discussion of Bentham and the panopticon, see *Discipline and Punish.*

40. "Rapport médical sur les bains d'Aix-en-Savoie pour l'année 1828," AD Savoie, 1FS 2803.

41. For a brief treatment of the relationship between eighteenth-century individualism, contamination theory, and the group bed, see Corbin, *Foul and the Fragrant,* 102. The design of the typical spa hospital, while it did feature a system of surveillance, circulation control, and individuation, was still far removed from the cellular spatiality that would characterize such places later in the nineteenth century. For a discussion of the cellular design and its social functions, see Foucault, *Discipline and Punish.* For a more traditional examination of hospital design, see Olivier Faure, *Genèse de l'hôpital moderne: Les hospices civils de Lyon de 1802 à 1845* (Paris: Presses Universitaires de Lyon, 1981).

42. AH Vichy, 1J.

43. AM Aix, I120.

44. The solution spa developers found in hospitalization would remain fundamentally unaltered well into the twentieth century, although segregating the poor was occasionally a politically contested practice when it was taken to mean that access to the medicinal virtues of mineral water had in fact been limited. Particularly in the wake of the Revolution of 1848, radical and certain liberal critics denounced the fact that French indigents had so little access to the medical benefits of the country's spas. In 1849, for example, a rare government official spoke out on behalf of increased indigent access to the spas. One Jules François, engineer and chief of mines for the *département* of the Vosges, in a published report of that year, contended that thermal spas should be completely open, in all of their facilities, especially to poor persons needing cures. For his passionate plea on this issue, see AN, F14 8278.

45. This description of spa interiors, authored by a *médecin d'eaux,* referred to thermal establishments in Europe generally. "Rapport médical sur la saison des bains d'Aix-en-Savoie, 1829," AD Savoie, 1FS 2803.

46. This description of private bath cabinets and *baignoires* is taken from the "Prospectus pour l'établissement d'une société d'actionnaires pour l'amélioration des bains d'Aix-en-Savoie, 23 July 1822, AD Savoie, 1FS 2801.

47. The *médecins d'eaux* of Aix-les-Bains reported that their basin was no longer used with any frequency by the middle 1820s. "Rapport de la commission administrative des bains d'Aix, 1824," AD Savoie, 1FS 2803.

48. "Prospectus pour l'établissement d'une société d'actionnaires pour l'amélioration des bains d'Aix-en-Savoie, 23 July 1822," AD Savoie, 1FS 2801. Too frequent bathing in this period was taken as a sign of invalidism. Daily baths often meant that one's health was fragile or even failing. Just to prepare a bath at home was a major endeavor, requiring the assistance of several domestics. For an interesting cultural, social, and medical history of domestic bathing in this period, see Léonard, *Archives du corps.*

49. In 1823 the doctors of Aix-les-Bains estimated that some three thousand baths were administered to *voyageurs* at their hotels and *pensions.* "Séance de la commission administrative des bains d'Aix, 26 April 1824," ATN Aix, livre 26. This type of bathing was a variation on a standard practice in many French urban centers of the period. In Paris and other major cities in the 1820s, bathtubs and the water for them were rented when needed. One of some 1,000 contractors, individuals, or companies whose business it was to lease collapsible tubs and warm water would be contracted for the specific date on which the rare bath was to be taken. As late as July 1852, the council on hygiene for the city of Nantes could note, "Simple baths are more an object of luxury than necessity; the vast majority of men and women have never taken a bath, and one can see that they are not at all worse for this lack." Léonard, *Archives du corps,* 119.

50. For a brief discussion of the genesis of spa architecture in France, see Institut Français d'Architecture, *Villes d'eaux en France,* 68–73. Because the new spas at Vichy and Luchon, completed in the first two decades of the nineteenth century, both featured central basins surrounded by private baths, the authors of *Villes d'eaux en France* argue that these establishments were more traditional than they were modern in their designs. I argue that the basins at these spas, which were never used for bathing, were strictly ornamental. Thus private bathing, not its collective and traditional counterpart, was the point of the Vichy and Luchon designs. The architects of these spas, even as they paid homage to certain conventional features in spa interior design, were clearly creating spaces that departed from tradition.

51. Ibid.

52. Ibid.

53. Report of 27 June 1818, AD Allier, series X.

54. "Rapport médical sur la saison des bains d'Aix-en-Savoie, 1829," AD Savoie, 1FS 2803.

55. Letter to the prefect of the Allier, 9 February 1819, AD Allier, series X.

56. "Séance de la commission administrative des bains d'Aix, 7 March 1817," ATN Aix, livre 26.

57. Ibid. Dismantled in the later early 1830s when the service requirements at the spa rendered it too inconvenient, the barrier at the midpoint of corridor E, nevertheless, was an important first step in the direction of more discreet bathing at Aix-les-Bains.

58. This phrase was routinely used by spa doctors and developers when referring to bourgeois bathers.

59. "Séance de la commission administrative des bains d'Aix, 7 March 1817," ATN Aix, livre 26.

60. Administrative surveillance was directed equally at the various personnel of a thermal establishment. Developers were universally concerned that service be conducted on an efficient and proper enough level to please their visitors. Reports from Aix-les-Bains in this period suggest that surveillance of this type was relatively successful. Aix's *économe,* M. Cochet, reported one such lapse to the commission in its meeting of 4 September 1829. "Today, at ten in the morning," the *économe* observed, "the porters Damois and

Magnin scuffled at the establishment's entrance and caused minor injuries to each other." Cochet further noted that the details of this altercation were communicated to him by one of the *huissiers.* After complaining that "Magnin is the source of daily unrest and altercations among the staff of porters," Cochet convinced the commission to suspend both of the errant porters for a period of two weeks. "Séance de la commission administrative des bains d'Aix, 4 September 1829," ATN Aix, livre 26. On another occasion, the watchful administration reprimanded one if its *doucheurs,* M. Joseph Philippe, for failing to extend the correct "*politesse* to a woman lodged at the Boiquin residence." Not only was this employee suspended, but the commission asked that he approach the offended guest with both an excuse and an apology. "Séance de la commission administrative des bains d'Aix, 28 July 1831." For this and scores of other examples of the spa's surveillance system at work against its employees, see ATN Aix, livre 26.

61. Ibid. Spa administrators of this period continued to worry about morality and sexuality even after installing new bath interiors and administrative safeguards. Indeed, the institution of solitary bathing only replaced one form of sexuality with another. Visual and physical contact, at least between opposite sex bathers, was next to impossible in the new spas. But these highly gendered, compartmentalized, and individuated facilities did far less by way of making masturbation or homosexual encounters impossible. To be sure, spa administrators took measures to combat these constructions of bath sexuality too. Indeed, spa privacy was always an inspected condition. Curists were seldom if ever left alone in their cabinets, and it was known that bath givers would enter cabinets without knocking. To avoid an even more dire set of sexual possibilities, curists were not left alone with a single bath technician either. Rather, these spa underlings almost always worked in pairs. While there is scant reason to suspect much misconduct on the part of bath takers or givers—and certainly spa administrators felt that their surveillance systems, rules, and design principles had guaranteed propriety in spa facilities—it is no doubt true that desires, fantasies, and suspicions of a sexual nature flourished in this privatized environment precisely because sexual practice of any kind had become such a taboo.

62. "Séance de la commission administrative des bains d'Aix, 1 July 1831," ATN Aix, livre 26.

63. Granville, *Spas of England,* 380.

64. Such uncharitable descriptions were legion in the private and public writings of spa doctors in the nineteenth century. These specific examples relate to the thermal spa at Bath, England. They come from Barbeau, *Life and Letters,* 53–54; and Granville, *Spas of England,* 378. England's Bath refused to "modernize" its facilities until the late 1860s. No doubt this hesitancy contributed to the great rise of the seaside holiday in England in the intervening years. Unlike the French case, the history of the English seaside has long been a topic of great academic interest. For the best general history of seaside resorts in nineteenth-century England, and particularly for an argument that links the decline of Bath to the rise of Brighton, etc., see Pimlott, *A Social History of the Englishman's Holiday.* A less scholarly complement that includes a number of good illustrations and caricatures from the nineteenth century is Hern, *The Seaside Holiday: The History of the English Seaside Resort.* Two more recent contributions to the literature consider the beginnings of the working-class presence at England's watering places, see J. Walton, *The Blackpool Landlady: A Social History,* and Walvin, *A Social History of the Popular Seaside Holiday.* Three fascinating, contemporary impressions of English coastal watering places in this period are Evans, *An Excursion to Brighton;* Harwood, *On the Curative Influence of the Southern Coast of England;* and Hutton, *A Description of Blackpool.*

65. Granville, *Spas of England,* 380.

66. Ibid.

67. "États des recettes de l'établissement thermal d'Aix-les-Bains de 1816 à 1904," AM Aix, I120.

68. Martin-Fugier, *La bourgeoisie,* 120.

69. AH Vichy, 3L3.

70. AD Allier, series X.

71. "Projet de décret sur l'exploitation, le service médicale, et la police des établissements d'eaux minérales naturelles," article 14, title 3 of article 19 of the law of 14 July 1856, AN, F14 8279.

CHAPTER FOUR

1. At Aix-Les-Bains, for instance, the doctors Despine, whose entrepreneurial, administrative, and architectural skills had created a profitable new spa, were prolific writers of promotional literature over a period of more than thirty years. Dr. Charles Despine's dissertation, filed at Montpellier, was itself a guidebook of sorts. See Charles Despine, *Essai topographique et médical d'Aix-en-Savoie et sur les eaux minérales* (Montpellier, An X). By the middle of the 1830s however, Charles Despine and his son Constant had begun a prolific career in guidebook writing that must have had very few equivalents. Their principal works, which were published in multiple and even annual editions, included *Bulletin des eaux d'Aix-en-Savoie* (Annecy: Burdet, 1836); *Manuel topographique et médical de l'étranger aux eaux d'Aix-en- Savoie; Indicateur médical et topographique d'Aix-les-Bains;* and, with Hyacinthe Audiffred, *L'été à Aix-en-Savoie: Nouveau guide pratique, médical, et pittoresque.*

2. Guides to certain French spas date to the seventeenth century. Dr. J.-B. de Cabias's *Les vertus merveilleuses des bains d'Aix en Savoie,* for example, was clearly an attempt by a local doctor to promote his curative techniques and the mineral waters on which they depended. Similar works were written in this period for Plombières and Vichy. European travel literature generally, of course, predates the seventeenth century. Travel guides were written for most of Europe's pilgrimage sights in the century prior to the Protestant Reformation.

3. Weekly meetings of spa administrators at Aix-les-Bains, where water doctors were eager administrators, prolific publicists, and willing investors, reveal no collective plan for promoting spas. At these meetings, in fact, there was no reference in the 1820s or 1830s to the promotional works of the spa's many doctors/authors. Promoters, it seems, worked on their projects independently of each other or of any grand campaign. ATN Aix, livre 26.

4. Constant Despine, *Manuel topographique,* 149–50.

5. Constant Despine, *Practical Guide to the Baths of Aix in Savoy with All the Necessary Information for Reaching Aix and Taking the Baths,* 29.

6. Dr. G. Mortillet wrote something like a standard line on spa personnel: "Tous portent un uniforme, l'inscription placée sur leur casquette indique à l'étranger leur emploi." *Guide du baigneur et de l'étranger à Aix-les-Bains,* 23.

7. *Chaises-à-porteurs* were used at many although not all French spas. They were also commonly seen at English spas. Their equivalents by the seaside, the peculiar bathing machines, were generally introduced in the 1830s too. For a discussion of the French seaside and bathing machines there, see Corbin, *Le territoire du vide: L'occident et le désir du rivage.*

8. Chasseloup, *Guide pittoresque aux eaux d'Aix-en-Savoie,* 32.

9. Pleasure was more than hinted at in the guides of this period too, but medicine was certainly their major focus. If most authors allocated brief chapters to a discussion of promenades and amusements, they devoted entire sections—sometimes including a dozen or more chapters per section—to detail the medical efficacy of their spas.

10. Even tiny pocket guides, which flourished after about 1850, routinely contained several pages of tables devoted to water analysis. All spas in the period had had their water sources assessed by the French Academy of Medicine.

11. On the French Academy of Medicine's efforts to increase the respect accorded to mineral water curing, see Weisz, *The Medical Mandarins: The French Academy of Medicine in the Nineteenth and Early Twentieth Centuries,* 133–48.

12. Chasseloup, *Guide pittoresque,* 13.

13. Forestier, *Le conseiller du baigneur,* 85.

14. Despine and Audiffred, *L'été à Aix-en-Savoie,* 192.

15. For an excellent account of the French discovery and reaction to the demographic transition of the middle and later nineteenth century, see MacLaren, *Sexuality and Social Order: The Debate over the Fertility of Women and Workers in France, 1770–1920.* In particular, the research of spa doctors on the question of feminine fertility and the larger issue of the French birth rate tended to focus on the links between nervousness, hysteria, and infertility. A sampling of this literature for the earlier period should include J. Brachet, *Traité complet de l'hypocondrie, Traité de l'hystérie,* and *Recherches de la nature et le siège de l'hystérie et de l'hypocondrie, et sur l'analogie et les différences de ces deux maladies;* Briquet, *Traité clinique et thérapeutique de l'hystérie;* Corlieu, *Études sur les causes de la mélancolie;* Pierre Dechaux, *Parallèle de l'hystérie et des maladies du col de l'utérus* (Paris: Baillière, 1873); and, for the later period, Barbaud, *Le nervosisme aux stations thermales, La femme aux trois grandes périodes de sa vie,* and *La puberté chez la femme: Étude physiologique, clinique, et thérapeutique;* Borel, *Nervosisme ou neurasthénie: La maladie du siècle et les divers moyens de la combattre;* and Pierre Dechaux, *La femme stérile* (Paris: Baillière, 1882).

16. Despine and Audiffred, *L'été à Aix-en-Savoie,* 188.

17. Ibid.

18. Ibid, 142. Many doctors claimed that tampering with the natural properties of water caused some of its active ingredients to be lost.

19. Guides of the later period, together with the reports that most spas filed with the state and the French Medical Academy, actually tried to chart the curative success of the spas. After detailing the total number of persons who had sought a cure in a given year, these charts broke down the larger cohort of malades according to specific medical complaint. Then, another chart showed the effects of the water cure on each cohort: Was the condition cured, improved, or nonresponsive? Such charts invariably showed a spa to be highly successful.

20. For a brilliant analysis of patient case histories as they were developed as textual dispatchers of empathy, together with other forms of "realism" in the eighteenth century, see Laqueur, "Bodies, Details, and the Humanitarian Narrative," 176–205.

21. Forestier, *Le conseiller du baigneur.*

22. Berthet, *Aix-les-Bains et ses thermes: Traité complet, descriptif, et thérapeutique.*

23. Despine and Audiffred, *L'été à Aix-en-Savoie,* 296–97.

24. On science and medicine and their collaborative characterizations of femininity, see Cynthia Eagle Russett, *Sexual Science: The Victorian Construction of Womanhood* (Cambridge: Harvard University Press, 1989).

25. I will discuss the changing place of bourgeois women with respect to commercial enterprise in chapter 5.

26. Other popular medical guides included Eberhard, *Le livre des gardes-malades et des mères de famille;* Lelièvre, *Médecine usuelle;* and Perussell, *Guide médical et hygiénique de la mère de famille.* Many household guides from the period also contained fairly detailed sections on family medicine.

27. For a discussion of family and home medicine in the eighteenth century, see Coleman, "Health and Hygiene in the Encyclopedia: A Medical Doctrine for the Bourgeoisie."

28. Millet-Robinet, *La maison rustique des dames,* as quoted in Hellerstein, Hume, and Offen, *Victorian Women: A Documentary Account of Women's Lives in Nineteenth-Century England, France, and the United States,* 294.

29. As Cora-Elisabeth Millet-Robinet wrote in her household manual of 1844, "she can then treat uncomplicated cases, which will not get worse if they are well cared for at the outset, and she can then judge when the time has come to call for a doctor's assistance." Hellerstein, Hume, and Offen, *Victorian Women,* 294.

30. For a fascinating theoretical and literary examination of the relationship between medical narratives and the nineteenth-century novel, see Rothfield, *Vital Signs: Medical Realism in Nineteenth-Century Fiction.*

31. On the tactical and social uses of female invalidism for the latter part of the nineteenth century, see Bram Dijkstra, *Idols of Perversity: Fantasies of Feminine Evil in Fin-de-Siècle Culture* (Oxford: Oxford University Press, 1988).

32. This is by no means a suggestion that medical literature or doctors had an estimation of women or their physiology that failed to conform to larger social currents. On the contrary, as Angus MacLaren and others have rightly argued, medical literature was a vital voice in the nineteenth-century discourse of disempowerment that relentlessly surrounded women. I am arguing, however, that women's medical literacy allowed them certain tactical powers within their marriages and their families. As MacLaren notes, sex was one aspect of married life over which a woman—who could claim to have any of sundry nervous conditions or maladies—could use medicine as a means of some control. For an insightful discussion of the relationship between doctors and bourgeois family life in nineteenth-century France, see MacLaren, *Sexuality and Social Order.*

33. MacLaren cites no less an authority on the nineteenth-century family than Michelet as one contemporary critic who felt that husbands were "helpless" before the medically sanctioned powers of their wives. Ibid., 48.

34. Huart, *Physiologie du médecin,* as quoted in MacLaren, *Sexuality and Social Order,* 78. For an interesting analysis of female hysteria in Flaubert's *Madame Bovary,* see Rothfield, *Vital Signs,* chap. 2.

35. Constant Despine, *Indicateur médical et topographique,* 189. Discussions of this sort strongly foreshadowed the debate over male neurasthenia that would so interest French doctors and society in the latter decades of the nineteenth century. As disinterested an authority as *La grande encyclopédie,* by the 1880s, could note that "Academicians, civil servants, and businessmen find in hydrotherapy an effective remedy for malaria *urban et mondaine.*" *La grande encyclopédie* (Paris: H. Lamirault, 1886), 457. Melancholia was also a common justification for a course of sea bathing in this period. See Corbin, *Territoire du vide,* 76.

36. Constant Despine, *Indicateur médical et topographique,* 189.

37. Chasseloup, *Guide pittoresque,* 13.

38. Ibid.

39. Ibid. Here again, there were many parallels to the ways in which seaside watering places were represented and medically understood. See Corbin, *Territoire du vide,* 76.

40. While there is a decided lack of research on bourgeois leisure practice in the first half of the nineteenth century, the vast corpus of scholarship concerned with work suggests that holidays were hardly of central importance to French males in this period. One study of the bourgeoisie of the North has suggested that bourgeois men routinely "boasted that they were the hardest workers in their factories or other enterprises—the first to arrive in the morning and the last to leave at night. . . . [T]heir devotion to industrial time, in which each moment brought a new acquisition, was such that they often surrendered seasonal vacations for work, while their wives and children went to spas." See B. Smith, *Ladies of the Leisure Class,* 21.

41. On women's authority with respect to family budgets, see Daumard, *Les bourgeois et la bourgeoisie en France,* especially p. 193.

42. Here Lombard is referring to Constant Despine, *Manuel topographique.*

43. Lombard, *Une cure aux bains d'Aix-en-Savoie,* 2.

44. Bonjean was at least a self-promoter in this work, although his writing on the bathing facility at Aix-les-Bains was indeed vast. At the bottom of the last page of his introduction to this work, the pharmacist saw fit to encourage his readers, "See my chemical analysis of the waters of Aix-en-Savoie, 1838, and my analysis of the Marlioz spring, 1857." Bonjean, *Guide de l'étranger aux eaux d'Aix-en-Savoie, Chambéry et leurs environs,* 3, 4.

45. L. Brachet, *Aix-les-Bains in Savoy: The Medical Treatment and General Indications.* This work-in-translation was published in French some decades earlier. In the 1880s, it joined scores of other books in a promotional drive to attract English and American patients to French spas.

46. Relations between spa doctors and regular physicians were by no means always good in the nineteenth century. On the contrary, family doctors, who typically earned far less money than their spa counterparts, regularly protested that *médecins d'eaux* engaged in patient-poaching.

47. Constant Despine, *Practical Guide,* 58, 59.

48. Ibid.

49. These statistics are cited in Martin-Fugier, *La bourgeoisie,* 120.

50. Ibid.

51. And this was, of course, a matter of degree. Doctors had long been entrenched at the spas of France, and many of them had labored throughout the eighteenth century in particular to codify and further rationalize their curative systems and techniques. For a discussion of medicalization at the seaside watering places of eighteenth-century England and France, see Corbin, *Territoire du vide,* especially his chapter entitled "La nouvelle harmonie du corps et de la mer," pp. 72-113.

52. The three-week *séjour,* which had been matter of social custom during the Old Regime, persisted as a medical underpinning of the French vacation throughout the nineteenth century and well into the twentieth.

53. The only real debate on the length of the *séjour* revolved around whether or not it was advantageous for curists to follow their stay at a spa with a so-called after-cure. Wealthy doctors of especially wealthy spa-goers tended to advise on behalf of a two-week rest, after the spa *séjour,* at any of Italy's coastal towns.

54. Wallon, *La vie quotidienne,* 191.

55. Discipline in spas, just like factories and other settings where it was installed in

the nineteenth century, was not merely a matter of following a clock. Chapter 2 suggests how surveillance, among other things, saw to the installation of discipline and control in French spas. For a thoughtful analysis of time-discipline in nineteenth-century French industry, see Michelle Perrot, "Three Ages of Industrial Discipline." A seminal work on factory discipline is Thompson, "Time, Work-discipline, and Industrial Capitalism." A good general account of discipline in the industrial revolution is still Pollard, "Factory Discipline in the Industrial Revolution."

56. Forestier, *Le conseiller du baigneur*, 62.

57. Ibid., 85.

58. Ibid.

59. The continued differentiation of hydrotherapeutics was a constant goal of France's Academy of Medicine throughout much of the nineteenth century. See Weisz, "Water Cures and Science: The French Academy of Medicine and Mineral Waters in the Nineteenth Century."

60. Patissier was the most influential hydrologist in France during the first half of the nineteenth century. For a discussion of his influence within the French Academy of Medicine, see Weisz, "Water Cures and Science."

61. Constant Despine, *Manuel topographique*, 167.

62. Ibid., 168.

63. A seminal exploration of the making of the clinical body is Foucault, *Naissance de la clinique*. For an equally wide ranging discussion of medical discourse with respect to the gendered body, see Laqueur, *Making Sex: Sexuality and the Body from the Greeks to Freud*. For an insightful discussion of the construction of a clinical body by eighteenth-century English obstetricians, see Cody, *The Politics of Body Contact: Disciplines of Reproduction in Britain, 1688–1834*.

64. L. Brachet, *Aix-les-Bains in Savoy*, 89.

65. Ibid., 90.

66. Ibid., 91, 92.

67. Berthet, *Aix-les-Bains et ses thermes*, 171.

68. Ibid.

69. This trend, however vast, was never organized at the state level or under the auspices of the French Academy of Medicine. Rather, individual spas and their medical corps instituted such policies more or less on their own. See Weisz, "Water Cures and Science," 401. Although less rigidly enforced at the seaside watering places of this period, medical consultations were certainly encouraged in conjunction with sea bathing both in France and in England. For a discussion of this, see Corbin, *Territoire du vide*, 82, 84, 89.

70. Section 2, article 9 of *Règlement et tarif de l'établissement thermal d'Aix-les-Bains* (Chambéry: Imprimerie de Deletraz, 1834), 10.

71. James Clark, *The Sanative Influence of Climate: With an Account of the Best Places of Resort in England, the South of Europe, etc.*, 27.

72. Chasseloup, *Guide pittoresque*, 13.

73. Noyer, *Lettres topographiques et médicale sur Vichy, ses minérales et leur action thérapeutique sur nos organes*, 191.

74. Arthur X, *Une saison d'eaux à Aix-les-Bains: album caricatural*, 4.

75. Forestier, *Le conseiller du baigneur*, 81.

76. Ibid.

77. Sparks, *The Riviera*, 158.

78. Ibid.

79. Corbin's discussion of medical regimens at the seaside watering places of France and England suggests that sea bathing, rather than being a therapeutic strategy that was to work in conjunction with a host of other prescriptions concerning diet, etc., was the sole prescriptive element in the seaside cure. In fact, Corbin notes, sea bathing was supposed to help one rediscover one's appetite. Corbin, *Territoire du vide*, 76.

80. Chasseloup, *Guide pittoresque*, 26.

81. Ibid.

82. Yeo, *Health Resorts and Their Uses*, 49.

83. Ibid.

84. Ibid.

85. Clark, *Sanative Influence of Climate*, 27, 28.

86. Noyer, *Lettres topographiques*, 195.

87. Yeo, *Health Resorts and Their Uses*, 367.

88. L. Brachet, *Aix-les-Bains in Savoy*, 9.

89. Chasseloup, *Guide pittoresque*, 26.

90. *La grande encyclopédie*, 457.

91. Linn, *The Health Resorts of Europe*, 11.

92. Barthès, *Guide pratique*, 282.

93. Ibid.

94. While doctors at the spas' seaside counterparts clearly had impulses in the direction of a regimented day, they, according to Corbin, typically allowed patients to make major decisions concerning what to do when not curing. Corbin, *Territoire du vide*, 82.

95. Yeo, *Health Resorts and Their Uses*, 367.

96. H. Weber, *Climatotherapy and Balneotherapy*, 364.

97. Yeo, *Health Resorts and Their Uses*, 367.

98. Ibid., 365.

99. Sparks, *The Riviera*, 158.

100. Noyer, *Lettres topographiques*, 195.

101. Ibid.

102. Ibid., 159.

103. Sparks, *The Riviera*, 158.

104. Corbin has shown that this was the case too with respect to seaside resorts: "En contrepartie, le curiste dispose de peu de liberté: le médecin a prescrit la saison, l'heure, la durée, le lieu de ses exercices; il a fixé le nombre de bains de saison." Corbin, *Territoire du vide*, 89.

105. For the bathing patterns of Aix-les-Bains in this period, see any of the published *Bulletins des eaux d'Aix-en-Savoie* that were written by the spa's medical directors. For the particular statistics cited in the text, see Vidal, *Notice historique et médicale sur l'hospice d'Aix en Savoie*, 36, AD Savoie, C51.

106. AD Allier, series X.

107. Dr. James Johnson, *Pilgrimage to the Spas* (London: Highler, 1841), 52.

108. Scheuer, *Guide pratique du baigneur*, 69, 70.

109. Barthès, *Guide pratique*, 238.

110. Johnson, *Pilgrimage to the Spas*, 52.

111. Spa doctors and the French medical community more generally did not entirely agree as to how mineral water worked upon/within the body's organs. Whether it was temperature, mode of delivery (i.e., baths, showers, vapors, massage, etc.), or mineral content, most water doctors of the nineteenth century believed that at least some of hydrother-

apy's success was derived from the skin's absorption of heavily mineralized water. For a concise summary of terms of the debate on the medical working of mineral water, see Vidart, *Considérations générales sur l'hydrothérapie.*

112. Johnson, *Pilgrimage to the Spas,* 60.

113. Ibid.

114. James, *Guide pratique aux eaux minérales,* 49.

115. Weber and Weber, *Eaux minérales et stations climatériques de l'Europe,* 365.

116. Chasseloup, *Guide pittoresque,* 27.

117. Ibid.

118. Bertier, *Compte-rendu des eaux thermales sulfureuses d'Aix en Savoie pendant la saison de 1857 suivi de considérations pratiques sur leur action curative,* 17.

119. Constant Despine, *Practical Guide to the Baths of Aix,* 31.

120. Ibid.

121. Ibid., 32.

122. Or, as one medical promoter from the early 1840s stated it in a newspaper advertisement for his spa, this treatment center was a "piscine d'eau thermale pour la natation et autres exercices gymnastiques." Advertisement published in Annecy newspaper, 2 May 1840, entitled "Notions sur les eaux minérales d'Aix-en-Savoie," AD Savoie, 1FS 2801.

123. On the use of cold water hydrotherapy in public hospitals and asylums in France, see Vidart, *De la cure d'eau froide à l'institut hydrothérapique de Divonne* and *Études pratiques sur l'hydrothérapie, ou traitement des maladies par l'eau froide.* For a discussion of cold water plunging at the seaside watering places of France and England, see Corbin, *Territoire du vide,* 89–96.

124. The greatest influence of Priessnitz in France can be found in Bigel, *Manuel d'hydrosupathie, ou traitement des maladies par l'eau froide suivant la méthode de V. Priessnitz à Graefenberg.* A second important work on cold water hydrotherapy is Baldou, *L'hydrothérapie, méthode rationnelle du traitement par l'eau froide, le régime, et l'exercice.* Perhaps the most widely read French specialist in hydrotherapy, Constantin James, was also a great champion of cold water cures. His notable work on the subject is *Études sur l'hydrothérapie, ou traitement par l'eau froide.*

125. Wright, *Six Months at Graefenberg,* 44. For a more sympathetic account of this and other cold water cures by a French champion of this treatment, see Rul, *Quatre ans à Graefenberg.* Corbin has shown that some of this disempowerment figured into the practice of sea bathing at the watering places of France and England, where bath technicians decided exactly when bathers were to be subjected to a "brutal immersion" in freezing cold sea water. Corbin, *Territoire du vide,* 89.

126. Wright, *Six Months at Graefenberg,* 45.

127. Weber and Weber, 311. For the standard medical texts on the hydrotherapeutic treatment of women's health, see Allain, *Études cliniques sur l'hydrothérapie;* Pigeaire, *Des avantages de l'hydrothérapie appliqués aux maladies chroniques et aux affections nerveuses;* Duvivier, *De l'hypocondrie et de la mélancolie;* and J. Brachet, *Traité complet de l'hypocondrie.* As Corbin has rightly argued, cold water bathing at the seaside was a punishing experience too. Bathers in this context experienced a strong sense of suffocation from the shock of their icy plunges. Corbin, *Territoire du vide,* 89, 90.

128. Annual Report of the Medical Director of Aix-les-Bains for the year 1828, AD Savoie, 1FS 2803.

129. Wright, *Six Months at Graefenberg,* 119.

130. Ibid., 119, 120.

131. Aix-les-Bains even had its *"division d'enfer,"* with separate bathing cells for men and women.

132. Bertier, *Compte-rendu des eaux thermales sulfureuses,* 17.

133. For a detailed description of mud baths at the spas of the 1830s and 1840s, see Constant Despine, *Manuel topographique,* 177–81.

134. Weber and Weber, *Eaux minérales,* 337.

135. Yeo, *Health Resorts and Their Uses,* 58.

136. Ibid.

137. Chasseloup, *Guide pittoresque,* 68.

138. Weber and Weber, *Eaux minérales,* 305.

139. Annual Report of the Medical Director of the Thermal Establishment at Aix-les-Bains, 1829, AD Savoie, 1FS 2803.

140. Statement of bath receipts for the period 1840–50, AD Savoie, 1FS 2805.

141. AD Allier, series X.

142. The frequency of the *douche massage* obviously varied, but many guides noted that a variety of different ailments were best combated by a dozen or more *douches* per *séjour.* Thus the average number of bathing operations per summer at the spas was far higher than the average number of summer visitors. At Aix-les-Bains in 1833, for example, 28,303 treatments were administered to only 2,913 people. AM Aix, I120.

143. Constant Despine, *Manuel topographique.*

144. Linn, *Health Resorts of Europe,* 90, 91.

145. Working at a spa was a family affair among many technicians. Registries of spa personnel in the nineteenth century clearly suggest that fathers passed their training onto sons and that mothers did the same with daughters. This well-paying and skilled labor often enticed up to three generations of an extended family to work at a spa.

146. Yeo, *Health Resorts and Their Uses,* 167.

147. Chasseloup, *Guide pittoresque,* 210.

148. Female patients were always attended to by female technicians and male patients were always attended to by male technicians.

149. Virtually no scholarly work has examined in detail the importance of seasonal work in the social and economic history of France's tourist regions. The well-recorded lives of spa personnel would certainly constitute one vital window into such a history. For a valuable example of this line of inquiry in the Austrian case, see Gamper, "The Impact of Tourism on Two Alpine Communities in Austria."

150. Freeman, *The Thermal Baths of Bath,* 255.

151. Lombard, *Une cure,* 16.

152. Weber and Weber, *Eaux minérales,* 312, 313.

153. Yeo, *Health Resorts and Their Uses,* 58.

154. One Albert Constant, in a 1856 report to the ministry of commerce entitled "Des eaux minérales dans leurs rapports avec l'économie publique," estimated that only two of every five persons on holiday actually took a medical cure. Constant's report is cited in A. Veyrat, *Compte rendu de la saison des eaux thermales pendant l'année 1856* (Chambéry: Imprimerie Nationale, 1857), 26. At Aix-les-Bains, for example, only 3,940 persons of an annual total of 7,617 made use of the thermal establishment in 1861. For contemporary comment on this statistic, see Bonjean, *Guide de l'étranger,* 19–20.

155. Weisz, "Water Cures and Science," 401.

156. Extremely ambitious spa doctors, like Louis Berthet of Aix-les-Bains, argued that spas should begin administering cures throughout the year, rather than just in the summer

months. Another common idea among doctors was to try to lengthen the average curists stay at a spa. See Berthet, *Aix-les-Bains et ses thermes*.

157. Ibid., 216.

158. Ibid., 12.

CHAPTER FIVE

1. "Acte de formation de la Société du cercle d'Aix-les-Bains 20 avril 1824" shows that all the doctors associated with the town's thermal establishment were also members of the casino's entrepreneurial sect. AD Savoie, BC 51.

2. E. Weber, *France, Fin de Siècle*, 189.

3. I am indebted to Leif Brown for his insightful discussions about public space and its capacity not just to moralize but to instruct in the ways of civility and gentility. The phrase "living etiquette book" is his.

4. I am not suggesting here that novels had not yet been written about spas. On the contrary, Jane Austin among many others had featured spas in novels of the later eighteenth and earlier nineteenth centuries. What I am arguing, however, is that using the novel as a promotional form was new to the period around midcentury.

5. Laussedat, *Une Cure au Mont-Dore;* Audiffred, *Quinze jours au Mont-Dore;* and Ferras, *Jean Bonnet à Luchon* were either partially written or directly overseen by a practicing spa doctor.

6. Aix's famous spa doctor, Louis Berthet, wrote *Le solitaire d'Aix-les-Bains* under the pseudonym Pierre de Mirlori (hereafter cited as Berthet). Dr. Constant Despine, who wrote numerous medical guides to Aix-les-Bains over a period of more than forty years, teamed up with Hyacinthe Audiffred to write *L'été à Aix-en-Savoie.*

7. On the bourgeois conception of nature in the period, and especially that conception's relationship to works of art, see Nicholas Green, *The Spectacle of Nature: Bourgeois Culture and Landscape in Nineteenth-Century France* (Manchester: Manchester University Press, 1990).

8. For a clear example of this narrative strategy in the case of Contrexéville, see Millet, *Une saison à Contrexéville.*

9. Barthès, *Guide pratique*, 35.

10. Virtually every guide to this spa written in the nineteenth century told the history of this woman, a friend of the Sardinian queen, who perished in a fall into a local river.

11. Barthès, *Guide pratique*, 43.

12. Forestier, *Des promenades d'Aix-les-Bains*, 123–25.

13. Ordinaire, *Aix en Savoie et ses environs pendant la saison des eaux*, 64.

14. Ibid. Concierges of spa casinos were famous for their role as facilitators of love *en séjour.* The concierge of Aix-les-Bains's casino in the 1850s, one M. Baptiste, was actually identified in guidebooks to that spa as someone who knew the name and relevant information about every unescorted lady in residence. See Achard, *Une saison à Aix-les-Bains*, 146.

15. Perhaps to convey the impression that their curists were legitimate rather than seasonal members of the leisure class, spa newspapers, in contrast to the hotel registries from which they gleaned their vital statistics, chose not to record the occupation of any curist listed on their illustrious rolls. This effectively disguised who was and was not middle class.

16. Achard, *Une saison à Aix-les-Bains*, 118.

17. My cursory examination of spa registries from this period strongly suggests that

same-sex singles tended to go on group vacations. Thus, unescorted middle-class women, whose public lives were severely limited even in Paris, could go on vacation together and live a relatively rich public life. See my analysis of this issue below.

18. Troupes of actors and singers seem to have taken up residence in the *villes d'eaux* for the duration of the thermal season. Most spas offered them free access to their bathing facilities during their tenure. The individuals who made up these troupes tended to work in several productions at a time. For the best primary sources on spa entertainment in this period, see the local and national newspapers of the *villes d'eaux*. In particular, see *Aix Bijou, Aix Cosmopolite, L'Écho d'Aix-les-Bains, L'Écho des villes d'eaux, bains de mer, et stations hivernales,* and *La Gazette des bains.*

19. Many casinos had listed their rules earlier in the century, but those lists of regulations had tended to be vague and oriented toward practical matters, such as when a facility was open.

20. Bourbon-l'Archambault casino rules from 1872, AD Allier, series X.

21. Ibid.

22. Berthet, *Le solitaire d'Aix-les-Bains,* 73.

23. Ibid.

24. These details about spa casinos, including the rules about *journaux* and attire, are found in Constant Despine, *Indicateur médical et topographique d'Aix-les-Bains,* 41. Less than twenty years before, a popularizer of the same spa casino described the society of this facility as one which needed no education in the casino's "secrets." Amédée Achard wrote in 1850, "The equal of these vivacious conversations and elegant manners could only be found among the best company of the faubourg Saint-Germain . . . [where] one hears not a single vulgar word uttered." *Une saison à Aix-les-Bains,* 105.

25. For a brief discussion of the symbolic place of the piano in bourgeois circles of the nineteenth century, especially pertaining to literature and the history of the family, see Michelle Perrot, *History of Private Life.* For an insightful exploration of the piano's place in bourgeois society as seen from the perspective of art history, see Eyerman, "Popular Representations of Women at the Piano, 1830–1848."

26. Ordinaire, *Aix en Savoie,* 122. Countless spa guidebooks of this era, in their descriptions of casino services, note the availability of dancing lessons.

27. *Aix-bijou: Chronique mondaine d'Aix-les-Bains,* 23 July 1885, BM Chambéry, B46.

28. Berthet, *Le solitaire d'Aix-les-Bains,* 10.

29. An example of this representation of a spa casino can be found in *Souvenir: Album historique et pittoresque d'Aix-les-Bains et ses environs.*

30. At Aix-les-Bains and Vichy in this period, for example, approximately one-sixth of the summer population opted for a full membership in the casino. Frieh, *Le grand cercle,* 141.

31. P. Perrot, *Les dessus et les dessous,* 316.

32. Ibid.

33. For a consideration of etiquette and social rituals surrounding public dining, see Alq, *Le Savoir-vivre dans toutes les circonstances de la vie.*

34. Ordinaire, *Aix en Savoie,* 66, 67.

35. Quoted in Institut Français d'Architecture, *Villes d'eaux en France,* 384.

36. Ibid., 378.

37. Ibid., 67.

38. The best work on the development of manners in European society is still Elias, *The History of Manners.* For a fascinating discussion of the importance of manners

to English elite and middle-class society in the nineteenth century, see Davidoff, *Best Circles*.

39. Ordinaire, *Aix en Savoie*, 116.

40. Berthet, *Le solitaire d'Aix-les-Bains*, 33.

41. In the week of 12 June 1870 at Aix-les-Bains, 79 single men arrived on vacation. This figure compared to 43 single women for the same period and 30 married couples. In this week, only 8 married couples brought their children with them to Aix. This week was by no means unusual in the composition of the visiting population at Aix or other large *villes d'eaux*. The very next week, for example, saw 103 single men as compared to 41 single women and 45 married couples. Similarly, the week of 26 June brought 161 single men, 71 single women and only 53 married couples. *Gazette d'Aix,* June–August 1870.

42. On the frustrations of middle-class men, see Philip Nord, *Paris shopkeepers and the Politics of Resentment* (Princeton, Princeton Univeristy Press, 1986).

43. *Gazette d'Aix,* June–August 1870.

44. As much scholarship on women in social spaces has suggested, unescorted women or even female groups had very little social freedom in public places of this period. For a compelling qualification of this widely shared view, see V. Schwartz, *The Public Taste for Reality: Early Mass Culture in Fin-de-Siècle Paris.*

45. Lenore Davidoff has convincingly shown how, at least in the English case, young men and women of the middle class had to plan their unions with the utmost care lest they find themselves unable to afford to make a proper show of themselves at home and in society. See *Best Circles*.

46. For three especially colorful examples of social "fraud" at the *villes d'eaux*, see Achard, *Une saison à Aix-les-Bains;* Audiffred, *Quinze jours au Mont-Dore;* and Berthet, *Le solitaire d'Aix-les-Bains.*

47. Despine and Audiffred, *L'été à Aix-en-Savoie*, 34.

48. For the miniature narrative about Antonia Lovenzi, see Despine and Audiffred, 35–48.

49. Émile Zola, *Au Bonheur des dames* (1883). Peter Gay offers an interesting discussion of the novel and its relationship to both modern sexuality and consumerism. See Gay, *The Tender Passion*, 313–15.

50. For a thoughtful analysis of caricature as a form of institutionalized opposition to the bourgeois social order of the July Monarchy, see Terdiman, *Discourse and Counter-Discourse: The Theory and Practice of Symbolic Resistance in Nineteenth-Century France,* especially chapter 3, "Counter Images: Daumier and Le Charivari."

51. Something of carnivalesque humor resided in the bodies and therapeutic situations that were sketched and commented upon in these books. It should also be said, however, that that something was vestigial and residual more that it was a genuine echo of the carnivalesque sensibility. No, these lower strata references, depictions of the world turned upside down and wild renderings of the human body as grotesque, were hardly universal in scope—most French people in this period had only the vaguest familiarity with spas and hydrotherapy, so they lacked the context in which to find humor in such sketches—nor were they especially festive in their presentation. Yet they differed from all other representations of the spa because they so thoroughly failed to participate in the construction of a clinical body. For the seminal discussion of the carnivalesque, see Bakhtin, *Rabelais and His World,* 11, 12.

52. Contained within a souvenir album entitled *Hydrothérapie sauvage.* Caricature de Cham. La saison des eaux, circa 1870s.

53. ATN Aix, uncataloged materials dated 1876.

54. On the cult of invalidism in this period, see Bram Dijkstra, *Idols of Perversity: Fantasies of Feminine Evil in Fin-de-Siècle Culture* (New York: Oxford University Press, 1986).

EPILOGUE

1. Postcard vendors abound throughout France, as anyone who has ever gone to a French flea market knows well enough. For a useful anthology of postcards related to one spa during the Belle Époque, see Bousquet and Neu, *Enghien-les-Bains en 1900: L'histoire du lac et des bains d'Enghien vue en cartes postales.*

2. Postcard of Marie Guillaume dated 21 September 1906. Personal collection of the author. All quotations of Marie Guillaume are from this source.

3. *L'Écho d'Aix-les-Bains,* 8 August 1909.

4. Ibid. Due to the frailty of this newspaper, I was unable to reproduce either advertisement for this chapter.

$\mathcal{B}ibliography$

ARCHIVAL MATERIALS

Archives Nationales, Paris

SERIES F8

F8 129 (reports and letters concerning spa development at state-owned thermal establishments, 1800–1815)

F8 236 (annual reports of the French Academy of Medicine concerning spas, 1900–1903)

SERIES F14

F14 8259 (dossier on public utility decrees at French spas and on problems associated with the acquisition of land for spa development)

F14 8260 (reports and financial records of public works and spa development, 1790s–1870)

F14 8261 (letters and reports, arranged by *département,* concerning state-owned spas, 1850s–1880)

F14 8262 (financial records of state expenses at Aix-les-Bains)

F14 8268 (letters and parliamentary reports concerning public utility decrees at state-owned spas, 1830–1850)

F14 8278 (letters and reports, arranged by *département,* concerning state-owned spas, 1850s–1880)

F14 8279 (letters and reports, arranged by *département,* concerning state-owned spas, 1850s–1880)

F14 8280 (letters and reports, arranged by *département,* concerning state-owned spas, 1850s–1880)

SERIES F17

F17 3688 (letters, reports, and assorted writings concerning the French Academy of Medicine's ongoing administrative interest in mineral water sources, 1890s)

Archives Départementales de la Haute-Savoie, Annecy

SERIES 4M

4M 231 (letters and reports concerning spa casinos)

SERIES 5M

5M 113 (reports and correspondence of the medical inspectors of the thermal establishments, 1861–1870, emphasis on Évian-les-Bains)

5M 121 (statistics and administrative correspondence concerning seasonal visitation to spas, 1895, 1900, and 1904)

5M 122 (correspondence, promotional materials, and administrative reports concerning the thermal establishments at Évian-les-Bains and Aix-les-Bains)

SERIES 11J

Fonds Despine, cartons 587, 613, 1243, 1244 (correspondence, medical registries, publication information, promotional materials, and miscellaneous papers concerning the family of spa doctors of Annecy and Aix-les-Bains, 1790s–1860s)

Archives Départementales d'Allier, Yzeure

SERIES X

Uncataloged (documents concerning thermal establishments generally; papers, visitor statistics, medical registries, medical reports, and economic information concerning the thermal establishments of the Allier)

Archives Départementales de la Savoie, Chambéry

FONDS SARDE

1FS 2800 (miscellaneous papers and reports concerning spa development in the Savoie, 1815–1819)

1FS 2801 (papers and reports concerning spa development and administration at Aix-les-Bains, 1821–1860)

1FS 2802 (statistics, building plans, and lists of rules for the thermal establishments of the Savoie)

1FS 2803 (letters and annual medical reports of spa medical inspectors of the Savoie)

1FS 2804 (lists of foreign visitors to Aix-les-Bains and miscellaneous administrative reports and letters, 1820s)

1FS 2805 (statistics relative to bathing practices at Aix-les-Bains, 1820s–1850s)

1FS 2820 (published lists of foreign visitors to Aix-les-Bains, 1820–1860)

1FS 2822 (letters and reports concerning admission and administration of indigent bathers at spas of the Savoie, 1820s–1860s)

1FS 2823 (letters and reports concerning indigents and hospital patients at spas of the Savoie, 1816–1860)

SERIES 92X

92X.96 (annual medical reports concerning the thermal establishments of the Savoie)

92X.97 (annual reports of the French Academy of Medicine concerning spas of the Savoie, 1891–1897)

92X.108 (rules of the thermal establishment at Aix-les-Bains, 1860s–1880s)

SERIES C

C51 (printed materials, guidebooks, and advertisements concerning the spas of the Savoie, 1802–1857)

C52 (guidebooks and printed reports concerning the spas of the Savoie, 1857–1876)

Archives Hospitalières de Bourbon-l'Archambault

SERIES A

1A (documents concerning the spa and the hospital of the Old Regime)

SERIES J

1J (deliberations of the administrative commission of the spa's hospital, nineteenth century)

2J (rules and regulations for the thermal establishment and the hospital, eighteenth and
nineteenth centuries)

SERIES L

Uncataloged (administrative correspondence)

Archives Hospitalières de Vichy

SERIES A

1A (correspondence and plans concerning the founding of the hospital at Vichy, eighteenth century)

SERIES E

6E (architectural plans and correspondence concerning public buildings in Vichy, nineteenth century)

SERIES F

1F (registry of patients, 1701–1756)

2F (registry of foreigners visiting Vichy, 1728–1753)

SERIES J

1J2 (rules for the administration of the thermal establishment, nineteenth century)

1J3 (rules for the administration of the thermal hospital of Vichy, 1839)

SERIES L

1L (registry of the deliberations of the administrative commission of the thermal hospital of Vichy)

3L3 (correspondence concerning indigents)

Archives Municipales d'Aix-les-Bains

SERIES I

1I20 (statistics relative to the summer population of Aix-les-Bains, 1816–1904)

Archives Municipales de Brisson-Saint-Innocent

FONDS DESPINE

Uncataloged dossiers (medical registries of the director of the thermal establishment at
Aix-les-Bains, 1780s–1840s)

Archives Municipales de Vichy

SERIES A

A2 (annual reports on the mineral water baths of Vichy, eighteenth century)

SERIES B

B12 (annual reports and correspondence concerning the hospital of Vichy, eighteenth century)

SERIES F

F2 (indigence reports and hospital admissions, 1792–1815)

Archives des Thermes Nationaux d'Aix-les-Bains

Livre 26 (minutes of weekly meetings of the administrative commission of the spa at Aix-les-Bains, 1817–1835)

Cartons 1–4 (miscellaneous materials concerning the thermal industry in the Savoie and in France generally)

ANNUAL MEDICAL REPORTS

Bulletin des eaux d'Aix en Savoie (1830s)

Compte-rendu des eaux d'Aix en Savoie (1850s–1860s)

Observations médicales sur les eaux d'Aix (1850s)

NEWSPAPERS

Aix bijou

Aix cosmopolite

L'Écho d'Aix-les-Bains

L'Écho des villes d'eaux, bains de mer, et stations hivernales

La Gazette des bains

MEDICAL JOURNALS

Annales d'hygiène publique et de médicine légale

Annales de la Société d'hydrologique médicale de Paris

Annales de l'hydrothérapie scientifique

Bulletin de l'Académie de Médecine

L'Europe thermale

La Gazette des eaux

Le Monde thermal

Revue des villes d'eaux

Revue d'hydrologie médicale française et étrangère

CONTEMPORARY BOOKS, GUIDEBOOKS, AND ESSAYS

Achard, Amédée. *Une saison à Aix-les-Bains.* Paris: Bourdin, 1850.

Alary, L. J. *Album des eaux thermales du centre de la France.* 1847.

Allain, Dr. L. *Études cliniques sur l'hydrothérapie.* Paris, 1856.

Alq, Louise d'. *Le savoir-vivre dans toutes les circonstances de la vie,* 2 vols. Paris: Bureaux des Causeries Familières, 1883.

Audiffred, Hyacinthe. *Quinze jours au Mont-Dore.* Paris, 1850.

———. *Un mois à Vichy.* 1851.

Baldou, Dr. L. *L'hydrothérapie, méthode rationnelle du traitement par l'eau froide, le régime, et l'exercice.* Paris, 1841.

Baradou, H. *Conseils médicaux aux personnes qui veulent faire usage des eaux de Vichy.* 1864.

Barbaud, Dr. C. *La femme aux trois grandes périodes de sa vie.* Paris, 1897.

———. *Le nervosisme aux stations thermales.* Paris: Jouvet, 1893.

———. *La puberté chez la femme: Étude physiologique, clinique, et thérapeutique.* Paris, 1897.

Barthès, P. *Guide pratique des malades aux eaux de Vichy.* Paris: Ballière, 1851.

Bassanville, Anaïs Lebrun de. *Almanach du savoir-vivre: Petit code de la bonne compagnie.* Paris: Plon, 1876.

———. *Code du cérémonial: Guide des gens du monde dans toutes les circonstances de la vie.* Paris: Dusquesne, 1867.

Beaurepaire, Compte Davet de. *Histoire et description des sources minérales d'Évian, d'Amphion, et du Chablais.* Paris, 1852.

Berthet, J.-L. *Aix-les-Bains et ses thermes: Traité complet, descriptif, et thérapeutique.* Chambéry: Putod, 1862.

——— [Pierre de Mirlori, pseud.]. *Le solitaire d'Aix-les-Bains.* 1861.

Bertier, Dr. L. *Compte-rendu des eaux thermales sulfureuses d'Aix en Savoie pendant la saison de 1857 suivi de considérations pratiques sur leur action curative.* Chambéry: Puthod Fils, 1858.

Bigel, Dr. J. *Manuel d'hydrosupathie, ou traitement des maladies par l'eau froide suivant la méthode de V. Priessnitz à Graefenberg.* Paris: Baillière, 1840.

Boirot-Desserviers, P. *Recherches historiques et observations médicales sur les eaux thermales et minérales de Néris en Bourbonnais.* 1822.

Bonjean, J. *Guide de l'étranger aux eaux d'Aix-en-Savoie, Chambéry, et leurs environs.* Chambéry: French Government Press, 1862.

Borel, Dr. V. *Nervosisme ou neurasthénie: La maladie du siècle et les divers moyens de la combattre.* Paris, 1894.

Boucher de Perthes, M. *Trois semaines à Vichy en août 1857.* 1866.

Bougy, Alfred J. de. *Évian et ses environs.* Geneva, 1852.

Brachet, Dr. J. *Recherches de la nature et le siège de l'hystérie et de l'hypocondrie, et sur l'analogie et les différences de ces deux maladies.* Paris: Gabon, 1832.

————. *Traité complet de l'hypocondrie.* Paris: Baillière, 1844.

————. *Traité de l'hystérie.* Paris: Ballière, 1847.

Brachet, Dr. L. *Aix-les-Bains in Savoy: The Medical Treatment and General Indications.* London: Renshaw, 1884.

Brainne, Charles. *Baigneuses et buveurs d'eau.* 1860.

————. *Vichy sous Napoléon III, son histoire, ses eaux, ses monuments, et ses environs.* Vichy: Bougarel, 1863.

Briquet, Dr. J. *Traité clinique et thérapeutique de l'hystérie.* Paris, 1859.

Cabias, Jean-Baptiste de. *Les vertus merveilleuses des bains d'Aix en Savoie.* Lyon: Roussin, 1623.

Carrère, Dr. J. *Catalogue raisonné des ouvrages qui ont été publiés sur les eaux minérales en général et sur celles de la France en particulier.* Paris, 1785.

Chasseloup, Dr. *Guide pittoresque aux eaux d'Aix-en-Savoie.* 1834.

Chiais, Dr. Jean-François. *L'action réductrice des eaux d'Évian sur l'acide urique et les corps voisins.* Paris, 1898.

————. *Les conditions de traitement d'Évian-les-Bains.* Paris: Baillière, 1906.

————. *L'eau d'Évian.* Paris: Baillière, 1903.

————. *Les eaux d'Évian dans l'arthritisme, la neurasthénie, la goutte.* Paris, 1896.

————. *La goutte à Évian-les-Bains.* Paris, 1900.

————. *Neurasthénie et goutte: Leur traitement par les eaux d'Évian.* Paris, 1891.

Clark, James. *The Sanative Influence of Climate: With an Account of the Best Places of Resort in England, the South of Europe, etc.* Philadelphia: Waldie, 1841.

Corlieu, Dr. A. *Études sur les causes de la mélancolie.* Paris: Baillière, 1873.

Debout, Dr. Albert-Émile. *Guide médical à Contrexéville.* Paris: Delahaye, 1879.

————. *Thirty-Five Years at Contrexéville.* London: Health Resorts Bureau, 1903.

Despine, Dr. Charles. *Essai topographique et médical d'Aix-en-Savoie et sur les eaux minérales.* Montpellier, An X, 1799.

Despine, Dr. Constant. *Indicateur médical et topographique d'Aix-les-Bains.* Annecy: Burdet, 1850.

————. *Manuel topographique et médical de l'étranger aux eaux d'Aix-en-Savoie.* Annecy: Burdet, 1834.

————. *Practical Guide to the Baths of Aix in Savoy with All the Necessary Information for Reaching Aix and Taking the Baths.* Paris: Masson.

————, and Hyacinthe Audiffred. *L'été à Aix-en-Savoie: Nouveau guide pratique, médical, et pittoresque.* Paris, multiple editions of the 1850s and 1860s.

Dubois, Amable. *Manuel du malade à Vichy.* 1860.

Durand, Leopold. *Traité historique des eaux et des bains de Plombières.* Nancy, 1748.

Duvivier, Dr. E. *De l'hypocondrie et de la mélancolie.* Paris, 1853.

Eberhard, E. *Le livre des gardes-malades et des mères de famille.* Paris, 1867.

Enduran, Ladoix. *Vichy: Flâneries d'un buveur d'eau.* 1845.

Evans, J. *An Excursion to Brighton.* 1821.

Ferras, Ernest. *Jean Bonnet à Luchon.* Toulouse, 1890.

Ferry, Jules. *Lettres de Jules Ferry, 1846–1893.* Paris: Calmann-Lévy.

Forestier, Dr. Auguste. *Le conseiller du baigneur.* Chambéry: French Government Press, 1857.

———. *Des promenades d'Aix-les-Bains ou le nouveau guide pratique, médical, et pittoresque. Vade-Mecum.* Chambéry, 1876.

Freeman, Dr. Henry. *The Thermal Baths of Bath.* London: Hamilton, Adams, 1888.

Gaudin, Célestin. *Carnet hygiénique et médical du baigneur à Vichy.* 1865.

———. *Vichy, au point de vue de l'hygiène et du traitement, mis à la portée des gens du monde.* 1865.

Goldsmith, Oliver. *The Life of Richard Nash of Bath.* 1762.

Granville, Dr. A. B. *The Spas of England and Principal Sea-Bathing Places.* London: H. Colburn, 1841.

Grellety, J. "Une cure thermale à Vichy pendant le dix-septième siècle," in *Revue Bourbonnaise,* 1884.

Guide du baigneur à Vichy: Saison 1866. Vichy: Wallon, 1866.

Harwood, William. *On the Curative Influence of the Southern Coast of England.* 1828.

Huart, Dr. Louis. *Physiologie du médecin.* Paris: Aubert, 1841. Quoted in Angus MacLaren, *Sexuality and Social Order: The Debate over the Fertility of Women and Workers in France, 1770–1920* (New York: Holmes and Meier, 1983).

Hutton, William. *A Description of Blackpool.* 1788.

James, Dr. Constantin. *Études sur l'hydrothérapie, ou traitement par l'eau froide.* Paris: Dusillion, 1846.

———. *Guide pratique aux eaux minérales.* Paris, 1855.

Langeais, Duchesse de. *Almanach du savoir-vivre et de la politesse.* Paris, 1869.

Laussedat, Louis. *Une cure au Mont-Dore.* Paris, 1868.

Le Bret, Eugène. *De l'institution des hôpitaux dans les stations thermales.* 1862.

Lecoq, H. *Vichy et ses environs, ou description des eaux thermales, et des sites qui les entourent, avec quelques considérations sur l'action médicale des eaux.* Vol 3 of *Description pittoresque de l'Auvergne.* 1836.

Lelièvre, Dr. *Médecine usuelle.* Paris, 1881.

Linn, Dr. Thomas. *The Health Resorts of Europe.* New York, 1893.

Lombard, Dr. H. C. *Une cure aux bains d'Aix-en-Savoie.* Geneva: Fick, 1853.

Maupassant, Guy de. *Mont-Oriol.* Paris: Gallimard, 1976.

Millet, Dr. Auguste. *Une saison à Contrexéville.* Paris, 1863.

Millet-Robinet, Cora-Elisabeth. *La maison rustique des dames.* Paris, 1844.

Mortillet, Dr. G. *Guide du baigneur et de l'étranger à Aix-les-Bains.* Chambéry: Perrin, 1855.

Nadeau, Louis. *Vichy historique.* 1869.

———. *Voyage en Bourbonnais, Moulins, Néris, Vichy, Bourbon-l'Archambault, et leurs environs.* Paris: Hachette, 1865.

Noyer, Victor. *Lettres topographiques et médicales sur Vichy, ses eaux minérales et leur action thérapeutique sur nos organes.* 1833.

Ordinaire, Dr. P. C. *Aix en Savoie et ses environs pendant la saison des eaux.* 1840.

Pariset, Mme. *Manuel de la maîtresse de maison, ou lettres sur l'économie domestique.* 3d ed. Paris: Audot, 1825.

Pascal, Jean *Traité des eaux de Bourbon l'Archambault selon les principes de la nouvelle physique.* Paris: Claude Jombert, 1699.

Patezon, Dr. J. *Guide aux eaux minérales de Vittel.* Paris, 1866.

Perussell, H. *Guide médical et hygiénique de la mère de famille.* Paris, 1882.

Pétin, Charles. *Des eaux minérales alcalines de Vichy.* 1843.

Piesse, L. *Vichy et ses environs.* 1854.

Pigeaire, Dr. J. *Des avantages de l'hydrothérapie appliqués aux maladies chroniques et aux affections nerveuses.* Paris: Baillière, 1847.

Quinsonas, Comte de. *Les embellissements d'Aix-les-Bains.* Aix: Bolliet, 1862.

Raulin, Dr. Joseph. *Traité analytique des eaux minérales en général, de leurs propriétés, et de leur usage dans les maladies.* Paris: Chez Vincent, 1772.

Rul, Dr. L. *Quatre ans à Graefenberg.* Paris, 1858.

Scheuer, Dr. Victor. *Guide pratique du baigneur.* Paris, 1854.

Second, Albéric. *Vichy-Sévigné, Vichy-Napoléon, ses eaux, ses embellissements, ses environs, son histoire.* 1862.

Souligoux, Léonce. *De l'examen organique et physiologique du malade pendant son séjour à Vichy.* 1869.

Souvenir: Album historique et pittoresque d'Aix-les-Bains et ses environs. Aix: Bachet, 1872.

Sparks, Dr. Edward. *The Riviera.* London: Churchill, 1879.

Spry, Dr. Joseph. *A Practical Treatise on the Bath Waters.* London: Longman, 1822.

Tanard, J. *Vichy descriptif et humoristique.* 1893.

Vichy anecdotique et la berlue: Tout Vichy y passera par un buveur. 1874.

Vidal, Dr. *Notice historique et médicale sur l'hospice d'Aix en Savoie.* Chambéry, 1853.

Vidart, Dr. Paul. *Considérations générales sur l'hydrothérapie.* Paris, 1849.

———. *De la cure d'eau froide à l'institut hydrothérapique de Divonne.* Paris: Chebruliez, 1852.

———. *Études pratiques sur l'hydrothérapie, ou traitement des maladies par l'eau froide.* Paris, 1855.

Weber, Dr. Hermann. *Climatotherapy and Balneotherapy.* London: Smith, Elder, 1907.

———, and Dr. F. Parkes Weber, *Eaux minérales et stations climatériques de l'Europe.* Paris, 1899.

Willemin, A. *Clinique médicale de Vichy pendant la saison de 1862.* 1863.

Wright, Henry C. *Six Months at Graefenberg.* London, 1845.

X, Arthur. *Une saison d'eaux à Aix-les-Bains: Album caricatural.* 2d ed. Aix, 1868.

Yeo, Dr. Isaac. *Health Resorts and Their Uses.* London: Chapman and Hall, 1882.

SECONDARY SOURCES

Ackerknecht, Ernest. "Medical Education in Nineteenth-Century France." *Journal of Medical Education* 1 (1957): 15–18.

————. *Medicine at the Paris Hospital, 1794–1848.* Baltimore: Johns Hopkins University Press, 1967.

Adams, Thomas M. *Bureaucrats and Beggars: French Social Policy in the Age of the Enlightenment.* New York: Oxford University Press, 1990.

Addison, William. *English Spas.* London: Batsford, 1951.

Agulhon, Maurice. *Le cercle dans la France bourgeoise, 1810–1848: étude d'une mutation de sociabilité.* Paris: Presses Universitaires de France, 1977.

————. *The Republic in the Village: The People of the Var from the French Revolution to the Second Republic.* Cambridge, Cambridge University Press, 1982.

Appadurai, Arjun, ed. *The Social Life of Things: Commodities in Cultural Perspective.* New York: Cambridge University Press, 1986.

Aubert, Jean. *En Auvergne: Les villes d'eaux autrefois.* Lyon: Horvath, 1993.

Auby, Jean-François. *Les eaux minérales.* Paris: Presses Universitaires de France, 1994.

Auslander, Leora. "The Gendering of Consumer Practices in Nineteenth-Century France." In Victoria de Grazia, ed. *The Sex of Things: Gender and Consumption in Historical Perspective.* Berkeley and Los Angeles: University of California, 1996.

————. *Taste and Power: Furnishing Modern France.* Berkeley and Los Angeles: University of California Press, 1996.

Bailey, Peter. *Leisure and Class and Victorian England: Rational Recreation and the Contest for Control, 1830–1885.* London: Routledge, 1987.

Bakhtin, Mikhail. *Rabelais and His World.* Cambridge: Cambridge University Press, 1968.

Barbeau, Alfred. *Life and Letters at Bath in the Eighteenth Century.* London: Heinemann, 1904.

Barber, Elinor. *The Bourgeoisie in Eighteenth-Century France.* Princeton: Princeton University Press, 1955.

Barnes, David. *The Making of a Social Disease: Tuberculosis in Nineteenth-Century France.* Berkeley and Los Angeles: University of California Press, 1995.

Barrows, Susanna. "Nineteenth-Century Cafés: Arenas of Everyday Life." In Barbara Stern Shapiro, *Pleasures of Paris: Daumier to Picasso.* Boston: Museum of Fine Arts, 1991.

Benedict, Barbara. "The Printed Resort: Erotic Consumption and the Gender of Leisure in Eighteenth-Century Spa Literature." Unpublished.

Bergeron, Louis. "French Industrialization in the Nineteenth Century: An Attempt to Define National Way." *Proceedings of the Annual Meeting of the Western Society for French History* 12 (1984): 154–63.

Black, Jeremy. *The British and the Grand Tour.* London: Croom Helm, 1985.

Bouloumie, Pierre. *Histoire de Vittel.* Paris: Maloine, 1925.

Bousquet, Jean-Pierre, and Jean-Paul Neu. *Enghien-les-Bains en 1900: L'histoire du lac et des bains d'Enghien vue en cartes postales.* Paris: COFIMAG, 1983.

Boussel, Patrice. *Histoire des vacances*. Paris: Éditions Berger-Levrault, 1961.

Brockliss, Laurence. "The Development of the Spa in Seventeenth-Century France." In Roy Porter, ed., *The Medical History of Waters and Spas*. Supplement no. 10 to *Medical History*. London: Wellcome Institute for the History of Medicine, 1990.

————. *French Higher Education in the Seventeenth and Eighteenth Centuries*. Oxford: Oxford University Press, 1987.

————. *Medical Teaching at the University of Paris, 1600–1720*. Oxford: Oxford University Press, 1978.

————. *The Medical World of Early Modern France*. Oxford: Oxford University Press, 1997.

Brown, Leif. "Golden Gate Park as Etiquette Book, 1870–1900." Unpublished.

Cameron, Rondo E. "Economic Growth and Stagnation in France, 1815–1914." *Journal of Modern History* vol. 30, no. 1 (March, 1958).

Carter, Edward C., ed. *Enterprise and Entrepreneurs in Nineteenth- and Twentieth-Century France*. Baltimore: Johns Hopkins University Press, 1976.

Certeau, Michel de. *The Practice of Everyday Life*. Berkeley and Los Angeles: University of California Press, 1984.

Chard, Chloe, and Helen Langdon, eds. *Transports: Travel, Pleasure, and Imaginative Geography, 1600–1830*. New Haven: Yale University Press, 1996.

Clark, T. J. *The Painting of Modern Life: Paris in the Art of Manet and His Followers*. Princeton: Princeton University Press, 1984.

Cody, Lisa. "The Politics of Body Contact: Disciplines of Reproduction in Britain, 1688–1834." Ph.D. diss., University of California, Berkeley, 1993.

Cohen, Erik. "A Phenomenology of Tourist Experiences." *Sociology* 3 (1979): 179–202.

Coleman, William. "Health and Hygiene in the Encyclopedia: A Medical Doctrine for the Bourgeoisie." *Journal of the History of Medicine and Allied Sciences* 29 (1974): 399–421.

Corbin, Alain. *L'avènement des loisirs, 1850–1960*. Paris: Aubier, 1995.

————. *Les filles de noce: Misère sexuelle et prostitution, dix-neuvième siècle*. Paris: Flammarion, 1978.

————. *The Foul and the Fragrant: Odor and the French Social Imagination*. Cambridge: Harvard University Press, 1986.

————. *Le territoire du vide: L'Occident et le désir du rivage, 1750–1840*. Paris: Aubier, 1988.

Cox, Edward. *A Reference Guide to the Literature of Travel*. Seattle: University of Washington Publications in Language and Literature, 1935.

Cunningham, Hugh. *Leisure in the Industrial Revolution, 1780–1880*. New York: St. Martin's Press, 1980.

Daumard, Adeline. *Les bourgeois et la bourgeoisie en France depuis 1815*. Paris: Flammarion, 1991.

————. "The Parisian Bourgeoisie, 1815–1848." In Andrew Lees and Lynn Hollen Lees, *The Urbanization of European Society in the Nineteenth Century*. Lexington, Mass.: Heath, 1976.

Davidoff, Lenore. *The Best Circles: Women and Society in Victorian Britain.* Totowa, N.J.: Rowman and Littlefield, 1973.

Davidoff, Lenore and Catherine Hall. *Family Fortunes: Men and Women of the English Middle Class, 1780–1850.* Chicago: University of Chicago Press, 1987.

Decorcet, G. *Vichy: Deuxième part, 1755–1895,* 1899.

Desgranges, Bernard. *Histoire des thermes de Luxeuil.* Luxeuil: Desgranges, 1981.

Dunot, P. *Le thermalisme.* Paris: Presses Universitaires de France, 1963.

Dupront, A. "Tourisme et pèlerinage, réflexions sur la psychologie collective." *Communications* vol. 10 (1967).

Elias, Norbert. *The Civilizing Process: The History of Manners.* Geneva: Urizen, 1939.

Fairburn, A. N. "The Grand Tour." *Geographical Magazine* 24 (1951): 118–27.

Féneyrou, Gaston. *La vie des eaux thermominérales.* Toulouse: Éditions Erès 1989.

Foucault, Michel. *Discipline and Punish: The Birth of the Prison.* Trans. Alan Sheridan. Paris: Gallimard, 1975.

———. *The History of Sexuality: An Introduction.* New York: Random House, 1978.

———. *Madness and Civilization: A History of Insanity in the Age of Reason.* New York: Random House, 1978.

———. *Naissance de la clinique.* Paris: Presses Universitaires de France, 1963.

Frieh, Geneviève. *Le grand cercle d'Aix-les-Bains: Histoire d'un casino.* Aix: Musumeci Éditeur, 1984.

Furlough, Ellen. *Consumer Cooperation in France: The Politics of Consumption.* Ithaca: Cornell University Press, 1991.

Gadd, David. *Georgian Summer: Bath in the Eighteenth Century.* Bath: Adams and Dart, 1971.

Gamper, Josef. "The Impact of Tourism on Two Alpine Communities in Austria." Ph.D. diss., University of California, Berkeley, 1982.

Gaudry, Joachim. *Histoire du barreau de Paris depuis son origine jusqu'à 1830.* Paris: Durand, 1864.

Gay, Peter. *The Tender Passion.* Vol. 2 of *The Bourgeois Experience: Victoria to Freud.* Oxford: Oxford University Press, 1986.

Gelfand, Toby. *Professionalizing Modern Medicine: Paris Surgeons, Medical Science, and Institutions in the Eighteenth Century.* Westport, Conn.: Greenwood Press, 1980.

Gerbod, Paul. "Les fièvres thermales en France au dix-neuvième siècle." In *Revue Historique,* no. 562 (April 1987).

Gerschenkron, Alexander. *Economic Backwardness in Historical Perspective.* Cambridge: Belknap Press, 1962.

Gillis, John. "The Cultural Production of Family Identities in Nineteenth-Century Britain." Unpublished.

Gillispie, Charles. *Science and Polity in France at the End of the Old Regime.* Princeton: Princeton University Press, 1980.

Goubert, Jean-Pierre. *The Conquest of Water: The Advent of Health in the Industrial Age.* Princeton: Princeton University Press, 1989.

———. *Malades et médecine en Bretagne, 1770–1790.* Paris: Klincksieck, 1974.

Guitard, E. "Le prestige passé des eaux minérales." *Société historique de la pharmacie* (1931).

Hamon, Philippe. *Expositions: Literature and Architecture in Nineteenth-Century France.* Berkeley and Los Angeles: University of California Press, 1992.

Hannaway, Caroline. "Medicine, Public Welfare, and the State in Eighteenth-Century France: The Société Royale de Médecine of Paris, 1776–1793." Ph.D. diss., Johns Hopkins University, 1974.

Harris, Ruth. *Murderers and Madness: Medicine, Law, and Society in the Fin de Siècle.* Oxford: Oxford University Press, 1988.

Harrison, Carol. "Honest Amusements: Voluntary Associations and Bourgeois Leisure." Paper presented at the Annual Meeting of the Western Society for French History, 1994.

Haug, James. *Leisure and Urbanism in Nineteenth-Century Nice.* Lawrence: Regents Press of Kansas, 1982.

Heath, Sidney. *In the Steps of the Pilgrims.* New York: Putnam's Sons, 1911.

Hellerstein, Erna Olafson, Leslie Parker Hume, and Karen Offen. *Victorian Women: A Documentary Account of Women's Lives in Nineteenth-Century England, France, and the United States.* Stanford: Stanford University Press, 1981.

———. "Women, Social Order, and the City: Rules for French Ladies, 1830–1870." Ph.D. diss., University of California, Berkeley, 1980.

Helme, J. *Les villes d'eaux et stations climatiques françaises.* Paris: Masson, 1939.

Hembry, Phyllis. *The English Spa, 1560–1815.* London: Athlone Press; Rutherford, N.J.: Fairleigh Dickinson University Press, 1990.

Hern, Anthony. *The Seaside Holiday: The History of the English Seaside Resort.* New York: Hilary House, 1967.

Hildreth, Martha L. *Doctors, Bureaucrats, and Public Health, 1888–1902.* New York: Garland, 1988.

Hufton, Olwen. *The Poor of Eighteenth-Century France, 1750–1789.* Oxford: Oxford University Press, 1974.

Hunt, Lynn. *Politics, Culture, and Class in the French Revolution.* Berkeley and Los Angeles: University of California Press, 1984.

———. "The Unstable Boundaries of the French Revolution." In Michelle Perrot, ed., *A History of Private Life: From the Fires of the Revolution to the Great War.* Cambridge: Harvard University Press, 1987.

———, ed. *The New Cultural History.* Berkeley and Los Angeles: University of California Press, 1989.

Institut Français d'Architecture. *Villes d'eaux en France.* Paris: Hazan, 1985.

Jamot, Christian. *Thermalisme et les villes thermales en France.* Clermont-Ferrand: Institut d'Études du Massif Central, 1988.

Jarrassé, Dominique. *Les thermes romantiques: Bains et villégiatures en France de 1800 à 1850.* Clermont-Ferrand: Institute d'Études du Massif Central, 1992.

Jones, Colin. *The Charitable Imperative: Hospitals and Nursing in Ancien Régime and Revolutionary France.* London: Routledge, 1989.

Kaplan, Caren. *Questions of Travel: Postmodern Discourses of Displacement.* Durham: Duke University Press, 1996.

Kendall, Alan. *Medieval Pilgrims.* London: Wayland, 1970.

Kindleberger, Charles P. *Economic Growth in France and Britain, 1851–1950.* Cambridge: Harvard University Press, 1964.

Krippendorf, Jost. *The Holiday-Makers: Understanding the Impact of Leisure and Travel.* London: Heinemann, 1987.

Kudlick, Catherine J. *Cholera in Post-Revolutionary Paris: A Cultural History.* Berkeley and Los Angeles: University of California Press, 1996.

Laberge, Anne. F. *Mission and Method: The Early Nineteenth-Century French Public Health Movement.* Cambridge: Cambridge University Press, 1992.

Lambert, Richard, ed. *Grand Tour: A Journey in the Tracks of the Age of Aristocracy.* New York: Dutton, 1937.

Landes, David. *Business and the Businessman: French Entrepreneurship and Industrial Growth in the Nineteenth Century, a Social Analysis.* Indianapolis: Bobbs Merrill, 1960.

———. "Religion and Enterprise: The Case of the French Textile Industry." In Edward Carter II, Robert Forster, and Joseph N. Moody, eds., *Enterprise and Entrepreneurs in Nineteenth- and Twentieth-Century France.* Baltimore: Johns Hopkins University Press, 1976.

Langenieux-Villard, Philippe. *Les stations thermales en France.* Paris: Presses Universitaires de France, 1990.

Laqueur, Thomas. "Bodies, Details, and the Humanitarian Narrative." In Lynn Hunt, ed., *The New Cultural History.* Berkeley and Los Angeles: University of California Press, 1989.

———. *Making Sex: Sexuality and the Body from the Greeks to Freud.* Berkeley and Los Angeles: University of California Press, 1990.

Larson, Magali Sarfatti. *The Rise of Professionalism: A Sociological Analysis.* Berkeley and Los Angeles: University of California Press, 1979.

Lecuir, Jean. "La médicalisation de la société française dans la deuxième moitié du dix-huitième siècle en France: Aux origines des premiers traités de médecine légale." *Annales de Bretagne* 86, no. 2 (1979): 321–50.

Leguay, Jean-Pierre. *Histoire d'Aix-les-Bains et sa région: Une grande station thermale.* Aix: Avenir, 1988.

Léonard, Jacques. *Archives du corps: La santé aux dix-neuvième siècle.* Paris: Ouest-France, 1986.

Livois, Rene. *Histoire de la presse française.* Vol. 1. Paris: Les Temps de la Presse, 1965.

Lynch, Katherine. *Family, Class, and Ideology in Early Industrial France: Social Policy and the Working Class Family, 1825–1848.* Madison: University of Wisconsin, 1988.

Looz, François de. *Néris de 1789 à 1914.* Tulle: Imprimerie Orfeuil, 1981.

MacCannell, Dean. *The Tourist: A New Theory of the Leisure Class.* New York: Schocken, 1976.

MacLaren, Angus. *Sexuality and Social Order: The Debate over the Fertility of Women and Workers in France, 1770–1920.* New York: Holmes and Meier, 1983.

Malcomson, Robert. *Popular Recreation in English Society, 1700–1850.* New York: Cambridge: Cambridge University Press, 1973.

Mangin, Nathalie. *La vie de société dans les villes d'eaux européennes de 1850 à 1914, Cosmopolitanisme et nationalisme.* Paris, 1994.

Margadant, Ted. *French Peasants in Revolt.* Princeton: Princeton University Press, 1979.

Martin-Fugier, Anne. *La bourgeoisie.* Paris: Grasset, 1983.

———. *La vie élégante ou la formation du Tout-Paris, 1815–1848.* Paris: Fayard, 1990.

Mauve, E. *Vichy avant la compagnie fermière, 1833–1853.* Moulins: Crépin-Leblond, 1935.

Mead, W. E. *The Grand Tour in the Eighteenth Century.* Boston: Houghton Mifflin, 1914.

Merriman, John. *The Agony of the Republic.* New Haven: Yale University Press, 1978.

Miller, Daniel. *Material Culture and Mass Consumption.* Oxford: Basil Blackwell, 1987.

Miller, Michael. *The Bon Marché: Bourgeois Culture and the Department Store, 1869–1920.* Princeton: Princeton University Press, 1981.

Morazé, Charles. *Les bourgeois conquérants: Dix-neuvième siècle.* Paris: A. Colin, 1957.

Murphy, Terence. "The Transformation of Traditional Medical Culture under the Old Regime." *Historical Reflection* vol. 16, nos. 2 and 3 (1989): 300–350.

Nye, Robert. *Crime, Madness, and Politics in Modern France: The Medical Concept of National Decline.* Princeton: Princeton University Press, 1984.

———. *Masculinity and Male Codes of Honor in Modern France.* Oxford: Oxford University Press, 1993.

O'Brien, Patrick. *Economic Growth in Britain and France, 1780–1914: Two Paths to the Twentieth Century.* London: Allen and Unwin, 1978.

Pagotto, Nicole. *Le thermalisme à Aix-les-Bains au dix-neuvième siècle.* Chambéry: Institut d'Études Savoisiennes, 1975.

Penez, Jérôme. *Dans la fièvre thermale. La société des eaux minérales de Châtel-Guyon, 1878 à 1914.* Clermont-Ferrand: Institut d'Études du Massif Central, 1994.

Perrot, Marguerite. *Le mode de vie des familles bourgeoises, 1873–1953.* Paris: Presses de la Fondation Nationale des Sciences Politiques, 1982.

Perrot, Michelle, ed. *A History of Private Life: From the Fires of the Revolution to the Great War.* Cambridge: Harvard University Press, 1990.

———. "The Three Ages of Industrial Discipline in Nineteenth-Century France." In John Merriman, ed., *Consciousness and Class Experience in Nineteenth-Century Europe.* New York: Holmes and Meier, 1979.

Perrot, Philippe. *Les dessus et les dessous de la bourgeoisie: Une histoire du vêtement au dix-neuvième siècle.* Paris: Fayard, 1981.

Peterson, M. Jeanne. *The Medical Profession in Mid-Victorian London.* Berkeley and Los Angeles: University of California Press, 1978.

Pimlott, J. A. R. *Englishman's Holiday: A Social History.* London: Faber and Faber, 1947.

Pinkney, David. *Napoleon III and the Rebuilding of Paris.* Princeton: Princeton University Press, 1958.

Pollard, S. "Factory Discipline in the Industrial Revolution." *Economic History Review* 16 (December 1963): 254–71.

Pomerol, Charles. *Terroirs et thermalisme: Les eaux minérales françaises.* Orléans: Éditions du BRGM, 1992.

Porter, Roy, ed. *The Codification of Medical Morality: Historical and Philosophical Studies of the Formalization of Western Medical Morality in the Eighteenth and Nineteenth Centuries.* Boston: Kluwer Academic Publishing, 1993.

———. *Dictionary of the History of Medicine.* Princeton: Princeton University Press, 1981.

———. *The Hospital in History.* London: Routledge, 1989.

———. *Literature and Medicine during the Eighteenth Century.* London: Routledge, 1993.

———. *Medical Fringe and Medical Orthodoxy, 1750–1850.* London: Croom Helm, 1987.

———. *The Medical History of Waters and Spas.* London: Wellcome Institute for the History of Medicine, 1990.

———. *Medicine in the Enlightenment.* Atlanta: Rodopi, 1995.

———. *The Popularization of Medicine, 1650–1850.* London: Routledge, 1992.

Rabinow, Paul, ed. *The Foucault Reader.* New York: Pantheon Books, 1984.

Ramsey, Matthew. *Professional and Popular Medicine in France, 1770–1830.* Cambridge: Cambridge University Press, 1988.

Rauch, André. *Les vacances.* Paris: Presses Universitaires de France, 1993.

———. *Vacances et pratiques corporelles: La naissance des morales du dépaysement.* Paris: Presses Universitaires de France, 1988.

Rearick, Charles. *Pleasures of the Belle Époque: Entertainment and Festivity in Turn-of-the-Century France.* New Haven: Yale University Press, 1985.

Reason, J. T. *Man in Motion: The Psychology of Travel.* London: Weidenfeld and Nicholson, 1974.

Redford, Bruce. *Venice and the Grand Tour.* New Haven: Yale University Press, 1996.

Robinson, H. *A Geography of Tourism.* Plymouth: MacDonald and Evans, 1979.

Rothfield, Lawrence. *Vital Signs: Medical Realism in Nineteenth-Century Fiction.* Princeton: Princeton University Press, 1992.

Schmidt, C. J. *Tourism: Sacred Sights, Secular Seer.* Stoney Brook: State University of New York Press, 1980.

Schwartz, Robert M. *Policing the Poor in Eighteenth-Century France.* Chapel Hill: University of North Carolina Press, 1988.

Schwartz, Vanessa. "The Public Taste for Reality: Early Mass Culture in Fin-de-Siècle Paris." Ph.D. diss., University of California, Berkeley, 1993.

Smith, Bonnie. *Changing Lives: Women in European History since 1700.* Lexington, Mass.: D. C. Heath, 1989.

———. *Ladies of the Leisure Class: The Bourgeoises of Northern France in the Nineteenth Century.* Princeton: Princeton University Press, 1981.

Smith, Valene. *Hosts and Guests: The Anthropology of Tourism.* Philadelphia: University of Pennsylvania Press, 1989.

Soboul, Albert. "The Classical Historiography of the French Revolution and Its Critics." *Proceedings of the First Annual Meeting of the Western Society for French History* 5 (March 1974): 87–98.

Terdiman, Richard. *Discourse and Counter-Discourse: The Theory and Practice of Symbolic Resistance in Nineteenth-Century France.* Ithaca: Cornell University Press, 1985.

Thierry, Lionel. *Le thermalisme dans la région Rhône-Alpes.* Grenoble: Université Joseph Fourier, 1991.

Thompson, E. P. "Time, Work-Discipline and Industrial Capitalism." *Past and Present* 38 (December 1967): 56–97.

Towner, J. "The European Grand Tour, circa 1550–1840: A Study of its Role in the History of Tourism." Ph.D. diss., University of Birmingham, Alabama, 1984.

———. "The Grand Tour: Sources and Methodology for the Historical Study of Tourism." *Tourism Management* 5 (1984): 215–22.

Turner, Victor. *Image and Pilgrimage in Christian Culture.* New York: Columbia University Press, 1978.

Vaughan, John E. "Early Guide Books as Sources of Social History." *Amateur Historian* vol. 5 (1961).

Veblen, Thorstein. *Theory of the Leisure Class: An Economic Study of Institutions.* New York: Modern Library, 1934.

Viard, Jean. *Penser les vacances.* Paris: Presses Universitaires de France, 1984.

Wallon, Armand. "Saisons de Vichy pendant la Révolution." *Bulletin sociologique, historique, et archéologique de Vichy,* 12.

———. *La vie quotidienne dans les villes d'eaux.* Paris: Hachette, 1986.

Walton, John. *The Blackpool Landlady: A Social History.* 1979.

———. *The English Seaside Resort: A Social History, 1750–1914.* Leicester: Leicester University Press, 1983.

Walton, Whitney. "Feminine Hospitality in the Bourgeois Home of Nineteenth-Century Paris." *Proceedings of the Annual Meeting of the Western Society for French History* 14 (1987): 197–203.

———. *France at the Crystal Palace: Bourgeois Taste and Artisan Manufacture in the Nineteenth Century.* Berkeley and Los Angeles: University of California Press, 1992.

Walvin, James. *Leisure and Society, 1830–1950.* London: Allen Lane, 1978.

———. *Beside the Seaside: A Social History of the Popular Seaside Holiday.* London: Allen Lane, 1978.

Watt, Francis. *Canterbury Pilgrims and Their Ways.* London: Methuen, 1917.

Weber, Eugen. *France, Fin de Siècle.* Cambridge: Harvard University Press, 1986.

————. "Gymnastics and Sports in Fin-de-Siècle France: Opium of the Classes?" *American Historical Review* 86 (1971): 70–98.

Weber, Max. *The Protestant Ethic and the Spirit of Capitalism.* London: Unwin University Books, 1930.

Weisz, George. *The Medical Mandarins: The French Academy of Medicine in the Nineteenth and Early Twentieth Centuries.* Oxford: Oxford University Press, 1995.

————. "Water Cures and Science: The French Academy of Medicine and Mineral Waters in the Nineteenth Century." *Bulletin of the History of Medicine* 64, no. 3 (fall 1990): 393–416.

Williams, Rosalind. *Dream Worlds: Mass Consumption in Late Nineteenth-Century France.* Berkeley and Los Angeles: University of California Press, 1982.

Wilson, Lindsay. *Women and Medicine in the French Enlightenment: The Debate over "Maladies des Femmes."* Baltimore: Johns Hopkins University Press, 1993.

Wright, Gordon. *France in Modern Times.* New York: Norton, 1981.

Zeldin, Theodore. *France, 1848–1945.* Vol. 2. Oxford: Clarendon Press, 1977.

————. *The Political System of Napoleon III.* New York: Norton, 1958.

Index

Academy of Medicine: governance of spa medicine, 119, 165n. 8; and research on spas, 93, 182n. 19. *See also* doctors; hydrotherapy; medicine; mineral water cures

advertising: caricatures in, 141–47; by doctors, 86–96; and hydrotherapeutic methods, 88–90, 99, 107–8; hygiene represented in, 81–82; medical testimonials in, 90–96; narrative immediacy in, 90, 95, 100–101, 123–26; and newspapers, 129, 136, 157; order represented in, 132; romance suggested in, 136–40; social and cultural performance as, 127; social mobility promised in, 135–36; spa novels as, 124–25, 135–36; and topographic narratives, 125–26; and women travelers, 136–38. *See also* bathing; bourgeoisie; class relations; consumer culture; doctors; economic development; gender; guidebooks; identity formation; medicine; newspapers; spa novels; spas; women

Aix-en-Provence, 15

Aix-les-Bains: and the bourgeoisie, 34–36; casino at, 58; and Despine family, 13, 45–46, 86, 95–96, 99; development of, 45–46, 57–64, 121, 168n. 63; doctors at, 13, 94, 99, 102, 121; and the French Revolution, 25–26; gambling at, 58; guidebooks for, 52, 86–87, 89, 94–96, 125–26; Haldimand Hospital, 73–75; hotels in, 58, 127–29; newspapers of, 129, pool at, in Old Regime, 20; postcards from, 155–56; provincial travelers to, 52; 135;

shower massages at, 113; societal composition of, in Old Regime, 22; in spa novels, 128, 135–37; spa renovation at, 78–83; spa rules at, 30; statistics for, 22, 43, 46, 52, 111, 136; urbanization of, 58; visitors to, in Old Regime, 22. *See also* advertising; architecture; class relations; doctors; economic development; entrepreneurialism; guidebooks; hospitals; hydrotherapy; indigents; mineral water cures; newspapers; spas

architects, spa, 59–62

architecture: complaints about, 71, 75; and gender, 76, 78, 80; hotel, 127–28; indecency of, 75, 81–82; landscape, 59–62, 132, 139; and privacy, 75–81; and order, 132; and surveillance, 71–74, 80–81, 127–28, 132; and urban planning, 59–65

aristocracy: in advertising narratives, 140; and medicine, 17; sociability at spas among, 21, 175n. 2; at spas, decline of, 52; —, in Old Regime, 16; travel by, 16; —, impact of French Revolution on, 27; and visitor lists, 52

Ax-les-Thermes, 13, 15

Bagnères-de-Bigorre, 13, 15, 17, 75

bain simple. *See* bathing

basins. *See* pools

bath cabinets: appearance at spas of, 78, 80, 179n. 50; bourgeois preference for, 75, 80, 107, 179n. 49; complaints about lack of, 75; gendered organization of, 76–81; propriety of, 75–76,